Praise for *The New Age of Empire*

"An uncompromising account of the roots of racism today."
—Kimberlé Crenshaw

"This book is a provocation. It is not meant to make us comfortable or inspired, but rather to remind us of the hard truth that the West was built on slavery, genocide, and colonialism—the bases of racial capitalism and modern empire. And as Kehinde Andrews argues, we are still living this imperial nightmare, still reaping the consequences of contemporary racialized violence and exploitation. The lesson: no freedom under racism, no future under capitalism, no justice without decolonization."
— Robin D. G. Kelley, author of *Freedom Dreams: The Black Radical Imagination*

"This book is a radical, necessary indictment of the racist structures that produced the current anti-Black world order. Historically rigorous and deeply researched, Kehinde Andrews writes with lucidity about the global tactics of Western imperialism, centuries ago and at present. His clear-eyed analysis insists upon the revolutionary acts of freedom we will need to break out of these systems of violence."
—Ibram X. Kendi, National Book Award–winning author of *Stamped from the Beginning* and *How to Be an Antiracist*

"Kehinde is a leader and a teacher who puts the Black Lives Matter movement into its historical and global context, and explains persuasively how it could shape our future. If you want to go beyond gestures and slogans and to the truth, this is the book to get you there."
—Russell Brand

"Professor Andrews takes the reader on a journey, and it isn't a comfortable one. Pick up this book and read it carefully. Once that is done, readers will be surely challenged, both in thinking and action."
—Dawn Butler, Labour MP for Brent Central

"Kehinde is a crucial voice, walking in a proud tradition of Black radical criticism and action."
—Akala

THE NEW AGE OF EMPIRE

THE NEW AGE OF EMPIRE

How Racism and Colonialism Still Rule the World

Kehinde Andrews

BOLD TYPE BOOKS

New York

Bold Type Books
116 East 16th Street, 8th Floor New York, NY 10003
www.boldtypebooks.org
@BoldTypeBooks

Printed in the United States of America

Originally published in February 2021 by Allen Lane / Penguin in Great Britain

First US Edition: March 2021

Published by Bold Type Books, an imprint of Perseus Books, LLC, a subsidiary of Hachette Book Group, Inc. Bold Type Books is a co-publishing venture of the Type Media Center and Perseus Books.

The Hachette Speakers Bureau provides a wide range of authors for speaking events. To find out more, go to www.hachettespeakersbureau.com or call (866) 376-6591.

The publisher is not responsible for websites (or their content) that are not owned by the publisher.

Set in Sabon LT Std

Print book interior design by Integra Software Services Pvt. Ltd, Pondicherry.

Library of Congress Control Number: 2020947282

ISBNs: 978-1-64503-692-0 (hardcover), 978-1-64503-690-6 (ebook)

LSC-C

Printing 1, 2021

For Assata, Kadiri, Omaje and Ajani

Contents

Foreword

Racism Is a Matter of Life and Death

Witnessing the police killing George Floyd in May 2020 was the straw that broke the camel's back, coming so close on the heels of the lynching of Ahmaud Arbery and state-sanctioned murder of Breonna Taylor. A wave of protest and rebellion was unleashed onto the streets in the United States, reminiscent of the hot summers of the 1960s, when racial tensions exploded and cities burned. Millions of people across the world joined the movement, protesting the experiences of racism that are all too common. Black Lives Matter came into vogue and was adopted by media companies, major corporations and even national governments. An optimism has been felt, that society is now ready to face up to the realities of racism. But rather than celebrating the new-found enthusiasm for talking about racism, we should approach with extreme caution. Unilever and L'Oréal loudly trumpeting that they were removing the word 'fair' from their skin-lightening products is the perfect metaphor for the meaningless change being offered in response to the moment. Rebranding a racist product is not a step in the right direction, it is a kick in the teeth to all those who suffer the impacts of White supremacy. We entirely miss the point if we believe that racism can be overcome with token gestures, commitment to diverse hiring practices or statements of brand solidarity. It is not mere coincidence that the latest wave of protests took hold during the lockdowns for the Covid-19 pandemic. The cynic in me will always be convinced that the lack of other news and places to go was a major factor in the mainstreaming of racial justice. We saw the exact same responses to the murders of Alton Sterling and Philando Castile in 2016 from Black communities across the globe, which somehow failed to grasp the attention of the ~~Whiter~~ wider public. But by the time the protests kicked off, the pandemic itself had already exposed the racism underpinning society.

Covid-19 tore through the West so completely that there were discussion about whether the virus was the 'great leveller' of conditions in society. When British Prime Minister Boris Johnson was hospitalized with the virus, we were reminded that no one was safe. Donald Trump, the most unlikely president of the United States, started taking the anti-malarial drug hydroxychloroquine, later proved to be ineffective, in an effort to protect himself. Facing the impending loss of tens of thousands of lives, nations went into unprecedented lockdowns, and even the most right-wing, neoliberal governments provided economic safety nets for families and business that would have won the approval of Marx. But the delusions of all being in it together, or that viruses do not discriminate, quickly fell apart as the evidence began to show that Covid-19 simply laid bare existing social inequalities. The poor, the vulnerable and ethnic minorities were all shown to be far more likely both to catch the virus and to die from it, in Britain and the United States. The surprise at these findings tells us just how little we understand racism, which is not about personal prejudice, but rather is a matter of life or death. Covid-19 targeted ethnic minorities, thanks in part to our heavy concentration in the inner cities; disproportionate rates of poverty; and over-representation in the ranks of key workers.[1] These same conditions mean that in both Britain and the United States minorities are more likely to suffer almost all chronic illnesses and conditions, including asthma from polluted neighbourhoods, diabetes and obesity because of food deserts, and the rest of the so-called 'comorbidities' that increase the risk of Covid-19 deaths. The result of these inequalities is statistics like Black men in England and Wales being up to four times more likely to die from Covid than their White 'counterparts'.[2] The brutal and uncomfortable truth is that racism takes years off a life and the ability to enjoy it. But the racial fault lines in the developed world are minor cracks compared to the devastating chasms of the value of life across the globe, and the response to Covid-19 reveals the logics of empire that continue to govern the world.

When the West was threatened with a staggering death toll, it was remarkable to see how quickly investment in and the development of a vaccine occurred. A vaccine within a year of the virus appearing would previously have been truly unprecedented but has been willed into existence. Malaria has existed for over a hundred years and claims the lives of 400,000 children annually, but there is still no reliable vaccination. If those children were dying in Europe, rather than Africa, the political will would have existed to find a cure. We saw the speed with which a vaccine was developed for Ebola once the disease left Africa and arrived in the United States. Even illnesses for which there are vaccines, that have been all but eradicated in the West, still claim lives in the Rest. Tuberculosis kills 1.5 million people annually. The primary logic underpinning the Western world order is that Black and Brown life is worth less.

The Covid-19 death toll will pale into insignificance compared to the loss of life annually due to poverty. Nine million people die around the world each year due to hunger. A child dies every ten seconds because they do not have access to food and water. These lives are almost exclusively Black and Brown. One of the main reasons that Covid-19 was not as devastating in Africa is because there are far fewer old people, because they die younger. In Nigeria, which has the largest population on the continent, only 2.5 per cent are over sixty-five, compared to over 15 per cent of the United States. In South Africa, one of the supposed success stories of the continent, more people die each year in the 30–34 age bracket than the 80–84 range.[3] Such a figure is unimaginable in the nation's former colonial ruler, Britain, where there are almost fifty times as many fatalities in the older age group. A virus that mainly kills old people was never going to be as much of a problem for a region whose life expectancy has just crept above sixty. Covid-19 brought the fear of life and death into the West that is the daily experience of billions around the globe.

For all the so-called aid dumped into the underdeveloped world, the problems of poverty remain entrenched. The majority of the progress of the much-lauded United Nations Development Goals, which sought to reduce world poverty by 2015, has been because of China's success. We still live in a world where a family of four, including children, farming tobacco leaves in Malawi for multinational corporation British American Tobacco can expect to earn £140 for a *whole year*.[4] These kinds of conditions are just as prevalent in the majority of the world, where people live in levels of poverty that we in the West can only imagine. We're so used to this reality that we forget it is no historical accident. There is a reason and a logic behind global poverty. Although you would never guess it from the analysis of the United Nations (UN), World Bank, International Monetary Fund (IMF) or Western governments, racism still governs the entire political and economic system. Truly addressing this inequality cannot be done without a transfer of wealth and resources that would be transformative to the West. As long as we delude ourselves with rebranding and tinkering at the margins we will never be able to address the issue of racism.

Introduction

The Logic of Empire

We urgently need to destroy the myth that the West was founded on the three great revolutions of science, industry and politics. Instead we need to trace how genocide, slavery and colonialism are the key foundation stones upon which the West was built. The legacies of each of these remain present today, shaping both wealth and inequality in the hierarchy of White supremacy. The Enlightenment was essential in providing the intellectual basis for Western imperialism, justifying White supremacy through scientific rationality. In other words, the West invented scientific theories to 'prove' the superiority of White people and acted as if they were truth. It is also in the Enlightenment that we can see the roots of the new age of empire, the universal application of colonial logic.

The breakdown of European countries' direct administration of their colonies made way for the United States to become the centre of empire. The UN, IMF, World Bank and World Trade Organization all play their part in administering colonial logic and neo-colonialism. In the new age of empire, the so-called independence of the colonies laid the groundwork for the emergence of an elite in the underdeveloped world who administer the system with brutal efficiency. Colonial logic has always incorporated the ladder of White supremacy, with some taking advantage of their superior positions in the racial hierarchy. We must consider how China has adopted Western approaches to enrich itself by plundering Africa for its resources. This feeding frenzy is not restricted to China but includes nations from across the underdeveloped world. If the former Third World cannot be relied on for solidarity the same is certainly true for the new so-called radicals of the Western left. Rather than

xiii

offering truly radical visions of the future we must consider how Whiteness pervades these movements that are continuations of racist progress. Following the 2008 financial crisis we are in a moment where the chickens are coming home to roost in the seat of empire. China is becoming a more efficient version of the West; the financial crisis further unleashed the forces of neoliberalism; and the children of empire are migrating into the old mother countries because of what the West has done to their homelands. The world looks different today than it did four hundred years ago but the same logic which were being embedded into the system then continues to shape the world in the image of White supremacy.

Before we delve into the book I want to draw attention to four aspects of the new age of empire that are not referred to by name again but are present throughout. The aim of the book is to build on these concepts and ideas in order to understand the logic of Western imperialism.

RACIAL CAPITALISM

In the new age of empire, the United States has become the centre of modern colonial power. The country likes to present itself as a victim of British colonialism, which freed itself from tyranny and now looks to do the same for the rest of the world. But this is a delusional fantasy. The United States is in fact the most extreme expression of the racist world order. Not only does the United States have its own history (and present) of colonial possession but its entire existence is based on the logic of Western empire. Built by enslaved Africans on land stolen through the genocide of the native inhabitants, the United States became a Garden of Eden for Europeans looking for wealth and opportunity. After the Second World War, the great European powers having exhausted themselves, the United States inherited its birthright as the leader of the new age. Now we have major institutions that manage globalization and maintain the logic of empire under the guise of 'development': the World Bank, International Monetary Fund and United Nations are all based in the US. This new regime is as effective as the European empires were at maintaining global White supremacy and colonial domination.

Racism is not only the glue that holds the system together but the material of which it is comprised. In his classic work *Black Marxism*, the late Cedric Robinson explained the nature of 'racial capitalism'.[1] On the domestic front we can see how these dynamics play out in the United States. Ava DuVernay's heartbreaking documentary *13th* brought a greater awareness of the extent of the racist problem of mass incarceration, which is so stark that one in every three African American boys born in 2001 is expected to spend time in prison.[2] The film takes its name from the Thirteenth Amendment of the US Constitution, which abolished slavery and 'involuntary servitude except as a punishment for crime whereof the party shall have been duly convicted'. After emancipation, African Americans were far more likely to be arrested and imprisoned, to be put to work in various forms of prison labour, and slavery was therefore maintained within the prison system. The fact that the state of servitude was maintained in the very amendment that ended slavery is a chilling reminder that there is no such thing as progress in racial capitalism.[3]

Michelle Alexander explained in *The New Jim Crow* how the 'war on drugs' following the crack epidemic took the problem of racialized incarceration and pumped it with steroids.[4] By racializing the drug crisis in the 1980s the United States government targeted Black communities, flooding neighbourhoods with police and incarcerating unprecedented numbers of people. This was a shared conservative and liberal project, with each side outdoing the other to seem 'tough on crime'. We should never forget that it was the so-called first 'Black president'[5] Bill Clinton who introduced the infamous Crime Bill in 1994 that was so pivotal in amplifying the impact of mass incarceration and which included three-strikes sentencing; flooding the streets with police officers; and a huge boost in funding for prisons. In the last forty years the United States prison population has ballooned by 500 per cent, almost exclusively by incarcerating predominantly African Americans for non-violent drug offences.[6] There is perhaps no better illustration of how racism works in the United States today, but also of how intertwined it is with capitalism. One of the drivers of mass incarceration is the privatization of the prison industry, which creates incentives to lock up historic numbers of people. Slave labour is also an economic incentive; there is no need to outsource if you can pay prisoners a few cents an hour for their toil. In 1994 the telephone company AT&T broke its workers' union action by laying off call centre workers and replacing them with prison labour. McDonald's, Macy's and Microsoft have all exploited prison labour, as well as countless more corporations across the United States. The US government has a Federal Prison Industries company, Unicor, producing a vast array of products including air filters and office supplies, that pays its workers between 23 cents and $1.15 an hour. Prior to 2011 its products were only sold within the public sector, but since that restriction was lifted Unicor has been selling goods and services with relish to private corporations. As well as the benefits of modern-day slave labour wages Unicor also touts that companies can stamp their products as 'Made in America' with pride. This is Third World wages for homemade produce, the embodiment of Trump's promise to 'Make America Great Again'. In the first half of 2018 alone Unicor had made $300 million worth of sales in goods and services across the public and private sectors.[7] Providing prison labour on the cheap is a form of corporate welfare: the state foots the bill for their incarceration and the companies make a profit off the lack of prisoner wages. Incarceration is expensive for the state – over $35,000 per prisoner per year in federal prison.[8] It seems like insanity for them to provide labour at this huge expense – until we remember that it fits perfectly into the logic of racial capitalism.

Veteran prison activist and scholar Ruth Wilson Gilmore explained how she first saw prisons a 'consequence of state failure' but had to learn they were actually a 'project of state-building'.[9] Billions of dollars spent on incarcerating a disproportionate number of Black people is not only corporate but social welfare. The major problem the United States has with its Black population is that they are now surplus to requirements. Slavery was the reason we were taken there in chains and that labour is no longer needed. During the era of the New Deal and national regeneration African American labour was needed once again to build the infrastructure and the promise of a new America. In the war years that followed African American labour was once again vital. But neoliberalism has cut public sector jobs and labour has either been outsourced to the underdeveloped world or mechanized. We are once again surplus to requirements, and it is no coincidence that mass incarceration coincided with the transition to Reaganomics. Neoliberalism is just a more extreme version of Western society, so racism was bound to be emphasized in an economic regime that steeply increases inequality. A major reason that the unrestrained individualism at the heart of the neoliberal project won at the ballot box is because there was no way that the body politic of the United States could survive if social welfare was dispensed to African Americans in the amounts needed, because the nation is so steeped in racism. A functioning welfare state, that at least dulled the harder edges of poverty, would probably cost the state less than mass incarceration in the long run. But we must remember that throughout the history of the West the state has been a mechanism for private enterprise to reap the benefits of racial exploitation. Various versions of the welfare state in different countries were but short-lived experiments in sharing the spoils of empire more fairly in the West. Racial capitalism makes the public happy for their tax dollars to be spent on caging the mostly Black and Brown, as corporations are then free to feast on modern-day American slave labour. And of course, all that profit will eventually trickle down to the average voter.

COLONIAL NOSTALGIA

'Make America Great Again' was a slogan built on colonial nostalgia, for a time when the logic of empire was much neater. Racial segregation; no civil rights legislation; respect for law and order; and unchecked United States dominance of the globe. Britain also experienced its own bout of yearning for the good old days. Once the nation had freed itself from the supposed shackles of the European Union in 2016, Whitehall officials fantasized about the prospect of the nation re-engaging with the world and establishing 'Empire 2.0'. The vote for Brexit was driven in large part by a colonial nostalgia to make Britain great again by returning to the days when Britannia ruled the waves. One of the main slogans from the Vote Leave campaign was 'Take Back Control' in order to return the nation to its former glories. Empire 2.0 was at least an acknowledgement that Britain was only ever 'great' when it ruled over an area so large that the sun never set on its dominions. Brexit, apparently, provided the opportunity to rekindle the country's abusive relationship with its former colonies.

Yearning for the glory days is not a new phenomenon in Britain, which has the Empire firmly embedded in its psyche. Almost 60 per cent of people believe that the Empire was 'something to be proud of', apparently either unaware of or uncaring about the centuries of slavery and brutality that Britain inflicted on other parts of the world.[10] Given this, it is unsurprising that the monarchy in general, and the Queen in particular, are extremely popular. Replete with crowns crusted in jewels stolen from various colonies, Her Majesty may be the premier symbol of Whiteness on this planet. Britain's former colonies remain part of the Commonwealth group of fifty-three nations, and the Queen is still the head of state of fifteen former colonies, a list that includes Jamaica, Australia, Canada and Belize. The royal family represents all the problems of elitism in Britain and privilege given to mediocre White people, with their only claim to their position being that they were born to rule. This is clearly not just a British problem, given the adulation the Queen receives from around the world. The popularity of Netflix's *The Crown* shows the cross-Atlantic appeal of imperial romance.

The idea of refashioning the Empire was problematic for an array of reasons. For a start, Britain lost the majority of its colonial possessions prior to joining the EU. In fact, the lack of an empire to exploit meant that Britain needed (and still needs) to be part of a large economic bloc to maintain its standing in the world. Many of its former colonies fought for their freedom and would not be happy to simply fall back under the thumb if Britain renewed its colonial ambitions. Not only that but India, at one point the jewel in the crown of the Empire, is now one of the fastest growing economies in the world, which Britain could not re-colonize even with force. The tables have turned so much that Indian company Tata took over what was British Steel in 2006. Whilst the 'Empire 2.0' episode did tell us just how much the colonial arrogance of the British ruling class remains, the Empire is never coming back, whatever the dreams of Whitehall officials.

The emergence of nations like India as leading world powers has bolstered the narrative that the West is in decline. The G20 forum for international economic cooperation, made up of the most apparently influential countries in the world, now includes South Korea, Japan, India, Indonesia, South Africa, Brazil, Argentina, Saudi Arabia and Turkey. Summit pictures are more reminiscent of a United Colours of Benneton advert than the imagery from the 1884–5 Berlin Conference, where European nations carved up Africa between them. China's rise in particular has shaken the West's confidence in itself and its prospects for continued global domination. This changing global arithmetic has led to many a think piece on the so-called decline of the West. In many ways Trump's election was driven by this desire to see White America at the forefront of global politics again, with his 'Make America Great Again' slogan. On the campaign trail Trump railed against globalization and in office has sparked trade wars with China to try and recapture the lost power of the United States. Running through all of this is the existential dread that the West has lost the battle for power, and that the underdeveloped world is leading the path into the future. But don't believe the hype. China's rapid economic development has been achieved in large part by exploiting their own poor and looting Africa in a disturbingly European fashion. Diversifying those dining on the spoils of empire does not change the menu and there is nothing new about some Black and Brown people taking advantage of a framework designed to exploit them. In other words, a handful of rich Nigerian students studying at Oxford does not change the system of oppression. Conditions in the underdeveloped world today are marked by the kind of poverty that those of us in the West could not imagine. To pretend we have moved into a post-racial dream is to ensure that the majority of Black and Brown people of the world continue to experience the Western nightmare.

So-called independence in the former colonies has provided for a privileged few to reap financial rewards from access to a slice of the Western imperial pie. A post-colonial elite have amassed wealth well beyond the dreams of even those doing relatively well in the West. There is also a growing middle class in the underdeveloped world who have some of the same opportunities as those in the West to spend money buying unneeded commodities. But their access and wealth are based on exploiting the same system that impoverishes the vast majority of those in the world who are Black and Brown. As I will discuss at length in Chapter 6, the multitude of 'dark mankind'[11] are not a homogenous mass but a varied group of people, many of whom have few qualms about using the hierarchical ladder of global White supremacy to pull themselves up on the back of those less fortunate.

All the old inequalities were simply built into the supposedly progressive system of international trade and law, ensuring that the West remained in an exploitative relationship to the former colonies. The new age of empire depends on corporations, unfair trade practices and puppet governments in the underdeveloped world, all of whom are perfectly happy to take their cut from selling off their population's assets and labour. The inclusion of the elite from the underdeveloped world has allowed for the mirage of progress in the new operating system. Institutions like the UN and the G20 even offer seats at the tables of power but, as Malcolm X warned us, 'sitting at the table doesn't make you a diner, unless you eat some of what's on that plate'.[12] If these leaders are meant to be representing their people then the question is not whether they are getting a taste of the delicacies of the West but whether their nations are being nourished. The stark reality is that the hierarchy of White supremacy is alive and well, with the White West at the head of the table and Africa lucky if it gets any scraps from the floor. Racism frames life in the new age of empire just as fundamentally as it did during the eras of slavery and direct colonization.

RACIAL PATRIARCHY

'Thinking intersectionally' means recognizing that there is no way to fully understand society without appreciating the interlocking oppressions that shape inequality. We must however recognize the roots of the concept in Critical Race Theory, Black Feminism and mobilizations such as the Combahee River Collective. It was by viewing the world from the standpoint of Black women that intersectionality was born, highlighting the nature of inequality. Unlike in some of the co-opted takes on intersectionality (which has been reduced to a buzzword in many academic and policy circles), it is impossible, in any genuine understanding, to remove racism from how we think intersectionally. A central thesis of this book is that White supremacy, and therefore anti-Blackness, is the fundamental basis of the political and economic system and therefore infects all interactions, institutions and ideas. My aim is to trace how White supremacy has been maintained and plays out in the various updates to Western empire. Discussions of genocide, slavery, colonialism, unfair trade practices and everything else we will consider all echo across the intersections of race, gender, class and other social divisions. But I have not generally touched the rich vein of vital work exploring the detailed intersections of racism and interlocking oppressions. If we see racism as the intersection then this book explores the junction but has not traced the roads that lead to it.[13] Scholars such as Kimberlé Crenshaw, Keeanga-Yamahtta Taylor, Patricia Hill Collins, Mikki Kendall and many other Black feminists have travelled these arteries and produced exceptional insights into the intersectional dimensions of oppression.[14]

It is essential to understand how fundamental patriarchy is to shaping the modern world. Academics have tended to locate class as the primary prism through which to understand society. But class relations in capitalism are produced out of the colonial logic of Western imperialism. Industrial labour is only possible because of the wealth generated from colonial exploitation. Without genocide, slavery and colonialism there is neither the wealth nor the resources for the supposedly revolutionary proletarian toiling in the European factory to come into existence. Therefore, Marx's hero of history is in fact a product of racism. Social classes existed before the dawn of the new age but were fundamentally transformed by the new system. But the patriarchy is different. It was not created by Western imperialism, although empire was propagated through it, via figures like the great male explorers Christopher Columbus and Vasco da Gama, who braved the new worlds and conquered the savages. Violence was the key ingredient in establishing Western empire, and sexual violence against women was a universal tool.

The foot soldiers of empire, colonial leaders and slave owners, all presided over patriarchal households where women were relegated to the domestic realm and unable to contribute fully to public life. White men were deemed to be at the top of the food chain of human beings while women were thought to be incapable of rationality because of their troublesome biology. So deeply ingrained were these ideas that Black men in the United States were allowed to vote (at least in theory) decades before the privilege was extended to White women. Gendered inequality remains a hallmark of empire, deeply seated in the West and around the globe.

The inspiration for this book came from a short video that I made for the *Guardian* called 'The West Is Built on Racism', which went viral. One of the responses to that was a tweet exclaiming that it was constructed on 'patriarchy too'. As fundamental as patriarchy is to the enactment of empire, this is not strictly true. The West is practised through patriarchy but is built on White supremacy. It is the expansion into the Americas and the exploitation of Black and Brown bodies and resources that enabled the West to come into being. I do not want to make the same mistake as Marx here in reducing other forms of oppression to the margins. To say that Western imperialism is practised through patriarchy does not diminish it, rather the opposite. Just as communism does not necessarily lead to the end of racism, overthrowing Western imperialism does not automatically dispense with patriarchy. It is perfectly possible to imagine a revolutionary future free from the West but governed by patriarchy. Equally important is the truth that patriarchy could potentially be abolished in a new iteration of Western imperialism, however unlikely that is.

Racial patriarchy lies at the heart of the new age of empire and tracing its practice is utterly essential. To do so means understanding that gender plays out at the intersection with racism in complex ways. For instance, whilst there is no doubt that women have experienced, and continue to experience, gendered oppression it is also true that those who are White accrue the benefits of colonial logic. Like the working classes in the West, women here are also spared the conditions of the underdeveloped world. For all the exclusions of women in the middle and ruling classes, they remain privileged compared to those poorer than them. While we remember the brave male pioneers of genocide, slavery and colonialism it was Queen Isabella of Spain who gave the green light to this new world 'discovery' and Queen Elizabeth I who launched Britain's industrial involvement in the slave trade when she assented to John Hawkins' mission on the slave ship *Jesus*. In the

Jim Crow South thousands of Black people were lynched by mobs of predominantly White men. Not only were many White women happy to join in the festivities around the strange fruit hanging from the poplar trees but their false accusations of rape and sexual misconduct against Black men often triggered the lynching in the first place. In the infamous murder of Emmett Till – a fourteen-year-old boy – Carolyn Bryant Donham had the 'decency' (or rather, the audacity) six decades later to admit she had made up her allegations against him.[15] Ida B. Wells, the African American anti-lynching activist, found support from White feminists of her day entirely absent because they did not view the murder of predominantly Black men as a feminist issue.[16] The failure to see how the issue of lynching was a result of racial patriarchy, and that the so-called 'protection' of White women was a central feature of anti-Black racism, was a major failing of White feminism at the time.[17]

If thousands of Black men are being lynched then the impact will inevitably be felt by Black women, who lose their partners, brothers, family and friends. An assault aimed disproportionately at Black men is therefore an attack on Black women, and vice versa. We can see the same process at work today with mass incarceration and the incredible levels of state violence that Black men are subject to. It is estimated that there are 1.5 million fewer Black men in the United States than there should be due to these effects. In Ferguson, the problem is so acute that there are 40 per cent fewer Black men than women.[18] Given this disparity we really should not be surprised that single parenthood rates are higher in African American communities, the result being that Black women with children are far more likely to live in poverty and to be evicted. This is not to mention the police violence and surveillance that invades communities in order to maintain the sheer number of African Americans in prison or on probation. Black women are also caught up in the same processes, and are far more likely to be arrested, jailed and killed than their White counterparts. In the UK we see exactly the same processes playing out, with Black men far more likely to be arrested and far less likely to be employed than their White counterparts. One of the results of this is a mirroring of higher rates of single parent households and poverty for Black women.

The assault on Black men is a result of the same racial patriarchy that subjugates Black women. Kimberlé Crenshaw explains that 'Black men are feared, Black women are despised.'[19] Europeans enslaved Africans because they believed we were subhuman, more beast than person. Black men were seen to be hypermasculine, with no intellect but instead full of brute force and dangerous sexual energy. In plantation societies like Haiti, around two-thirds of the enslaved were men, and 80 per cent of the Africans enslaved by the British were male, because the nature of the labour required the savage brute.[20] Deeply woven into these racist ideas was the brute sexual force of the beast, something that had to be restrained after emancipation. Black men were, and remain, very publicly assaulted. Beaten, whipped, lynched, and gunned down by police. Black women were also subject to all these crimes, but the primary mode of their oppression has been behind closed doors. They have been subjected to sexual violence, either in the house on the plantation or at the hands of the police in the present day. They have lived with the impact of poverty, evictions and steep health inequalities. As well as conforming to the public/private sphere split in terms of how we are oppressed, racial patriarchy also changes traditional expectations for men and women.

Sexual violence was not reserved for women, but was also meted out to enslaved African men as away to pacify and control them on the plantation. Rape and castration were common punishments used to control the savage beast. The enslaved were prevented from marrying and families were subject to being sold at the whim of their 'owners'. During slavery the nuclear family was essentially legislated against. After emancipation the idea of the male breadwinner was difficult to maintain due to high male unemployment, a process that has been exacerbated with mass incarceration. The right, in both Europe and the United States, criticizes Black communities for lacking the supposedly 'correct' familial structure, when it is racial patriarchy that makes the supposed ideal more elusive.

In Britain, one of the reasons that Black women were encouraged to emigrate from the Caribbean to work as nurses was so that White women could be put back into the home after their taste of work during the War. While White feminism was bemoaning the role of the housewife, Black women were being conscripted into the labour force. There was nothing novel about this. Women were incorporated into plantation society in order to put them to work. Ideas about gender were transformed when intersecting with race and were not simply re-enacted on different bodies.

Intersectionality is not about adding up various oppressions, but rather accounting for the interplay of race, gender, class and other divisions.[21] There have been attempts to treat an analysis of racism in intersectionality as optional but this completely undermines the concept.[22] Racism is always there, an ever-present factor shaping the way we relate to each other and society. There is no way to understand how patriarchy plays out for Black, White or Brown women without considering the colonial logic of Western imperialism. For instance, rape was permissible on the plantations because Black women were seen as subhuman, not only the property of the master but chattels who had no rights that needed to be respected. White women were also subject to rape, but there really is no comparison to the systemic sexual violence used against the enslaved. Thomas Thistlewood, for example, was a Brit who worked his way up the slavery system in Jamaica, starting as an overseer in 1750 and eventually owning his own plantation. He is notable only because he kept a diary of his barbarous exploits that remains a testimony to the horrors of slavery. He kept a log of the 3,852 sexual 'encounters' he had in his sorry life, the majority of those being with enslaved Africans.[23] The fact that there appears to be debate as to whether these were consensual tells us just how poor understandings of both race and gender are in society. Thistlewood documented his subjection of numerous women to repeated rapes, none of which were considered crimes because of their racial status as slaves. Women do not escape colonial logic because of their gender. The same is true of White women, who benefit from Western imperialism.

The liberalization of gender roles in the West is built on the same benefits from empire as those which accrued to the working classes. Gendered inequalities in the underdeveloped world are not a result of backward attitudes that can be undone with some Western education but are rooted in the political and economic system. For instance, when child mortality is high there is a need to have large families because the chances are some of the children will not survive. The role of women then becomes largely reproductive, delivering as many children as possible to ensure that the family can continue. Children are also necessary as labourers because pay and conditions are so poor. When women's roles are seen as wholly reproductive, this intensifies a public–private dichotomy where the man is seen as the breadwinner, the earner. It should be no surprise then that boys are more valuable in such societies because they can work rather than reproduce. The liberalization of gender roles in the West was dependent on improving child mortality rates because this meant that women could afford to have fewer children, safe in the knowledge they would likely survive to adulthood. In the underdeveloped world, where we have seen child mortality rates decrease in recent decades, there has also been a decrease in the number of children per woman, reducing the maternity imperative. If current trends continue, with improved access to health, we will reach 'peak child' in 2057 when the average number of children per woman globally will be two (down from over five in 1950), meaning that the population will not continue to grow exponentially.[24] It is because of the riches bestowed on the West from imperialism that women's equality is at an advanced stage.

We have not even mentioned how the riches stolen from the underdeveloped world allow for higher wages, the welfare state and therefore no need for child labourers to make ends meet. Contrary to popular belief, girls not being able to go to school in the underdeveloped world is not the same problem as the gender pay gap, thanks to the differing ways they experience womanhood, due to the intersection of race and gender. Women in the West are simply battling for equality of access to the resources leached from the underdeveloped world, the exploitation of which is a direct cause of why girls around the globe have poorer access to schooling.

The New Age of Empire focuses on tracing the colonial logic of the West and explores how Whiteness is embedded into the political and economic system. In doing so I have not specifically engaged in how the application of empire is gendered. Tracing the histories and legacies of racial patriarchy is central to a complete understanding of Western imperialism, but such a task would require at least another book, and more likely several. It is my hope that this book can be useful for taking that vital work forward.

POST-RACIALISM

If the greatest trick the devil pulled was convincing the world he does not exist, then the proudest achievement of Western imperialism is the delusion that we have moved beyond racism, that we are in a post-racial society. We are assured that the real people losing out are not minorities, or those in the underdeveloped world, but White people who are being left behind by a changing world. It is multiculturalism, immigration and globalization that are all conspiring to hold White people down. In this climate the right have even managed to hijack the legacy of Martin Luther King.

On the forty-seventh anniversary of the infamous 'I have a dream' speech Glenn Beck, a quasi-fascist talk radio host who had previously declared Obama 'a racist who hates White culture', took thousands of mostly White Tea Party supporters to the steps of the Lincoln Memorial, invoking King's famous speech.[25] He even brought along one of King's nieces, Alveda King, to burnish his post-racial credentials. The march was in order to 'restore the honor' of the US by turning to God and also to raise money for a charity providing finance to the children of special forces killed in action. Alveda King's address urged the audience to 'focus not on elections or on political causes but on honor, on character . . . not the color of our skin', as well as supporting Beck's vision that 'there is one human race . . . we are not here to divide. I'm about unity.' She really twisted the post-racial knife when she announced the reason she was speaking was to 'honor' her uncle.[26] Malcolm X denounced the 1963 March on Washington as a 'farce', a 'circus with clowns and all', due to its integrationist 'love thy enemy' approach.[27] After this debacle he is probably teasing a furious King with taunts of 'I told you so.'

King's speech must be one of the most abused political statements of all time. A militant campaigner for racial justice who was widely unpopular when he died, has been transformed into the cuddly uncle

(Tom) of the nation, used to ease the conscience of White America. The mechanism for this whitewashing of King is primarily the most famous soundbite from his dream that his 'four little children will one day live in a nation where they will not be judged by the color of their skin but by the content of their character'.[28] Rather than viewing this comment in the context of trying to solve racial inequality, it has been turned on its head to avoid addressing the very issues that King spent his life fighting against.

The yearnings for the good old days of empire or Jim Crow could be used to indicate that there has been a fundamental shift, that we actually are in a post-racial moment thanks to all the progress that has been made over the last fifty years. Nothing could be further from the truth. Critical Race Theory (CRT) emerged in the United States in the late eighties precisely because those involved in key civil rights reforms realized just how limited they were.[29] So successful was the civil rights movement that the United States now has affirmative action, something unimaginable in Britain. But for all the successes, and the likes of Jay-Z having too much money and too little sense to work with the NFL, the nation remains a beacon of racial inequality. Segregation is more of a problem today than after the landmark Brown vs Board of Education decision; poverty is still a blight on Black communities; the police continue to gun down the Black population; and there are new problems like mass incarceration that have made apartheid-era South Africa the correct analogy for the US race problem.[30] Britain is no better, with stark racial inequalities in every area of social life; police brutality and abuse of power; steep economic differences; health inequalities; and unemployment.[31] If you want one statistic to tell you the scale of racial injustice in Britain then the fact that over half of the juvenile prison population is from an ethnic minority should send shudders down your spine.[32] It is not just that we are making no strides towards freedom but as Derrick Bell, one of the founders of CRT explained, 'what we designate as "racial progress" is not a solution to that problem. It is a regeneration of the problem in a particularly perverse form.'[33] By creating enough opportunity for a Black middle class, and dare I say Black professors, to exist we have given fuel to the lie that everyone can make it if they would only just try hard enough and ignore the chips on their shoulders. This of course is utter nonsense for those of us discriminated against in the West and an even more ludicrous suggestion if applied to the underdeveloped world. The purpose of this book is to put the final nail in the coffin of the post-racial narrative, illustrating just how fundamental the racist logic of empire remains in shaping the world.

I

I'm White, Therefore I Am

'Of course the Enlightenment was racist,' I responded to Emily Maitlis on the BBC television show *Newsnight*, when asked about the intellectual movement that underpins Western society. It was 2017 and I was debating the School of Oriental and African Studies (SOAS) student union's campaign demanding that 'the majority of philosophers' taught on their courses should be from Africa and Asia. Rather than questioning why the intellectual production of a narrow parade of dead White men was ever deemed a suitable basis of knowledge to understand the regions, the students' mild demands caused an uproar in sections of the British media and the university establishment.[1] The head of philosophy at SOAS called the demands 'rather ridiculous'[2] and a slew of right-wing commentators lined up to decry the 'crackpot' head of the union and the generation of 'snowflake students' who were too wrapped up in their security blankets of political correctness to understand the real world.[3] The backlash against the SOAS movement was part of a wider reaction to the student-led movements that asked 'Why is my curriculum White?' and campaigned to 'decolonize the university'.[4] As one of the founders of the first Black Studies degree in Europe I was there to give a counterpoint to the tired Eurocentric dogma that cherishes the Enlightenment as though it were holy.

The Enlightenment of the seventeenth and eighteenth centuries emerged from Western Europe and the United States and is the intellectual basis of the modern world. Condemning the sacred foundations of Western knowledge as racist did not go down well with either the establishment or a large segment of the Twitter commentariat, but I wasn't exaggerating for greater impact. My words were simply an honest and indisputable assessment of the intellectual movement. In his criticism of the SOAS students, my adversary in the debate Sir Anthony Seldon, vice-chancellor of the University of Buckingham and author of numerous biographies of British prime ministers, accidentally hit the nail on the head. I couldn't have put it better myself – he said that 'we need to understand the world as it was and not to rewrite history as some might like it to have been.'[5] If we were to do this then we would understand the Enlightenment as the racist intellectual project it was, and how culpable the ideas it produced are in creating the unjust world we inhabit.

These debates are not simply academic. The world can only ever be as equal as the knowledge it is built upon. The Enlightenment emerged at a time when Europe had laid waste to much of the world through genocide and slavery and was asserting its dominance through colonial expansion. The arrogance of its thinkers was only possible due to the violence of the first version of Western empire. The 'great thinkers' found themselves on top of the world as a result and theorized about their apparent supremacy. One of their purposes was to provide the justification for the genocide, slavery and colonialism that were utterly indispensable to Western progress. The Enlightenment was pivotal in the shift into the new age of empire: it provided the universalist, supposedly rational and scientific framework of knowledge that maintained colonial logic. It is heresy to question the dead White men because their bodies of work lie at the foundation of the current unjust social order. To push them aside would lead to the system crashing down. Understanding how the Enlightenment and racism cannot be separated is the first step in truly appreciating that colonial logic still governs the world today.

YOU KANT BE SERIOUS

In the history of European thought we are presented with all the positive aspects of the sainted philosophers and none of the negative. There is perhaps no better example of this Whitewashing of the record than Immanuel Kant. I never realized how cherished an icon Kant was until I pointed out he was racist on television. Apparently, criticizing

Kant is the academic equivalent of questioning the morality of Jesus. His *Critique of Pure Reason* is offered not only as the basis for anti-racism but as the atonement for the sins of all mankind. I was surprised to find out that so many held the man and his work so dear, or that they had even read it. What is abundantly clear is that few have read Kant's extensive writing on race, where his racism is simply a matter of historical fact.

Even a scant review of his work would reveal Kant as a violent and ugly racist who saw 'humanity at its greatest perfection in the race of the Whites'. Kant's writing career spanned the second half of the eighteenth century, after the genocide of the natives in the Americas and during the peak of the transatlantic slave trade. He generously acknowledged that 'the yellow [Asian] Indians do have a meagre talent' but asserted that the 'Negroes are far below them and at the lowest point are a part of the American peoples'.[6] His belief that the 'Negro' was 'lazy, indolent and dawdling'[7] was not just used to disparage Black people but also to justify enslavement. Kant even used his pseudo-scientific approach to advise the most efficient way to beat the 'indolent' Negroes to get them to be productive labourers. He explained that it was best to

> use a split bamboo cane instead of a whip, so that the Negro will suffer a great deal of pains (because of the Negro's thick skin, he would not be racked with sufficient agonies through a whip) but without dying . . . the blood needs to find a way out of the Negro's thick skin to avoid festering.[8]

Prior to writing this book I had always known that the idea you can separate Kant's racism from his intellectual output is nonsense, but to see it so clearly illustrated in his own words is shocking. The devil really is in the detail. Not only did he use his 'intellect' to devise ways to inflict torture on Africans, his work was some of the most influential in creating the modern idea of so-called races and White supremacy.[9]

He outlined four different races based on biology and climate: White; the Negro; the Hun (Mongol or Kalmuck); and the Hindu or Hindustani.[10] He detested Native Americans the most but thought they were a 'Hunnish race . . . not yet fully acclimated'.[11] For Kant, geography was the key determining factor in racial categorizations. He argued that all the 'inhabitants of the hottest zones are, without exceptions, idle'.[12] These declarations about the different races were not separate from his moral philosophy but an integral part of it. For Kant, through 'moral geography' it was possible to grasp the true nature of what it meant to be human. His pursuit was to find an 'inner nature upon which to found moral existence'.[13] But, for him, this was not possible without the exterior of moral geography, because he thought the climate shaped the extent to which the different races possessed the talents necessary for moral development. Importantly, these climates produce biological adaptions that become fixed as different races even if people move to other parts of the world.

Kant's explanation of how 'blackness' emerges is the perfect example of his racial logic:

> The growth of the spongy parts of the body had to increase in a hot and humid climate. This growth produced a thick, turned up nose and thick, fatty lips. The skin had to be oily, not only to lessen the too heavy perspiration, but also to ward off the harmful absorption of the foul, humid air. The profusion of iron particles, which are otherwise found in the blood of every human being, and, in this case, are precipitated in the net-shaped substance through the evaporation of the phosphoric acid (which explains why all Negroes stink), is the cause of the blackness that shines through the epidermis.[14]

These supposed biological differences are used to explain why Black people are incapable of being fully and rationally human. In terms of attempting to understand reason and moral existence, Kant writes off those who are not White. We've already discounted 'Negroes', and remember he saw Native Americans as even less useful. Of the 'Hindus' Kant argued that they can be 'cultivated to the highest degree but only in the arts and not in the sciences. They never achieve the level of abstract concepts.'[15] It is for this reason that Kant focused his discovery of the state of rational human nature in Europe; he firmly believed that 'the White race possess *all* the motivating forces and talents *in itself*; therefore we must examine it more closely.'[16] If ever you need a quote that explains the Eurocentric curriculum you will not find a better one. We have only covered a few of Kant's pronouncements on race but already it is abundantly clear that they are not just racist, but absurd.

In order to defend his racial theory of climate Kant produced theories about the blood of 'Negroes'. He also believed that 'Hindus' had a lower body temperature and therefore cold hands and that the 'long slitty, half closed eyes' of the 'Hun race' came from living in the snow and then migrating to East Asia.[17] His declarations about the races were supposedly based on evidence but he never collected any of this first-hand and relied on the accounts of Europeans who actually ventured out to meet the savages. One of the most dishonest defences of Kant that is also used to defend the rest of the racist Enlightenment thinkers is when we are told that the 'evidence available' to him at the time supported his racist theories.[18] This is vitally important because it maintains the delusion that science is based on logic and reason. But as the evidence changes, so does the science, and therefore Kant was just a hostage to his time. We see this argument even today in the idea that advances in genetic science are all we need to undo racism; we have the proof that race is not real so we can all move on.[19] But we should reject this notion out of hand. There was plenty of 'evidence available' that directly contradicted Kant's ideas, he just chose to select the accounts that suited his twisted agenda. Towards the end of his career in 1788 he wrote an article where he specifically chose to dismiss the claims of abolitionist James Ramsay, who had spent time with those of African descent and could testify to our humanity, and elevated the accounts of the pro-slavery James Tobin, who stressed our laziness and stupidity.[20] What made this even more remarkable is that Kant's work is part of his response to a challenge from the anthropologist Georg Forster, who had first-hand experience of the supposed savages and criticized Kant for his use of colonial stereotypes.[21] Forster was interested in seeing whether Kant's theories could offer a notion of humanity to the enslaved, and Kant responded by advancing pro-slavery arguments.[22]

His racial philosophy was not based on evidence, but a particular – racist – view of the world, which produced an absurd racial theory. But it gets worse: at times Kant's ideas cross the threshold into the ludicrous. His racial theory was so universal that he theorized it reached 'as far as into space'. He genuinely supposed that 'the intelligence of creatures on different planets depends on the distance of the planet from the centre of gravity: the closer the planet is to the sun, the mentally lazier its inhabitants.'[23] Kant's pronouncements are so wrong-headed and bizarre that it should make us question his entire intellectual output. Trying to salvage the *Critique of Pure Reason* from the wreckage of his racial theory is like looking for coherent moral philosophy on a far-right conspiracy YouTube channel.

Nevertheless, Kant still has an array of defenders who contort themselves into various untenable positions to stand by their man. The most obvious example of doublespeak I came across was a defence in an academic work of his racial theory on the grounds that it 'is not racist simply because it claims that there are superior and inferior races'. Apparently, a theory is only racist if it relies on a 'culpable neglect of evidence . . . or expresses or encourages contempt or disregard for people because of the race they are alleged to belong to'.[24] The fact that Kant's theory of race is guilty of both of these is lost on the authors. Most defenders of Kant avoid trying to make excuses for his obviously racist theory and focus on his other works, essentially arguing that his universalist moral philosophy eventually makes him an outspoken critic of slavery and colonialism.

It is certainly true that in his latest writings Kant condemns colonization. In the *Groundwork of the Metaphysics of Morals* he says that 'even if a "superior" society encounters "savages" it is not justified in settling on their land, even with the motivation of spreading civilization.'[25] But to pretend this makes him some kind of anti-racist takes a special kind of short-sightedness. Kant came to the realization that non-Europeans have rights that should be respected, but this is perfectly compatible with his racial theory. In fact, as late as 1788, just a few years before the *Metaphysics of Morals*, he reaffirms that the 'Negro . . . holds the lowest of all remaining levels by which we have designated the different races'.[26] These two positions are in no way contradictory; it is entirely possible to believe that apes should have dominion over their habitat and be free from the gun of the poacher. It is also reminiscent of the uncomfortable reality that, during the Victorian period in Britain, black-and-white minstrel shows were a central part of the British abolitionist movement. 'White men in blackface delivered anti-racist speeches' from the stage in performances that criticized slavery whilst embracing the stereotypes that made it possible. If even avowed abolitionists upheld racial hierarchies, this demonstrates just how inescapable they were, and remain, to understanding the world.[27]

Kant is just one philosopher, but he is an important starting point because his work has all the ingredients that are so potent in the regimes of knowledge that underpin and maintain the current unjust social order. His concept of so-called universal human rights also laid the foundation for the United Nations and the European Union. He is so vigorously defended because he is one of the most important architects of the new age of empire.

THE ENLIGHTENMENT AS WHITE IDENTITY POLITICS

It is no coincidence that the architects of the Enlightenment were White men who had very exclusive views about race, class and gender. In the effort to deflect from the movement's inherent problems there has been a move away from seeing the Enlightenment as a unified whole. We are directed to the English, Scottish, French and American versions and the debates within and between them.[28] But the West is founded on collusion beyond national borders while pretending to maintain nationalist sovereignty. Intellectual production is certainly no exception, and while there has obviously been plenty of quite heated debate, there is consensus on the key issues. No concept is more important to the West than race, so it is no surprise that on the central premises the dead White men who represent the foundation stones of knowledge sang from the same sordid hymn sheet.

Racial science arose as a discipline to explore the superiority of the White race, and it is telling that basically all the key Enlightenment thinkers were architects of its intellectual framework. Voltaire (in France) believed that 'none but the blind can doubt that the Whites, the Negroes, the Albinoes [sic], the Hottentots, the Laplanders, the Chinese, the Americans, are races entirely different.'[29] Hegel (in Germany) thought that 'Negroes are to be regarded as a race of children who remain immersed in their state of naïveté. They are sold and let themselves be sold without any reflection on the rights or wrongs of the matter.'[30] John Locke (in seventeenth-century England) believed that 'Negroes' were the product of African women sleeping with apes and therefore that we were subhuman.[31] David Hume (in Scotland) was 'apt to suspect the negroes and in general all the other species of men (for there are four or five different kinds) to be naturally inferior to the Whites'.[32] One of the architects of the Greatest Democracy on Earth™, Thomas Jefferson (in the United States) believed that Black people 'whether originally a distinct race, or made distinct by time and circumstances, are inferior to the Whites in the endowments of both mind and body'.[33] All agreed that race was real and defined in biology that determined the extent to which a people could claim full humanity. The racial hierarchy that the Enlightenment produced is best summed up by the botanist Linnaeus' (who has a university in Sweden named after him) classification of the human species:

> *Europaeus albus*: ingenious, white, sanguine, governed by law; *Americanus rubescus*: happy with his lot, liberty loving, tanned and irascible, governed by custom; *Asiaticus luridus*: yellow, melancholy, governed by opinion; *Afer niger*: crafty, lazy, careless, black, governed by the arbitrary will of the master.[34]

White in this metric is right and even Johann von Herder, who was first Kant's student and later his rival, and is often 'either quoted . . . in defence of the struggle against racialism or ignored',[35] presented the same beliefs (albeit more poetically):

> the perfect human form found a site on the coast of the Mediterranean, where it was capable of uniting with the intellect, and displaying all the charms of terrestrial and celestial beauty to the mind, as well as to the eye . . . Here figures were conceived and executed, which no admirer of Circassian beauty, no Indian or Cashmirian artist, could have invented. The human form ascended Olympus, and clothed itself in divine beauty.[36]

Certainly there were differences in how each of these esteemed scholars understood what exactly race was. Whether or not the different races were from the same original source was the first dispute. Polygenists believed that there was more than one original man and that the races were completely distinct, whereas monogenists believed there to be one original source of humanity, but that White people represented the most developed, advanced incarnation of man. Voltaire and Hume were polygenists, who could not conceive of the lesser races having any relation to the perfection of Whiteness. The word *mulatto* was applied to those of mixed heritage because scholars such as Voltaire believed they were a 'bastard race' produced by the same type of inter-species breeding as the mule, the offspring of a horse and a donkey.[37] In perhaps the most obvious example of these great intellectuals ignoring all available evidence, Voltaire was among a number of his contemporaries who argued that just like mules, 'mulattoes' were infertile because they were the combination of two different species.

Whilst the monogenists believed that all races were part of a broader human family, this did not mean that their concepts were any less racist. Georges-Louis Leclerc, Comte de Buffon, one of the most notorious racial theorists, believed in the single human family and that 'if Africans were imported to Europe, their colour would gradually change and become "perhaps as White as the native" of Europe.'[38] Later, this idea was picked up by the monogenist-in-chief, Charles Darwin, who incorporated it into his theory of evolution. To support this hypothesis Darwin was not the first to cite the 'considerable evidence showing that in the Southern states the house-slaves of the third generation present a markedly different appearance from the field slaves'.[39] Apparently these theorists overlooked the rape of the enslaved by slave-masters as a far more logical explanation for the successively lighter skin tones. This is surprising not only because it is fairly obvious, but because it would have put a nail in the coffin of the polygenist notion that 'mulattoes' could not breed. But that is precisely the point: whichever side of the debate these so-called intellectuals fell on, they were jointly contributing to the same cause. Buffon believed in shared descent and also that slavery was justified on the grounds that 'Negroes' were 'so naturally lazy' that they were in a 'violent state' if not subject to forced labour.[40] Darwin's theory of evolution was the perfect, supposedly scientific scheme to prove the superiority of Whites. Man evolved from apes, and Africans, with their differently shaped bodies and skulls, were evidence of the chain of human

9

progression. The search for the so-called missing link between man and ape was in reality a discussion of which African people most closely resembled monkeys. Distinct races observed from supposedly scientific evidence are a key feature of White supremacy. These ideas permeate the Enlightenment and bled into the Eugenics movement that gave the theoretical basis for the Holocaust. There is a reason that Adolf Eichmann, who was executed for crimes against humanity, 'appealed to Kant in justifying his behaviour'.[41]

Racial science was not some marginal concern at the corners of European philosophy, it was an integral component of its intellectual framework. See how coldly Darwin justifies the imperial conquest by the West that cost the lives of tens of millions:

> When civilized nations come into contact with barbarians the struggle is short . . . New diseases and vices are highly destructive; and it appears that in every nation a new disease causes much death, until those who are most susceptible to its destructive influence are gradually weeded out; and so it may be with the evil effects from spirituous liquors, as well as with the unconquerably strong taste for them shown by so many savages.[42]

Darwin was simply building off the established intellectual order. Hegel had already declared the natives of the Americas a 'vanishing, feeble race', and asserted that 'when brought into contact with brandy and guns these savages become extinct'.[43] Whilst John Stuart Mill had proclaimed that 'despotism is a legitimate mode of government in dealing with barbarians, provided the end be their improvement'.[44]

To think rationally is what separates man from beast, and the whole basis of the Enlightenment is that rational thought is the sole possession of the White man. Even the idea of bringing light to the world – that Europe is the beacon to shine its torch on the dark and savage corners of the globe – is instructive. For, whatever their disagreements, the dead White men were unified in the belief that Europe was the foundation through which knowledge was spread. As Herder explained, 'The *Negro* has invented nothing for the *European* . . . From the region of well-formed people we have derived our religion, our arts, our sciences, and the whole frame of our cultivation and humanity.'[45] This is nothing short of White identity politics, racist propaganda to boost the collective self-esteem of Europe. The truth is that Europe was not superior to the rest of the world in the fifteenth century. If anything, the only part of the world in a Dark Age during that period was Europe, and it was only through violence and the murder of hundreds of millions that the West established its superiority. Imperial violence created the blank slate, the intellectual *terra nullius* (empty land) from which the Enlightenment thinkers emerged with their claims to a unique form of rationality and understanding.[46] Had the world not been built in the image of White supremacy the racial intellectual framework of the Enlightenment would have been impossible. It was self-evident that the natives of the Americas were inferior because they had been exterminated. 'Negroes' were obviously closer to livestock than humans because they were enslaved. Indians had nothing noteworthy to contribute because the West had already plundered their societies. It is from the rubble of colonial slaughter that supposedly universal reason emerges. Enlightenment thinkers claimed that to be rational, to think, to be human, was to be European. In other words, 'I'm White, therefore I am', and the imperial world at their feet was all the empirical evidence they needed to justify this claim. To sustain this belief, the truth about knowledge, science and reason had to first be erased.

Kant once noted Hume's challenge for 'anyone to cite a simple example in which a Negro has shown talents', arguing that 'not a single one was ever found who presented anything great in art or science or any other praiseworthy quality'.[47] In the twenty-first century it should not be necessary to offer a corrective to such racist fantasies. Unfortunately, I have been involved in far too many conversations with supposedly educated people to know that the idea that Europe produced science and reason is all too alive and well. So let's take up Hume's challenge and take it further. Not only can we find plenty of examples of talented 'Negroes', but the foundation of the knowledge we have today lies almost exclusively outside the West.

DECOLONIZING KNOWLEDGE

At the end of the fifteenth century Europe had been largely isolated from the rest of the world for centuries, ever since the collapse of the

Roman Empire. The region was in a Dark Age dominated by religious dogma and feudal repression, and aside from the crusades into the Muslim world had little thought of, or interest in, conquering the globe. This was the age when Christian beliefs supposedly explained the universe, and located the earth at the centre of Creation. Such beliefs limited the European imagination, most notably the idea that the world was flat and that to travel over the horizon would lead to falling into the abyss. As I will discuss, 1492 marked the beginning of the West, but importantly it also coincided with the fall of the empire that Europe most directly drew its intellectual tradition from. Columbus's maiden voyage was delayed until the Spanish had conquered Al-Andalus and driven the Moorish Empire out of Spain.[48] For the 700 years prior to this, a large part of the south of the country had been ruled by a Muslim empire that stretched out of North Africa. In fact, by the early eighth century the Muslims occupied over 5 million square miles of land, an area larger than the Roman Empire.[49] Only once they were defeated could the West begin its path to global domination.

By all accounts the Moorish occupation of southern Spain brought unparalleled levels of progress and development to the region. Prior to the Moors it had been ruled by the Visigoths who were so brutal and barbaric that the locals welcomed their foreign invaders as liberators. More than half the population had recently (707–9) died in a famine. When their Muslim saviours arrived they brought with them eastern 'sophistication' including the development of canals, irrigation techniques and farming expertise as well as relative luxuries like toothpaste, hairstyling and cutlery.[50] Córdoba became a centre of knowledge and learning under the Moors and in the tenth century a university famous for astronomy was founded in the legendary Mezquita. In her book *The Map of Knowledge* historian Violet Moller gives us an indication of just how far advanced the Muslim world was compared to Europe during this period:

twelfth-century scholar Bernard of Chartres [France] was proud of the twenty-four books he owned, but, in 1258, the city of Baghdad boasted thirty-six public libraries and over a hundred book merchants. The largest medieval library in Christian Europe, at the Abbey of Cluny, contained a few hundred books, while the royal library of Córdoba had 400,000.[51]

Throughout the Muslim Empire learning flourished and cities like Baghdad competed for the honour of being the capital of knowledge production. Ophthalmology, medicine and astronomy all thrived. In ninth-century Baghdad scientists studying at Caliph Al-Ma'um's 'House of Wisdom' could calculate the circumference of the world to within 400 miles of modern measurements using astronomy. The algorithms that determine so much of twenty-first century life are named after the Persian scholar Al-Khwarizmi, and for the concept of zero we owe a debt to Hindu intellectual Bramahgupta's *Siddhanta*, which was written in the seventh century. These are simple truths in direct contradiction of Enlightenment thinkers' ideas that only Europeans were capable of abstract thought. So central was the Muslim world to scholarship that Christian scholar Paul Alvarus of Córdoba lamented in the ninth century that 'all talented young Christians read and study with enthusiasm Arab books; they gather immense libraries at great expense . . . they have forgotten their own language'.[52]

At the heart of the intellectual tradition in the Muslim world was the acquisition and writing of books. After the fall of the Roman Empire there was little left of the once-great library in Alexandria or of the key texts essential to preserving knowledge. It was scholars in the Muslim world who went about securing and translating the classic texts as well as adding to them with new discoveries. Arabic became the language of knowledge until the fifteenth century. Once Europe asserted its dominion this was no longer allowed to be the case. Erasure of non-Europeans was at the core of the Western project in terms of both actual slaughter and symbolic destruction. After Granada was conquered by the Spanish, the powerful Cardinal Ximenéz de Cisneros, in his position as part of the Spanish Inquisition, organized a book burning on an almost unimaginable scale. In the city's main square almost 2 million Arabic books were incinerated because he thought that to 'destroy the written word is to deprive a culture of its soul, and eventually its identity'.[53] Although the books were burnt, their content was not always lost. Latin translations had been made to Europeanize the knowledge, the Arabic names changed to Latin ones.

Ibn Sina, an eleventh-century Persian scientist credited with being the founder of modern medicine, became Avicenna. Abbas al-Zahrawi, who pioneered surgical techniques in Córdoba in the tenth century, was transformed into Abulcasis. By burning books and libraries and Whitewashing history, Western intellectual thought was able to start from a clean slate of White supremacy. It is likely that the Enlightenment scholars genuinely believed they had inherited their knowledge solely from Europe, given the source material they were working from.

Tracing the history of knowledge through the Muslim world is important but also has limitations. For a start we could also explore the knowledge produced in the rest of Asia: China has had unbroken civilization for thousands of years. Then there's the indigenous knowledges of the Americas and Australia. The other major limitation is that this narrative ends up leading back to Greece, where the texts that the Islamic scholars were translating and building upon were largely produced. We could therefore add in the Muslim world and still end up with a Eurocentric foundation of knowledge. In *The Map of Knowledge*, from which I have drawn many of the above examples, it is exactly this intellectual geography that is reproduced. This is made worse by the exclusion of Timbuktu in what is now Mali, which was at the heart of Muslim scholarship from as early as the twelfth century when the University of Sankore was founded. By the sixteenth century the university had grown to teach 25,000 students and the library was one of the largest in the world, with hundreds of thousands of manuscripts.[54] The erasure of Africa from intellectual history continues in the book when the only Egyptian city that appears in it is Alexandria during its occupation by the Roman Empire. After reading it you could be forgiven for thinking that Egypt played a negligible part in the history of knowledge, when nothing could be further from the truth.

Prior to Greek civilization, Egypt reigned as the centre of progress for thousands of years. The Greeks learned from the Egyptians and even their 'cult of the Gods'.[55] Egypt was undoubtedly well advanced in science before Greece was. The pyramids alone are testimony to the civilization's scientific achievements. In school we learn that Archimedes discovered pi in the third century BC, but if you divide half the perimeter of the Great Pyramid of Giza, built over 2,000 years earlier, by its height, the number you come to is an approximation of pi. It is clear that the level of development in Egypt far outstripped anything in Europe at the time: even scholars in early Europe agreed that the Egyptians, and before them the Ethiopians, produced developed civilizations whilst Europe was in a stage of 'deep barbarism'.[56] Just as Europeans Whitewashed the Muslims out of their intellectual history, so the Greeks did the Egyptians. The most excruciating example of this was Imhotep (c. 2700–2611), the great Egyptian scientist and one of the earliest founders of medicine, who became worshipped as Asclepius by the Greeks. Historical Whitewashing would be bad enough, but in the 1999 film The Mummy Imhotep is the character they choose to raise from the dead, and depicts an evil monster who wants to rule the world. Imagine watching a movie where Aristotle comes back to life to destroy the world and you have the scale of intellectual sacrilege we are dealing with. As if defaming a dead scholar was not enough, the film also managed to reproduce the commonplace racist depiction of the ancient Egyptians by Hollywood.

Imhotep was played in the film by Arnold Vosloo, an actor who grew up in apartheid South Africa. Usually, ancient Egyptians are misrepresented as the Arabs who dominate the area today. In Vosloo's case they browned-up an actor classified as White by the apartheid regime. As I will discuss in Chapter 2, Egypt is sealed off from 'Africa proper' in the intellectual imagination. We are told its inhabitants were not part of Black Africa but rather the Mediterranean, so that it can be annexed into the Western tradition of intellectual thought. The truth is that though the country, and North Africa, is now predominantly Arab this was not the case at the time of the ancient Egyptian civilization. The Arab invasion of North Africa occurred in the seventh century, in the same move that saw the Moors take over southern Spain. In his classic work The African Origin of Civilization, African intellectual Cheik Anta Diop forensically delivers the evidence in terms of sculptures, artwork and history that the ancient Egyptians were Black. He explains that 'whenever the Egyptians use the word "Black" (khem) it is to designate themselves or their country: Kemit, land of the Blacks.'[57] He also traces Egyptian civilization back to Ethiopians who migrated north. The reality that maths, science and medicine were being practised across Africa centuries before the Greeks imagined any of them to be possible is undeniable. By focusing on the written word recorded in books we have ignored the truth that 'Africa is home to mathematical bodies of knowledge so vital they provide the bedrock of modern computing'.[58] In her excellent book *Don't Touch My Hair*, Emma Dabiri uses the patterns encoded in African hairstyles as evidence of complex mathematical formulas that have been used on the continent for centuries. For instance, in braiding patterns widely used in Africa for centuries we can see a representation of infinity. This may not sound particularly important, but the concept of infinity was so far beyond the comprehension of the Greeks it was associated with 'paradox and pathology'.[59] In 1877, European scholar Georg Cantor tried to represent the concept but was denounced as a heretic and ended his days in an asylum. His treatment, even in the so-called age of reason, harks back to how scientists were treated in fifth-century Greece: 'In 415, a mob of Christian zealots murdered the philosopher and mathematician Hypatia. Believing her to be a witch they flayed her alive with oyster shells.'[60] Whilst infinity is commonplace in traditional African hairstyles, village design and clothing, it took centuries for the West to catch up.

It was also not as though the Enlightenment thinkers needed to go far to find evidence of Black intelligence: there was plenty of it, they simply chose to ignore it. In direct response to Hume's challenge that Kant used as evidence for Black inferiority we can present Thomas Fuller, an enslaved African in eighteenth-century Virginia. He was so talented in mathematics that he could 'accurately count the hairs in a cow's tail, or the number of grains in bushels of wheat or flax seed' doing 'complex astronomy-related calculations that today would be done by computers'.[61] Fuller imported his mathematical genius into the United States from his education in West Africa before he was stolen into slavery. He was just one of countless examples of Black excellence that Europeans were well aware of but which were always discounted, interpreted as some kind of exception that proved the rules of racism. For example, Phyllis Wheatley was taken into slavery around 1760, but rose to become a world-renowned poet. Still, Thomas Jefferson discounted her talent, arguing that it was impossible to 'find that a black had uttered a thought above the level of plain narration; never saw an elementary trait of painting or sculpture . . . Religion, indeed, has produced a Phyllis Wheatley; but it could not produce a poet.'[62] Of course Wheatley was just parroting White skills through her rigorous training, rather than being capable of actually producing poetry. In direct conflict to everything we are told about Western science, time and again the great thinkers of the time ignored the clear empirical evidence around them in order to protect the superiority that lay at the heart of their White identity politics.

In Jefferson's case this was particularly egregious given that he not only owned enslaved Africans but subjected one of his 'property' to long-term sexual abuse. Jefferson's so-called relationship with Sally Hemings began when she was fourteen and his abuse of her continued for years. She bore him several children, who were freed, but Hemings remained Jefferson's captive until he died. Jefferson's 'affection' for Hemings and his children did not dissuade him from his White supremacist philosophy. Notwithstanding his obsession with Hemings, he asserted the 'superior beauty' of the White race; that Black people gave off a very strong and disagreeable odour; and that Black women preferred sleeping with orang-utans than with Black men.[63] These ideas were ideological, and the available evidence was twisted to fit his diseased view of the world.

As should by now be obvious, the central thesis of the Enlightenment – that knowledge and reason spreads out from Europe – is entirely bogus. It is not an exaggeration to say that Europe is responsible for very few genuinely new ideas and made its advances by building on an inheritance of knowledge derived from other parts of the world. Science, maths, medicine, reason and even political organization all have their roots in the world outside the West, while Europe had a scant awareness of these concepts. Even racism was not a novel European idea. As I will discuss in Chapter 2, the Arab slave trade pre-dates Europe's, and when Columbus started enslaving the natives of the Americas it was for markets in the Muslim world. As we have seen in this chapter, Western racial science codified the idea of White supremacy based on biological superiority to the so-called lesser races. But in the fourteenth century the Tunisian scholar Ibn Khaldun was hundreds of years ahead of the dead White men in declaring that Africans 'have little [that is essentially] human and have attributes that are quite similar to those of dumb animals'.[64] Before we get too carried away, although the West may not have birthed the idea of racism, it found its prosperity by exploiting the concept to its fullest.

On the one hand, it is important to destroy the notion of the Enlightenment as some unique achievement of Western civilization, to recognize that it was built on a foundation of global knowledge. But we should not give up on the idea that it is an utterly transcendent intellectual tradition upon which the success of the West is built. It may be exclusive, wrong and racist but that is simply the nature of the West. Without the racial intellectual framework inherited from the Enlightenment the current version of Western empire would be impossible. Decolonizing the curriculum has to mean more than being a bit critical of Kant or adding some diversity to reading lists. If, and this is a big if, we want to build an anti-racist society we need to completely rethink the underlying basis of the knowledge that produces the world.

WHITE WORLD SUPREMACY

The global economy today is built in the image of White supremacy that was so neatly outlined by the Enlightenment thinkers. Africa is the poorest continent on earth, while the countries with White majorities are the richest. We only need to look at Linnaeus' ladder of the species to understand the political and economic system. These debates are not simply about the past, because the Enlightenment shapes our present: a society can only be as fair as the knowledge it is built on, and established Western intellectual thought is rooted in racism. The most frustrating aspect of the way in which the Enlightenment is used is that we are told to believe 'it is reason that will enable us to solve the problem', if only we can just shine light on the relevant evidence.[65] Absent from this propaganda is the reality that Western concepts of reason can never be the solution to the problem of racism they helped to create and continue to maintain. Ignorance was never the issue: Western reason is based on White supremacy, the idea that those at the top of the racial hierarchy have the monopoly on knowledge. Freeing ourselves from the very nature of this intellectual framework is essential.

One of the main areas used to illustrate the positive contribution of the Western intellectual framework is the arena of human rights, which is deeply invested in the Enlightenment tradition.[66] Key documents like the US Bill of Rights and the French Revolution's Declaration of the Rights of Man are celebrated as the sacred texts of our freedoms, which are guaranteed by the human rights agenda. It is in this narrative that Locke, Hume, Kant, Voltaire and Hegel are applauded for their heroic theories of individual rights and freedom. The only problem is that you cannot separate their theories of rights from their racism, which goes to the core of their intellectual output.

A case in point is the American framework of rights. All men were apparently created equal – apart from Black men, of course. When the founding fathers were designing the Bill of Rights at the 1787 Constitutional Convention in the newly formed United States, they came upon the issue of representation for states based on population. The Southern states wanted to ensure that their slave populations could be used to give them representational power in the new nation. But a beast could obviously not be taken to be equal to a White person, and could certainly never vote. Therefore it was agreed that each of the enslaved would account for three-fifths of a White full human being. A dissenting voice from Massachusetts' Elbridge Gerry objected 'why should their representation be increased to the southward on account of the number of slaves, [rather] than [on the basis of] horses or oxen to the north?'[67]

It was not only race that limited rights in the United States:[68] full rights were granted solely to those who were wealthy, White and male. It should be no surprise that it was only that same group who were able to access university education at the time, where they created a framework of knowledge and rights that only their kind could enjoy. Yale, one of the most prestigious universities in the world, takes its name from Elihu Yale, a slave trader who also enriched himself in colonial India. There is perhaps no better representative of the unbreakable links to colonial violence and knowledge, but Yale is by no means alone.

The racist nature of inclusion in democracy is not incidental; it was embedded in those who were creating the concept of rights. Full participation in humanity was reserved for White and wealthy men while everyone else's rights were contingent. We could presume that extending rights only to White people was based on the erroneous assumption that other so-called races were not human, and that now that those notions have been (largely) cast aside these universal rights can be applied to all the human family. While that might be a comforting idea, it is a dangerous one, and ignores the basic framework of both knowledge and the political and economic system in the last 200 years.

When the Enlightenment is presented as the architect of the anti-imperialist movement it is on the basis that the movement eventually accepted that freedom means tolerating the diversity, or pluralism, that makes up humanity.[69] Ultimately, this is the position Kant arrives at in his later works. Whereas previously he used his 'moral geography' to justify the enslavement of the savages, he later saw that even though the natives were inferior they too possessed rights. But to pretend that this transformed his basic position is delusional. Kant essentially believed that 'special protection' was needed for the 'child-like' races, who could not be trusted to look after themselves.[70] We become accepted into the human family but forever frozen in a state of nature, destined to remain a step below in the racial hierarchy. We have the right to life, but the standard of that life was never thought to be at the level of the enlightened European. So, not only does Kant contribute to the theory of racial hierarchy, he also outlines a moral universalist philosophy that can be summed up most neatly in Kipling's idea of the 'White man's burden'. Here we can see the fatal weaknesses in the framework of human rights. It emerged at a time when it was understood that only White men were fully human citizens and that everyone else was deserving of rights according to their place in the hierarchy of 'moral geography'. Diderot 'praised the primitive and rejected the civilized . . . specifically celebrat[ing] the sexual freedom of Tahitians'.[71] Reminiscent of Rousseau's idea that savages lived in a state of nature which was purer than the rational world of Europeans, there was a celebration of their perceived basic and carnal instincts. In this framework the Tahitians have the right to maintain their supposedly backward ways of life, stuck for ever historically as the happy, smiling natives at peace with a world they do not truly understand.

I've seen these ideas at play countless times when having discussions about global poverty. Well-meaning volunteers to the underdeveloped world often come back fulfilled by the work they have done and contented with the idea that the people they have met have been so 'happy' with their lives. When you ask about the grinding poverty and conditions in which the natives struggle, you are chastised for applying 'Western' ideals. In the Enlightenment framework, humanity is not universal, it is contextual, allowing us to provide a completely different set of standards of individual rights across the world.

As seen in the example of the original US Constitution, property was at the foundation of how rights were granted. The same was true in Europe, where in order to vote, to have full rights, you had to be White, male and have money. Even White women only had a set of individual rights which disqualified them from taking part in democracy. The classed basis for the franchise is important too, because this economic limitation to rights is still in place today. There are no longer economic restrictions directly placed on voting rights in the West and most countries around the world have some sort of voting system. But wealth is indispensable to the kind of rights you will be afforded. Take for instance the UN Convention on the Rights of the Child that offers universal rights to young people around the globe. Article six has two parts, firstly that 'every child has the inherent right to life' and secondly that all 'parties shall ensure to the maximum extent possible the survival and development of the child'. Sounds reasonable enough, but look more closely: the 'maximum extent possible' is wildly different depending on where you live. In the West child deaths are extremely rare and most often occur in tragic circumstances. However, a child in the underdeveloped world dies every ten seconds because they have no proper access to food and water. The UN Convention *in theory* stresses the rights of those children, but in practice absolves signatories from ensuring those rights are achieved, due to their economic circumstances. That is the cultural pluralism which is the hallmark of Enlightenment reason.

It is a diversity that we accept all the time, whenever we enjoy the benefits of sweatshop labour or purchase smartphones powered by minerals stolen out of Africa's ground. Because living standards are so much lower in the underdeveloped world, we have normalized a different framework of reality. When children's rights are discussed in the West, apart from in the context of abuse, the topics are about the right to play or to not have too much stress from exams. In the under-developed world they are still stuck on the basic right to life. Vitally, these different economic conditions are racist. It is no coincidence that the poorest countries are the darkest ones. The West created a racial global order and then built a framework of rights that would maintain the status quo.

A major vehicle for maintaining this uneven pluralism of rights is the nation state. Sovereign nations were meant to deliver rights through their constitutions and their representative democracies. Hopefully, it is easy to see how this enshrines the unequal global order, making it the responsibility of the nation state only to provide rights for its citizens. If nations were empires, like Britain, then the colonial populations were subject to a different set of rules and rights.[72] It was Kant who first imagined a supranational collection of states to govern world affairs, something akin to the UN. It is the UN that has to ratify national sovereignty but, in testimony to the elastic nature of nation states, the only consistent aspect of their definition is that they have been legally recognized as individual states.[73] Rather than being natural systems of organization, nation states are containers used to control the political order. While the UN may look democratic from the outside, with its one-member-one-vote in the General Assembly, the organization is governed by fiat from the Security Council, with four of the five permanent members – France, the United States, Britain and Russia – being White Western countries. China is the exception whose economic might could not be ignored. This is again the cultural pluralism of rights: all nations have a right to a seat at the table, but only the preordained ones get to decide what to eat.

Worse still, by operating under the framework of universal rights, the West is free to moralize over its superior democracy and human rights records compared to the underdeveloped world. The solution to the problems of impoverished nation states is explained as the deficit of rights and freedom: if only they had more democracy and good governance, then of course they would prosper. The failure to provide economic freedom and basic rights belongs to the nation state and the West has absolved itself of all responsibility. The West has maintained its control over the world by Balkanizing Africa into individual nation states so that it can be more effectively managed and controlled.[74]

This would appear to be contradictory to the universalist moral philosophy but, as we have seen, the only aspect of these ideas that is universal is that the globe should be exploited on the principle of White supremacy.

Ultimately, the problem of the human rights framework is its perceived focus on the individual. The Enlightenment search for the moral agent, the rational core of humanity, was based on finding the uniqueness at the heart of man. This is usually taken to mean that what is true for one accounts for all, and therefore we are presented with a universal theory that elevates all humanity. As we have discussed, this is untrue. Human nature was theorized to be influenced by the external (racial factors) which determined the talents that people had to reach human potential. Full, rational, moral humanity was not understood as something that all humans achieved, only those with White skin. Therefore, the individual could be understood only through their race and through their gender. It is for this reason that there was no contradiction in Jefferson declaring that 'all people were created equal' whilst owning Africans. He saw them as 'Negroes', chattels, not in the category of human. All of the founding texts upon which the human rights framework was built were designed as the rights of White men. Within the West these rights have been extended, to some extent, to those who are not White and male. But countless Black people killed by the police would strongly contest their right to life. To be a full human being is still defined in Whiteness, the unquestioned right to freedom and prosperity that even the most privileged minority can only dream of. It remains the case that those who reside in the underdeveloped world are not afforded these rights. African migrants are left to drown crossing the Mediterranean; sweatshop workers in Asia are subject to medieval conditions; migrants in Latin America are brutalized on their journeys to find freedom; and Black and Brown children die by the second. The architecture of a society that creates these injustices is the Enlightenment and its universalist philosophy. The transition of Kant from adviser of slave drivers to opponent of colonialism is important because it marks the shift from the first version of Western empire, one that was rooted in violence and direct control, to the emergence of the updated system.

The Enlightenment was a product of the first stage of Western imperialism, with slavery and colonialism clearing the ground for its intellectual project. It then provided the intellectual bridge to the new age of empire, which maintains colonial logic but has clothed itself in the legitimacy of democracy, human rights and universal values. It is essential that we unlearn the distorted view of history that we have been conditioned into. We will explore the truth of how the West brutally established its imperial dominance before the dawning of a new, more enlightened, age of empire. To do so means starting at the beginning of the tale, in 1492 when Columbus sailed the ocean blue.

2

Genocide

In the wake of protests following the murder of George Floyd statues of Christopher Columbus became a target. Across the United States monuments were beheaded, vandalized, torched and even torn down entirely.[1] The anger at Columbus shows the power he still holds in the psyche of the nation, as does President Trump's 4 July speech celebrating the Italian as the person who 'discovered America'.[2] The reverence for Columbus has a long history, particularly in Colorado, which is where the Columbus national holiday celebrations first started.

In 2016 Denver City Council announced they would be celebrating Indigenous Peoples' Day rather than marking Columbus Day. This came about as a result of decades of activism, notably in 1992 when, minutes before it was due to start, the Columbus Day parade had to be cancelled because 500 protestors descended on the scene.[3] Halting the march in Denver was seen as a key victory for the activists because the idea of celebrating Christopher Columbus with a public holiday first came from Denver. Angelo Noce, an Italian immigrant to the city, persuaded the state to adopt Columbus Day in 1907 as a mark of recognition, given the significant discrimination that Italians were facing in the United States at the time.[4] It took until 1937 for the celebration to be adopted nationally, although this wasn't due to Columbus being controversial – on the contrary, Columbus is one of the most venerated figures in the United States. Most US cities have monuments in his honour as well as streets and major institutions named after him. There is a Columbus city in Ohio, and the United States seat of government is housed in the District of Columbia. The beatification of Columbus is remarkable, considering that he never set foot in what is now the United States of America.

Protests against Columbus Day have been going on for decades, because in 1492 Columbus sailed the ocean blue, and when he got off the boat unleashed a reign of genocidal terror on the indigenous people he supposedly 'discovered'. Notwithstanding his historical role as slave trader and mass murderer, Columbus Day continues to be celebrated, but the tales told to schoolchildren may as well begin 'Once upon a genocide'.[5]

European expansion into the Americas was vital to the development of the West. And yet explorers like Columbus did not 'discover' a new and empty land to be exploited. When they arrived, they found millions of people living in complex societies who needed to be erased in order to create the clean slate necessary for Western progress. The genocide in the Americas is without precedent, wiping up to 99 per cent of the natives off the face of the earth. The bodies of those slaughtered are the foundation of the current social order. Westward expansion was the key that unlocked the bounties of European domination. Slavery, colonialism, industry, science and so-called democracy are all indebted to the tens of millions sacrificed at the altar of 'progress'.

Although the genocide in the Americas was by far the largest in human history, it is rarely commented on. It is consigned to the dustbin of history as Western commentators decry genocide as the possession either of evil regimes like the Nazis or of supposedly backward peoples in the underdeveloped world. In truth, the West was birthed by genocide and relied on the slaughter of millions of Black and Brown bodies to develop and enrich itself. You cannot separate genocide and the West, which is by far the most brutal, violent and murderous system to ever grace the globe. Rather than come to terms with the centrality of genocide to the West it is understood as a process alien to the progressive society built on science. Understanding genocide through the lens of the evil perpetuated by Nazis, or backward savages in Rwanda, allows the West to maintain its moral superiority. In truth both examples were products of the West, born out of the logic of empire. In order to appreciate this history we need to undo the lies at the heart of how the West understands itself.

ONCE UPON A GENOCIDE

This fairy tale revolving around Columbus has some key elements that we need to dismiss. The first is that when Columbus mistakenly came across the Americas, when he was in fact looking for India, he *discovered* the land. Not only were there indigenous peoples across the Americas, there is clear evidence that Africans had visited and settled long before Columbus took his wrong turn. The Olmec civilization in Latin America made statues with clear African features at least 2,500 years before Columbus made his journey; remains of Africans have also been found in Olmec territory, along with Egyptian artefacts, in the Americas.[6] The finding of narcotics from the Americas in Egyptian mummies in 1992[7] was roundly criticized mostly because of the disbelief that Africans could have made it to the continent before Europeans. Despite a wealth of evidence, scholars have been deterred from tracing these connections for fear of career suicide.[8] It is only because of the conceit of Western ideas of supremacy that we ignore the history of global travel and interaction that far pre-dates European exploration. In fact, prior to Columbus departing on his third voyage to the Americas King Juan of Portugal had told him that Africans had a trade route to the region from Guinea, and Columbus confirmed this with the indigenous people when he arrived.[9] The notion that Columbus made a discovery is based on the White supremacist logic of knowledge. If a people live in a place and there are no Europeans around to witness it, contrary to Western beliefs, they still exist.

Central to the idea of discovery is the notion that the Americas were sparsely populated by pre-civilization natives who, even if we accept their existence, are discounted because of their savagery. I must admit that this myth is so embedded in how we understand the world that until I started researching for this book I had assumed that the population numbers were very low, though I obviously rejected the savagery part. But the midpoint estimate for the number of people who lived in the Americas when Columbus landed is 72 million.[10] The sheer number of people who inhabited the region is evidence that the image of the backward native is one of colonial fiction. Latin

America was home to empires like the Aztecs, with cities and civil-izations that dwarfed anything Europe had to offer. When Columbus landed on what was then named by Europeans, Hispaniola, rather than finding so-called primitives, he encountered a complex society that had a strong history of civilization and social order. Columbus did the most damage to the island that today is made up of Haiti and the Dominican Republic. The Taino and Arawaks who inhabited the islands had developed centuries of civilization, were experts in agri-culture and lived in harmony with the land. From first contact in 1492 up until 1509, when Columbus ceased to run the island, the popula-tion of native Taino went from a midpoint estimate of 8 million to just 100,000,[11] and by 1542 there were only 200 left. The scale of death has no parallel in human history.[12]

Alongside grossly under-portraying the numbers of indigenous people erased by Europeans, the bulk of the deaths are attributed to disease. It is certainly true that illness was a major killer of tens of millions. Indigenous populations did not have immunity to European illnesses like smallpox and flu and these spread rapidly. But it would be wrong to excuse the invaders for their accidental murder of mil-lions. For one, there is no doubt that the invaders could see the result of their presence and the deadly impact of their germs. Evidently there were no steps made to stop the spread of disease, because genocide was the logic of the European invasion. Instead throughout the ensuing period of history we see the exact opposite, with germ warfare being used to spread deadly diseases to eradicate indigenous populations. For instance, during a siege by Native Americans of Fort Pitt (now Pittsburgh) in 1763, Sir Jeffrey Amherst, commander in chief of the British forces, suggested that the indigenous people should be pur-posefully infected with smallpox 'by means of [infected] blankets as well as to try every other method that can serve to extirpate this execrable race'. Captain Ecuyer, of the Royal Americans, a colonial regiment of the British Army, later noted that 'we gave them two blankets and a handkerchief out of the smallpox hospital. I hope it will have the desired effect.'[13]

As well as biological warfare contributing to the spread of disease, we have to take into account the impact of the reign of colonial ter-ror that Europeans executed. Columbus was particularly brutal in his colonization of Hispaniola. After his initial voyage he returned to the island in 1493, invading with a band of mercenaries and man-eating dogs who rounded up the natives and subjugated them violently by 'hacking, roasting, burning and working them to death'.[14] Columbus instituted a law of tribute which meant that if a native did not meet their quota of collected gold they would have limbs chopped off. The brutal conditions in which the indigenous people were forced to live made their succumbing to disease inevitable. Starved of access to their usual diet, sanitary conditions and traditional ways of healing, the Taino were unable to resist illness. There is no doubt that European diseases would have taken a toll, but their genocidal impact was only possible in the context of colonial brutality.[15]

It is impossible to overstate, or even imagine, the scale of violence that Columbus inflicted on the Taino people. From the outset he saw them as subhuman, godless creatures who were to be used as fodder to enrich himself and his Spanish benefactors. After he realized he had ended up in entirely the wrong place and that the bounty he imagined did not readily exist, Columbus exploited the Taino, using them to find gold in newly constructed mines, and as commodities in themselves, becoming one of Europe's first slave traders. In an example of the inhumanity and horror induced by Columbus, in 1495 his mercenaries rounded up 1,600 Taino. Five hundred and fifty were taken in chains and sold into slavery in Spain and 650 were shared out between the Spanish colonists. The remaining 400 were set free but were so terrified that their tormentors would change their mind, according to Michele de Cuneo, one of Columbus's men, many of the women with 'infants at the breast . . . left their infants anywhere on the ground and started to flee like desperate people'.[16] This is the terror that you are celebrating when you elevate Columbus to a hero worthy of naming buildings and cities after, erecting statues of, or marching in a parade in honour for. Columbus sparked the deadliest period in human history; it did not take long for other European powers to fully immerse themselves in the genocidal method.

Britain entered the Americas later than the Spanish and Portuguese, who had an early monopoly over the region. But when the British did get involved, they built on what their fellow Europeans had developed. In order to establish themselves they had to overcome fierce resistance from the indigenous populations. In contrast to the picture book story of backward and disorganized natives, the indigenous people were extremely organized and resisted Europeans to the bitter end. Hilary Beckles, in his book *Britain's Black Debt*, explains that one of the reasons that Britain's first slave colony was Barbados in 1630 is because the island had largely been abandoned by the native Kalinago people.[17] The Kalinago caused hell for the Europeans through their resistance and organization. They mostly left Barbados to build strongholds on St Vincent and Dominica, where they maintained resistance and launched raids on other islands. For example, in 1640, the Kalinago attacked Antigua, killing at least fifty people and kidnapping the governor and his family. Resistance accelerated the genocidal impulses of the invaders, who viewed the Kalinago as enemies of Europe.

Due to the disruption of British commercial interests on plantations in the Caribbean in 1675 '"several merchants of London" addressed the Lords of Trade and Plantations in support of Governor [of Barbados] Stapleton's extermination plan . . . to destroy the barbarous savages'.[18] The genocidal war with the Kalinago continued for a century, replete with expeditions and massacres of men, women and children. In 1795 this resistance was eventually broken on the stronghold of St Vincent and 5,000 Kalinago were transported by the British to the island of Baliceaux. Within four months a third had died from starvation and the rest were left to eventually die off in horrendous conditions.

Massacres and removals were a pattern seen across the region, creating an industrial method of death that cleared the path for European advancement. This genocidal approach to conquest is the hallmark of Western development, and an absolutely essential ingredient to building the modern world. Columbus is an All American hero because he paved the way for the nation to develop. In keeping with Columbus's model, the indigenous people were almost erased from the land with a complete lack of regard for their lives.

During the American Revolutionary War, General George Washington launched the Sullivan Expedition to break the resistance of Native American Iroquois who had taken up arms for the British.

With typical brutality, he ordered a scorched earth policy with his expressed intent to 'lay waste all the settlements around, with instructions to do it in the most effectual manner, that the country may not be merely overrun, but destroyed.'[19] More than forty villages were destroyed and those who remained alive fled to Canada. This conquest was vital to victory and for establishing the US nation state. We see the same logic present in later efforts to expand the nation: the indigenous population of California was reduced from an estimated 310,000–750,000 in 1800 to just 18,000 in 1907. This was done in part through brutal massacres by death squads. In one such event around 1868 at Mill Creek, Norman Kingsley led a massacre of the Yahi Yana so sustained that he changed his gun mid-shooting because his rifle 'tore up' the bodies so badly, 'particularly the babies'.[20] A few years earlier, during the massacre of the Southern Cheyenne at Sand Creek in 1864, a Colorado death squad led by former minister John Chivington raided a village shooting at unarmed men, women and children, following them to the Sand Creek as they fled. Around 150 civilians were slaughtered, and the following scene took place:

> One poor woman, heavy with child, fell behind the others racing up the stream bed. Soldiers killed her too. Then one of them cut her open, and pulling out her unborn baby, he threw the little one down on the earth bedside her.[21]

Native Americans were erased from their lands and eventually moved onto reservations where they would be unable to interfere with the development of the United States. In keeping with the celebration of the genocidal Columbus, this period in American history is valorized in folklore. There is a whole genre of Cowboy movies that show the brave frontier folk battling savages and outlaws in order to make their way in the Wild West. The fairy-tale representation of this history, with the hardworking Europeans bravely taming the frontiers, provides the necessary comfort blanket for people looking back today. Rather than being the heroes of this history, the new Americans built their nation on genocidal slaughter. To recognize this would mean honestly accounting for the racist foundations of the nation.

THE FOUNDATION OF THE WEST

Atrocities in the Americas were not carried out because of some pathology within the European settlers. Erasing the natives was a necessary foundation upon which to build the development of the West. The expansion out of Europe was an essential step in the creation of industrial capitalism because it provided all the ingredients for the modern world.

Columbus's voyage was supported by the Spanish because he promised to bring back riches, and it was this pursuit of gold that drove the horrendous labour conditions for the natives of Hispaniola, which decimated the population. Later, it was the Gold Rush in the United States which accelerated expansion west. Rather than gold, Columbus stumbled into a far more valuable resource necessary for the West: the land itself. The Americas provided the territory necessary for the production that fuelled the development of industry. As I will explore in the next chapter on slavery, the key commodities that powered the Industrial Revolution were produced in the Americas. Cotton and sugar in particular were of outsize importance to capitalist growth. Colonizing the region was a pre-condition for slavery: once the natives were made extinct the transatlantic slave trade began, to provide the labour that built the modern world.

When Columbus accidentally landed in the Americas, Europe was behind most of the world. Religious dogma, war and a Dark Age had caused European development to stagnate. Europe did not dominate the world in the fifteenth or even the sixteenth century. It was the wealth produced from the Atlantic system that propelled the West to the position it is in today. Gold and silver from the mines of Brazil allowed European countries to amass wealth and make inroads into the East, which was far richer, more developed and powerful than Europe at this time. It was the profits from the Atlantic that allowed Europe to come to dominate the globe, leading the way in industry and science. But none of this was possible without the genocide in the Americas. Europe could not spread into the West and allow the indigenous people to remain on the land. They had to be cleared away to create the blank slate on which the West could be built.

Think of the Industrial Revolution, so much a part of the progressive myth the West tells about itself. I will never forget my A-level History course on the subject: the perfect example of schooling as propaganda. We learned about the accepted causes of industrial progress, which included the ingenuity of European scientists, capital investment, and also a population boom that meant there was more demand for goods and therefore the market had to work out ways to respond. At this point I did not know the specifics but I did wonder how it was possible that transatlantic slavery was not part of the discussion, given it was happening at the time and was extremely important to the economy. My teacher's response was very clear. We would be ignoring any discussion of either slavery or colonialism because it 'wasn't in the textbook' and 'definitely wouldn't be in the exam'. But if we want an honest assessment of the Industrial Revolution it is impossible to separate industry from colonial violence and genocide. Just consider the issue of population increase that was so central to providing the demand for industrial production.

The Americas were not just a cash-cow, they became an extension of Europe. Millions of Europeans flooded into North and South America, leaving space for population growth in Europe. If increased demand was a key driver of industrialization, there is no honest way to discuss this without including the expansion into the West. As more commodities were needed, science and industry had to transform to keep up with demand. I cannot imagine my teacher's response had I asked how it was possible for Europeans to expand into territory that had tens of millions of native inhabitants. Cooperating with the indigenous peoples, sharing land and coexisting could never have produced the modern world. In a very concrete way the genocide in the Americas cleared the way for the population explosion of Europeans and the political and economic systems which sustained them.

Worshipping at the altar of Columbus is tragically the appropriate response, given his role in founding the West. It is not an accident that he is adulated because nothing that we currently have would have been possible without his so-called discovery of the Americas. To pretend that there is some way to celebrate the birth of the United

States that is free from the history of genocide is perhaps worse than the delusional mainstream narratives of its beginnings. Not holding a parade, or taking down every statue of Columbus, would not alter the rotten foundations of the current world order. In a perverse way, both sides of this debate are attempting to present a distorted view of the nation. Pro-Columbus forces want to play down the negative aspects to ease collective guilt, whilst the anti-Columbus faction is hoping to eliminate the colonial nostalgia that makes it difficult for minorities to feel at home in the nation. There are many versions of this debate relating to all the horrors upon which the West is built. But recognition of atrocities does not change either their history or legacy. Acknowledging the barbarity of the West is meaningless unless we are committed to undoing the system that was created by it. If you are proud to be an American, Brit, European, or whatever else, and feel that there is some utility in this wicked system then you should proudly celebrate Columbus and all his genocidal contemporaries. They forged the way for the West, burning, hacking, roasting and enslaving their way along the path to the modern world. We can have theoretical debates about whether genocide was a necessary condition for Western development; in some alternate universe perhaps Europeans and the natives are coexisting in capitalist harmony, but in our reality, the foundation stone of the West is the tens of millions of bodies of the indigenous people of the Americas. If you fly the flag for the West then every last one of your heroes is drenched in blood. No amount of atonement can alter this basic fact.

SETTLER COLONIALISM IS GENOCIDE

As uncomfortable as it may be to acknowledge, settler colonialism in the Americas was an essential feature of Western development (it is not coincidence that the United States is the richest Western nation), and it is a method of imperialism that 'destroys to replace'.[22] Elimination of the native population became a necessary feature once the invading population became too large. Land and resources were taken away from the natives, making their survival almost impossible. In the United States, for example, the killing of buffalo for hides by Europeans drastically reduced the stock of food available to the indigenous population.[23] Destroying indigenous peoples' way of life ultimately led to conflict, and this resistance was used as an excuse to annihilate the troublesome savages. The pattern that we saw with Kalinago resistance in the Caribbean has been repeated so often that it should be treated as a fundamental process of modernity. Europeans needed land, the indigenous population resisted its seizure, and so they were exterminated. It is a pattern that can be seen across the history of Western colonialism around the globe.

When the British settled in Tasmania, an island off Australia, in the nineteenth century, they eradicated between 4,000 and 7,000 of the indigenous population, including all of those who were 'full-blooded natives'. Visiting after the native genocide was almost complete, the British Reverend Thomas Atkins attributed the '"almost extinct" condition of the Aborigines to the "universal law in the Divine government" that "savage tribes disappear before the progress of the civilized races"'.[24] This violence was essential to Enlightenment ideals of progress and White supremacy in civilization. The genocide accelerated after a native rebellion in 1826: extermination was the method chosen to quell resistance. The remainder of the indigenous population were forcibly removed to a reservation on Flinders Island, where the conditions were so dire that by 1847 only forty-six remained alive.

Exactly the same process occurred with the Yuki of California, whose population was reduced from between 5,000 and 20,000 to just 300 by 1864. An article in the *San Francisco Bulletin* in 1856 justified the slaughter of the Yuki by explaining that 'extermination is the quickest and cheapest remedy, and effectually prevents all other difficulties when an outbreak [of Indian violence] occurs.'[25] Wherever Europeans settled and populated in mass numbers the policy of the British in Australia, *terra nullus* or 'empty land', was enforced, regardless of the existence of native populations. In places like the United States, Latin America and Australia, where settler colonialism took hold and millions of Europeans migrated, the genocide of the indigenous population was almost total. Space is, after all, finite.

In Australia a debate has been ongoing over whether genocide is the correct term to use for the treatment of the Aborigines. Tasmania is often cited as a classic case study in genocide, but in Australia there has been extreme reluctance to use that label for the nation's actions. At the height of the so-called 'history wars' between historians and right-wing commentators, Prime Minister John Howard decried the usage of the term as 'outrageous'.[26] Australia likes to see itself as a bastion of liberal values and multicultural tolerance, preferring to imagine a deluded version of history rather than the ugly truth that it is a 'nation founded on genocide'.[27] As with every other example of settler colonialism, genocide was a necessary feature of creating the Australian state. The British did not find empty land but a population who had been there for tens of thousands of years. Britain's entry and domination of the land led to the same patterns of destruction we saw in the Americas. It is estimated that in 1788 there were between 750,000 and 1.2 million Aborigines and by 1900 only 75,000 remained.[28] After the British settled in Melbourne in 1835 the native population dropped from more than 10,000 to less than 2,000 in eighteen years – a decline of over 80 per cent.[29] So stark were the consequences of British settlement that in the ten years to 1849 there were only ten children born amongst all the native tribes in the area. In Queensland alone it is estimated that the death toll of indigenous people during the frontier period was at least 50,000.[30]

In terms of dodging accusations of genocide there is the common refrain that much of this death was accidental. Disease or competition for food was what led to the expiration of the Aborigines – an unintended consequence of industrial progress. We should pour as much scorn on that notion as possible. Not only did British settlement lead to the extinguishing of countless Aboriginal lives, the settlers knew exactly what they were doing and intended that very outcome. The first governor of Western Australia pronounced in 1835 that the Aborigines must 'gradually disappear' and that nothing could 'prevent the ulterior [sic] Extinction of that Race'.[31] In 1913 the Australian Prime Minister Billy Hughes celebrated that the inauguration of the new national capital at Canberra was 'taking place "without the slightest trace of that race we have banished from the face of the earth"'.[32] Australians were well aware that annexing the land meant the destruction of the Aborigines and had no problem watching a 'backward' race extinguish itself in the face of Darwinian progress.

Just as in the United States, the settlers were also a key factor in perpetuating genocide.

Between 1860 and 1895 in Alice Springs approximately 20 per cent of the Aboriginal population was lost to disease but 40 per cent to what the colonists called 'dispersal', a practice that involved clearing the land of the natives with the use of force and shootings.[33] Queensland was notorious for settler violence, supported by the Native Police Force, who created an 'environment of terror which governed the lives of Aboriginal people'.[34] Thousands were slaughtered, a subject that the British High Commissioner, Arthur Hamilton Gordon, raised with British Prime Minister William Gladstone in 1883. He was troubled by the culture of terror in Queensland:

> The habit of regarding the natives as vermin, to be cleared off the face of the earth, has given the average Queenslander a tone of brutality and cruelty . . . I have heard men of culture and refinement . . . talk, not only of the wholesale butchery . . . but of the individual murder of natives, exactly as they would talk of a day's sport, or having to kill some troublesome animal.[35]

Such barbarity was not reserved for Queenslanders. In 1824 martial law was declared in Bathurst, west of Sydney, to deal with the problem of Aboriginal resistance. At a public meeting one of the largest sheep farmers declared that 'the best thing that could be done, would be to shoot all the blacks and manure the ground with their carcases, which was all the good they were fit for!' At the same meeting it was 'recommended likewise that the Women and Children should especially be shot as the most certain method of getting rid of the race'. After martial law was declared the Aborigines were savagely attacked, which led to brutal inhumanities such as this event recounted by L. E. Threlkeld, a missionary at the time:

> A large number were driven into a swamp, and mounted police rode round and round and shot them off indiscriminately until they were all destroyed! When one of the police enquired of the Officer if a return should be made of the killed, wounded there were none, all were destroyed, Men, Women and Children! But forty-five heads were collected and boiled down for the sake of the skulls! My informant, a

Magistrate, saw the skulls packed for exportation in a case at Bathurst ready for shipment to accompany the commanding Officer on his voyage shortly afterwards taken to England.[36]

Such colonial brutality is the foundation stone of Australia, which could not have come into being without it. Genocide deniers can point to the fact that some in the leadership of the British Empire felt uncomfortable about the violence, and blame the slaughter on individual acts of the settlers. In theory the Aborigines were subjects of the British Crown and therefore extended protections. After one of the most notorious massacres, at Myall Creek, New South Wales in 1838, the perpetrators were eventually found guilty of murder and hanged for killing twenty-eight Aborigines. But it appears as though this massacre became notorious because it was one of the very few times that any murderers were punished. In fact, the case had to be re-tried after they were first acquitted and the perpetrators maintained that 'they were not aware that in destroying the aboriginals they were violating the law . . . as it had . . . been so frequently done in the colony before.'[37] The reality is that slaughter was an essential part of nation building: the state was happy to turn a blind eye and to participate in it when necessary.

It is not as though an enlightened country emerged from this foundation of colonial genocide. Australia maintained the logic of empire and continued to treat its Aboriginal population as less than human. In 1956 in the Maralinga Lands in South Australia, Aborigines were removed from their lands to make way for atomic bomb tests. They were left wandering the desert and many died from starvation and thirst. Conditions were so bad that parliament commissioned a report, which condemned the awful fact that Aborigines were going 'blind and dying from thirst' in a nation as rich as Australia. But the report was dismissed as alarmist by politicians and the right-wing press. In an ominous sign of what was to come, none other than a young Rupert Murdoch flew in to investigate and found that the report was '"hopelessly exaggerated" and that "these fine native people have never enjoyed better conditions"'.[38] Aboriginal life was, and in many ways continues to be, expendable in the pursuit of Australian so-called progress.

The more controversial dimension of the Australian genocide is the very clear attempt to biologically absorb the Aborigines, or to put it another way, to breed them out of existence. In Western Australia the 1936 Native Administration Act outlawed the marriage of so-called 'half castes' with supposedly 'full bloods', language steeped in the ideas of racial science. A. O. Neville (ironically titled 'Chief Protector of Aborigines') was clear that the aim of this law was that Australia would be able to 'forget that there ever were any aborigines'.[39] This followed a precedent set by the Department of the Interior, which prohibited Aborigines from interracial 'mating', but also from sexual union with women of 'part aboriginal blood'. They were making 'every endeavour to breed out the colour by elevating female half-castes to the White standard'.[40] In both law and policy this aim was being driven by the state. Neville explained the policy of using so-called 'half castes' in domestic service:

> Our policy is to send them out into the white community, and if a girl comes back pregnant our rule is to keep her for two years. The child is then taken away from the mother and sometimes never sees her again. Thus these children grow up as whites, knowing nothing of their own environment. At the expiration of the period of two years the mother goes back into service so it really does not matter if she has half a dozen.[41]

The region's records from this period corroborate the impact of this sordid abuse of Aboriginal women. They reveal 'a remarkably high rate of pregnancy for girls indentured to service, especially those sent to the cities'.[42]

None of this should be surprising, given how Australia treated the children of Aborigines. Between one in three and one in ten Aboriginal children were removed from their families between around 1910 and 1970.[43] Those of mixed descent were particularly preyed upon, given the intent to breed out the natives. The award-winning 2002 film *Rabbit-Proof Fence*, based loosely on a true story of three young girls who ran away and made it back to their families, documents this history of abuse. Most were not so fortunate, and the legacies of the damage done are still being felt. So commonplace was the practice of removing children and placing them with White families that when researcher Colin Tatz paid a research visit to the Retta Dixon Home in Darwin in 1962 he and his wife were offered an Aboriginal child for the one-time price of just 25 guineas. So accepted was the practice that 'they didn't blanch at the prospective "sale"' but drove around for an hour contemplating the offer.[44] (In a chilling parallel, in the United States and Canada in the nineteenth and twentieth centuries there were policies of removing native children from their families and placing them in boarding schools in order to assimilate them into Western culture.)[45] The debate about whether the policy of removing children from their parents was genocidal is essentially pointless: the intent was to forcibly assimilate the Aborigines into Australian life in order to extinguish them. It was part of the broader history of the nation where at both the local and national level for the majority of the twentieth century the state enforced a policy aimed at eventually destroying any trace of the Aborigines.[46]

The question of whether we apply the genocidal label to Australia matters so much because we need to shake ourselves out of the usual delusions we apply to the term. One of the objections to using the term is that it supposedly diminishes the unique suffering of Jewish people during the Holocaust. If incidental killing, or frontier violence, or mating policies are equated with the death camps and systematic slaughter of the final solution, we are somehow devaluing the horror of what the Nazis did. The notion that the violence suffered by Jewish people at the hands of the Nazis is unique only holds true if you discount the suffering, torture and brutality meted out to those who are not considered White. There is no questioning the horrors of the concentration camps, but to elevate the Holocaust to the status of primary evil done in the world has the added advantage of meaning that our eyes are averted from the brutality that Europe inflicted across the globe. Race cannot possibly be the defining logic if White people suffered the worst crime against humanity. It also allows Western nations to distance themselves from evil: Australia is progressive because it is *not* Nazi Germany. To compare the two is therefore heresy because it shatters the mirage necessary to maintain the nation's distorted image of itself. In truth the colonial logic of empire was at work in the destruction of both the Aborigines and Jewish people. The Holocaust was the logic of empire brought into the heart of Europe.

Before we deal in depth with the Holocaust, it is important to trace the genocidal roots of the final solution to German colonialism in Africa. German treatment of the natives in their colonies is particularly instructive and, given the events of the twentieth century, also hugely influential in how we understand the roots of modern genocide.

After the First World War, as a consequence of defeat, Germany was stripped of its colonies. Due to this it is easy to overlook Germany as a colonial nation, but make no mistake, the country was a major player in imperialism, particularly in Africa. What are now Namibia, Tanzania, Rwanda, Cameroon and Togo were part of the German Empire until Germany's defeat in the War. South-west Africa was initially seen as a place that Germans could settle in, and as the British had done in India a private company, the Society for German Colonization, was established to lead the charge. The private enterprise's progress was slower than expected, in large part because of the resistance of the indigenous population, who did not roll over and allow German conquest. As Chancellor, in 1891 Bismarck bought shares in the company, nationalizing the colonial effort and imposing the full force of the German Empire on the region.

At the turn of the twentieth century the Germans found themselves at a military disadvantage to the native Herero and Nama people, who outgunned them and were skilled fighters on horseback. This did not prevent the colonizers from appropriating land, raping women or forcing the natives into work. The practice of rape was 'so common that German settlers had names for it: *Verkafferung*, or going native, and *Schmutzwirtschaft*, or dirty trade'.[47] When the Herero and Nama rose up against the Germans in 1904 the invaders were ill equipped to win a war, either conventional or guerrilla. As we have seen elsewhere, genocidal logic prevailed. In the *Schrecklichkeit* (extermination) order to his officers, General Lothar von Trotha proclaimed at Osombo-Windimbe, on 2 October 1904:

> All Hereros must leave the country. If they do not do so, I will force them with cannons to do so. Within the German borders, every Herero, with or without weapons . . . will be shot. I shall no longer shelter women and children. They must either return to their people or I will shoot them. This is my message to the Herero nation.[48]

After being slaughtered in the thousands, the Herero were on the run and the Germans purposely forced them to retreat into the desert, fully aware of what the consequences would be. Thousands perished in the harsh conditions and the remainder were rounded up and put into concentration camps. Of the 35,000 Herero forced into such camps between 1904 and 1906 it is estimated that only 193 survived.[49] At least 70,000 Herero and 30,000 Nama were slaughtered by the Germans in just this two-year period, devastating the population. Overall, fighting, hunger and disease killed around 250,000 Africans as a result of German campaigns to stop rebellions in their southern African colonies.[50]

In the present day, the populations have returned to what they were before the genocide but the fact it took a hundred years tells us the scale of the annihilation. The case of the Herero and Nama people of Namibia has recently been in the spotlight because their present-day leaders sued Germany in the United States for reparations for this genocide in 2017. The reparations suit aims for historical redress for the mass slaughter and uses the $90 billion paid to the survivors of the Jewish Holocaust as its precedent.[51] Linking the atrocities in Namibia to the Holocaust is important because German actions in Africa were the precursor to the mass murder of Jewish people almost half a century later. All the ingredients existed: concentration camps, racial science, and of course genocide. The annihilation of the Herero and Nama was the first genocide of the twentieth century, and it provided the blueprint for what was to come.

The genocide was committed in large part by up to 14,000 soldiers and became part of the folklore of the German nation. As though it were a routine holiday destination, 'a host of photographs [were] taken, and made into picture postcards of soldiers sent with greetings from afar and representing anything from concentration camps, over [sic] emaciated prisoners in chains to execution scenes'.[52] Gustav Frenssen's 1906 novel *Peter Moors Fahrt nach Südwest* was a gruesome celebration of the horrors of the genocide told as an adventure of the German Empire. Not only was it translated into several languages (including English), it sold 400,000 copies in Germany up until 1945 and became standard school reading from 1908 until it fell out of favour with the fall of the Nazi regime.[53] Genocide in Namibia set an important precedent for the nation that may well have been a necessary pre-condition for the Holocaust.

THE HOLOCAUST IS MODERNITY

During the Second World War the lawyer Raphael Lemkin coined the term genocide. He was of Polish Jewish descent and lost almost fifty family members to the Nazi Holocaust that devastated Europe, so it is no surprise that he dedicated his life to defining and creating a legal framework for the prevention of genocide. Up until this point there was no conceptual or legal definition of the mass slaughter of particular groups and he based the word on the Greek *genos* (for tribe, race or family) and Latin *cide* (killing), explaining that genocide was the 'crime of destroying national, racial or religious groups'.[54] The horrors of the Holocaust reshaped much of the way that we think about the world, including defining generational slaughter.

Undoubtedly the annihilation of 6 million Jewish people by the Nazis is one of history's worst atrocities. The manner in which families were rounded up, forced into concentration camps and gassed to death as the 'final solution' left a sickening trail of destruction. 'Never again' rightly became the mantra across Europe after seeing the consequences of genocidal logic in Germany. But the way that we understand the Holocaust detracts from an honest assessment of genocide and its fundamental role in shaping the West.

Sociologist Zygmunt Bauman wrote *Modernity and the Holocaust* in 1989, which upended how we view the genocide. Having fled from the Nazis himself he was keenly aware of the brutality and significance of the Holocaust but disturbed by the mainstream narrative. British Historian Everett Hughes was typical of the dominant account:

> The National Socialist Government of Germany carried out the most colossal piece of 'dirty work' in history on the Jews. The crucial problems concerning such an occurrence are (1) who are the people who actually carry out such work and (2) what are the circumstances in which other 'good' people allow them to do it? What we need is better

knowledge of the signs of their rise to power and better ways of keeping them out of power.[55]

If we understand the Holocaust in this way then the genocide is an aberration in complete contrast to the progressive ideals of Western development. Hitler and his gang of Nazis are the bogeymen of history, pure evil in human form, whose type need to be prevented from seizing power by any means necessary. Evil is located at the individual level and soul searching is done to work out why so many people followed their sinister tune.

Rather than seeing the Holocaust as an aberration, going against the principles of the West, Bauman argued that

> The Holocaust was not an irrational outflow of the not-yet-fully-eradicated residues of pre-modern barbarity. It was a legitimate resident in the house of modernity; indeed, one who would not be at home in any other house.[56]

In other words, to see the Holocaust as the result of evil people who are not modern is to miss the point. The logic of the Holocaust is *the logic* of Western development. When we acknowledge this we can see the fallacies within the dominant approach to 'never again'. As we have already seen in this chapter, while the Holocaust was a horrendously brutal genocide, it does not stand alone in human history and certainly not within the formation of the West. Since 1492 genocide has been a key organizing principle of the rise of Western modernity, from the annihilation of tens of millions in the Americas and the Caribbean, to the almost total eradication of the Aborigines in Tasmania. The Holocaust represents colonial practices coming into play in Europe. Africans, Asians and indigenous people being slaughtered by Europeans did not trouble the psyche of the West, but seeing colonial violence enacted on White bodies meant a complete rethinking of long-held paradigms of race and power. Jewish people were racialized into a subhuman position using the same racial science that justified colonial brutality.

The fact that the term genocide only came to exist in the West during the Holocaust is testament enough to the problem. Systematic killing of hundreds of millions of 'savages' in the colonies did not merit the creation of a new concept. There was unfortunately very little that was remarkable about mass murder of the Black and Brown. As is evident from even the smallest glance at history, the genocide of the Herero and Nama in Namibia is the grandfather of the Holocaust. But in the cases seeking for reparations against Germany the government continues to resist calling the indiscriminate slaughter a genocide. In a perverse way they are correct to do so. The reason that the concept of genocide was not conceived of in the West until the Holocaust is that the term does not apply to those deemed subhuman, and the inhumanity of those that the Europeans encountered was presumed from the outset.

In 1550 the question of whether the indigenous people of the Americas 'had a soul or not' was put to a theological trial in Valladolid. Bartolomé de las Casas and Juan Ginés de Sepúlveda debated the issue, with las Casas eventually prevailing in his proposition that although the natives were backward they nevertheless had a soul and so could be Christianized.[57] Prior to this declaration it was assumed that the natives were subhuman and therefore their annihilation and enslavement by Europeans was perfectly acceptable. Las Casas had been arguing for the rights of the indigenous Americans for years but at this point there was no doubt in the European mind that Africans were inhuman beasts, more akin to animals than humans. In fact, las Casas argued that indigenous slave labour could be replaced with savage beasts from Africa. Transatlantic slavery was one of the single most barbaric and murderous of systems and was justified by the belief that Africans were not people.

It should come as no surprise then that even when the atrocities committed in the colonies were so egregious that they turned the stomachs of Europeans, their perpetration did not lead to any conceptual change in the West. As reward for organizing the Berlin Conference of 1884–5 that literally carved up Africa and divided it between the European powers, King Leopold II was granted the Congo Free State. We have already seen many examples of the European presumption that inhabited land was the possession of the colonizers. But this was a step beyond the usual: Congo was the personal possession of Leopold, who engaged his own private army to rule the region.[58] The result was perhaps one of the most extreme and brutal colonial regimes, one that stands out even in the horrors of the time.

As a direct result of Leopold's reign from 1885 to 1908, approximately 10 million, or half of the entire population of Congo were killed. Leopold's atrocities were crafted in the furnaces of Enlightenment thought, which led him to actually believe he was on a noble mission. He declared that 'to open to civilization the only part of our globe which it has yet to penetrate, to pierce the darkness which envelops entire peoples, is, I dare to say, a crusade worthy of this century of progress.'[59] Massacres, starvation and extreme physical cruelty accounted for the mass loss of life, but even in current literature there is debate about whether the deaths amounted to genocide.[60] In the twisted logic of Western scholarship, the intent to wipe out the population is seen as a vital ingredient for mass deaths to qualify as a genocide. In Congo much of the murder was done in efforts to get the natives to work rather than to erase the population. But when we consider the horrific brutality of Leopold's regime it should be obvious that if we do not consider it a genocide, that is only because of a deeply problematic definition of the word.

Congo is rubber rich and Leopold made a fortune extracting it. In a macabre similarity to Columbus four centuries earlier, he forced the locals to collect his bounty with horrific tactics. Not meeting your quota meant the amputation of your hand, even for small children. A particularly, but not uncommonly, gruesome account from a sub-agent of the Anversoise Trust, which Leopold set up to rule in Congo, told the story of being

> sent into a village to ascertain if the natives were collecting rubber, and in the contrary case to murder all, including men, women and children. We found the natives sitting peaceably. We asked them what they were doing. They were unable to reply, thereupon we fell upon them all, and killed them without mercy. An hour later we were joined by X—, and told him what had been done. He answered, 'It is well, but you have not done enough!' Thereupon he ordered us to cut off the heads of the men and hang them on the village palisades, also their sexual members, and to hang the women and children on the palisades in the form of a cross.[61]

Obviously, Leopold did not want to annihilate all the natives because if he did he would have no one to do his labour. Settler colonialism was not an option for a state owned by one man. But to debate whether the acts that led to the deaths of 10 million people are genocide demonstrates the conceptual problem at the heart of modernity. Black and Brown death simply is of less value intellectually. The definition of genocide is taken from the Nazi aim to eradicate *all* Jews and if we accept that as the definition of genocide then it would not apply in the case of Congo. But the fact that we have no word to account for the killing (intentionally or otherwise) of millions of people shows how little thought went into the problem of colonial genocides.

It is also noteworthy that, alongside the Holocaust, Lemkin repeatedly cited the Armenian genocide in 1915 as a motivator for a new language surrounding ethnic violence. The Armenian genocide was also horrendous: up to 1.5 million Armenians were slaughtered by the Ottoman Empire in Turkey, over fears that they would join the war effort against the Empire, which was allied with Germany in the First World War.[62] But it is telling that the systematic murder of a Christian minority by a Muslim empire would be central for the conceptual framework of the term genocide. There is no doubt in Western philosophy that the Christian victim has a soul and is therefore worthy of conceptual consideration. Colonial slaughter like that in Congo has not, and maybe could never have had the same impact on Western thought.

Apart from the sheer scale of the brutality, events in Congo stand out because they drew widespread condemnation from the rest of Europe. An international campaign to end the regime of terror in the Free State emerged to bring an end to the slaughter. In 1908 the Belgian parliament bowed to pressure and took Congo away from the sole control of Leopold. But before we celebrate this as some momentous victory and turning point in Europe's relationship to the peoples of the colonies, we should tread with extreme caution. No doubt the massacres, rapes, and mutilation of children had an impact and brought home the realities of other nations' own colonial brutality. But Edmund Morel, a British journalist who was one of the leading anti-Leopold campaigners, was honest in his objections to the Free State. As well as humanitarian concerns he was deeply troubled that Leopold's private fiefdom was a 'destruction of [the] commercial relationship between the European and the African'.[63] Not only was Leopold disrupting free trade in the region with his monopoly of Congo, in his excessive brutality he was endangering the colonial relationship between Africa and Europe. The British have always favoured an approach to colonial exploitation that left enough room for them to pretend they were doing the savages a favour by nobly picking up the 'White man's burden' to civilize the world. Mutilated children and mass killings put that fantasy beyond reasonable reach. Leopold had his playground taken away, but the exact same relationship of exploitation and a more managed brutality continued in its place. The rest of Europe also carried on with empire without the reality of their genocidal logic ever hitting home. That was impossible, until victims who we consider to be White were caught within the very same mechanisms.

Nazis justified the Holocaust using the same racial science that legitimized genocide, slavery and colonialism in the colonies. Germany was at the forefront of racial science because of its genocidal approach in South West Africa. At a ceremony in Berlin in 2018, Germany handed back human remains including nineteen skulls from Africans in the region, but still holds 1,000 skulls it took between 1884 and 1915 to conduct scientific experiments.[64] The archive of knowledge for scientific racism was built of such macabre colonial exploits that provided rigorous 'evidence' of the inferiority of Africans. Notorious Nazi scientist Eugen Fischer, whose work influenced Hitler's Nuremberg Laws, cut his teeth researching in Namibia in 1905 during the genocide. He created a device to categorize the 'races', a box with thirty different strands of hair from blonde to black, with colour and texture often meaning the difference between 'life and death'.[65] In a testament to how widespread these ideas were, he gave this device to Karl Pearson, who was one of the people who invented the field of statistics, at University College London in 1908. Pearson was the protégé of Francis Galton who pioneered the study of eugenics, which aimed to create a superior human family by breeding only the best stock and sterilizing the poor and non-White. These ideas of 'racial hygiene' were mainstream and powerful in the early twentieth century. Tens of thousands of poor and minority women in America were put through enforced sterilization and the notion of lesser peoples was used to limit immigration into the United States from Eastern European nations deemed to produce those of spoiled stock.

Jewish people became subject to the same genocidal logic as natives in the colonies because they were rendered subhuman by racial science.

Galton made it clear that 'Jews are specialised for a parasitical existence', and the eugenicists agreed that they were on a lower ladder of human development.[66] The Nazis were not only influenced but also inspired by the network of Western scholars in esteemed universities who provided the 'evidence' that Jews were less than human. They even copied the US sterilization laws as one of the first steps to eliminate the backward race. The Holocaust was the logic of race brought to bear within Europe. Racism is as essential to the West as water is to human beings, so in looking to explain the Holocaust we should not look for reasons outside the system itself.

Bauman explains that only modernity could produce the Holocaust, because of notions of scientific rationality developed in the Enlightenment. Annihilating 6 million people over the course of a few years required an efficiency and cold-blooded ruthlessness perfected in Western development. Nazi scientists studied the most efficient methods to kill, devising the most effective gas for the desired effect. The process of massacre in gas chambers resembled the bureaucratic mechanisms of the assembly line. Race was used to determine that Jewish people were subhuman and capitalist bureaucracy was enacted to dispose of the unwanted people. Race, bureaucracy, science and rationality, all key principles of modernity, came together to produce a genocide, one of the key mechanisms for the development of the West. The uncomfortable truth is that the Nazis did not undermine the governing principles of the West, they took them to their extreme, with deadly consequences. The simple 'never again' rhetoric misses the mark so widely because it presents the West as the solution, when in fact it was the system that was the problem all along. The call is coming from inside the house that produced the Holocaust, and we can see this same logical fallacy with how modern-day genocides are understood.

POST-COLONIAL GENOCIDE

Between April and July 1994 approximately 1 million Rwandans were massacred in the worst genocide since the Holocaust. At its conclusion 70 per cent of the Tutsi (who were the primary target for annihilation) in the country had been killed.[67] Images of Africans butchering other Africans with machetes cast the genocide as being derived from a barbarism that went decidedly against the progressive values of the West. A tribal blood feud between the Hutus and Tutsis perfectly fits the narrative of savage Africa, unable to resist urges for violence and division. The West, and the United States in particular, faced a lot of criticism for not intervening in the violence sooner and for their reluctant to term the slaughter a genocide. Declaring a genocide would have included a responsibility to react, and the West was reluctant to do so. Rwanda had no strategic relevance and the United States had already suffered an embarrassment in Somalia in 1993, immortalized in the film *Black Hawk Down*, where a US helicopter was hit with a rocket-propelled grenade. Bill Clinton, who was president at the time of the Rwandan massacre, admitted in an interview with CNN in 2013 that the slow response cost lives, saying, 'If we'd gone in sooner, I believe we could have saved at least a third of the lives that were lost. It had an enduring impact on me.' Whilst on a state visit to Rwanda in 1998 he apologized for the error, blaming a lack of awareness:

> It may seem strange to you here, especially the many of you who lost members of your family, but all over the world there were people like me sitting in offices, day after day after day, who did not fully appreciate the depth and the speed with which you were being engulfed by this unimaginable terror.[68]

It was in fact incredibly strange for the president to claim ignorance, when it was later revealed that the US government knew the scale of the slaughter almost immediately. Although the administration did not use the word publicly until 25 May, at least as early as 23 April internal memos to the government warned of the need to 'stop the genocide', and the words 'final solution' were used to describe the situation to officials.[69] Worse still, both the CIA and US officials were well aware of the escalating tensions before the genocide and the US provided arms to neighbouring Uganda in full knowledge that these were crossing into Rwanda.[70] All sorts of pragmatic and cynical reasons existed for the US in particular, and the West in general, to sit on their hands whilst the Tutsis were being exterminated. But the fact that the United Nations only officially designated the systematic annihilation of one ethnic group a genocide in *February 2014* is a testament to the conceptual problem of genocide in the colonies. As we have seen throughout this chapter, the deaths of the Black and Brown do not matter in the formation of the West. Genocide is a category reserved for the human and even in the twenty-first century our presence in that category has to be argued for.

The hand-wringing over the delayed response from the West in preventing the genocide is also problematic. It is entirely disempowering to portray the West as the benevolent hero in a tale of African savagery. Here again we can see the narrative of the 'White man's burden' being to civilize the colonies. We can also see the same conceptual error as we did with the Holocaust: that the Rwandan genocide was anti-Western, caused by tribal barbarity. In reality, the unspeakable horror of Rwanda was entirely a production of Western imperialism.

Hutus and Tutsis existed as distinct groups long before colonization by Europe, a process which began in earnest in 1890 when Germany was granted the region. Belgium also had an early influence in Rwanda due to the lack of clarity over borders until 1900. Although the different ethnic groups existed and there were tensions between the minority Tutsis and majority Hutus, the Europeans institutionalized and racialized these differences into solid absolutes that meant a person's tribe determined their role in the colony. Missionaries began this process, with one of the first schools being opened in 1905 by Father Classe, who explained that the purpose was to 'turn the Tutsi, the "born rulers" of Rwanda into an elite "capable of understanding and implementing progress"'.[71] The school was solely for Tutsis and if a stray Hutu was educated their instruction was in Swahili rather than the supposedly more civilized French. Once the Belgians took over the colony in 1916 they fully implemented a system of division that included forced labour for Hutus and a regime in which the highest local administrator was always a Tutsi chief. The 1933–4 census cemented the institutionalization of this policy by categorizing the population as either Tutsi, Hutu or Twa (another ethnic group in the region). It was not an arbitrary decision to elevate the Tutsi over the Hutu in Rwanda, but one rooted in racist ideas that the Belgians institutionalized.

To explain the scientific superiority of Africa historically, European scholars had to create racial mythologies. Burning books or Whitewashing the names of scholars would only go so far. Hegel is famous for drawing a distinction between European Africa and Africa Proper, but there is a long history of that idea. We should reject the term sub-Saharan Africa out of hand because it is built on the premise that proper Africa is where the savage Black people live and the north is inhabited by a different, more civilized race. This belief was etched onto Rwandan society by way of the Tutsis tending to be taller and lighter-skinned that the Hutus, a physical difference that was seized upon as proof of their superiority. When the Belgians colonized Rwanda they did so believing the Hamitic myth that a Tutsi was a 'European under a black skin' rather than an African.[72]

Ham is a biblical character, the son of Noah, who saw his father naked and drunk. As punishment for embarrassing him in front of his other sons, Noah cursed Ham's son Canaan to be the 'servant of servants'. The curse of Ham was used to justify both the Arab and European enslavement of Africans because Ham's descendants were understood to have Black skin and the curse of servitude became linked to their colour.[73] However, the Hamitic myth takes the same story and turns it on its head. In the version applied to Rwanda the Tutsis were claimed as the descendants of Ham cast into the wilderness in order to prove they were *superior* to real Africans. Based on anthropological studies, including of course examination of skulls, it was concluded that all inhabitants of Africa were not created equally, and the Hamites were identified as Caucasians with black skin. As academic Mahmood Mamdani explains,

> Every sign of 'progress' on the Dark Continent was now taken as evidence of a civilizing influence of an outsider race. This race of civilizers, it was said, were Caucasians who were black in color without being Negroid in race.[74]

Unfortunately, both the Hutu and Tutsi leant into this racialization of their differences. Tutsis largely accepted the benefits of being the privileged colonial class and the Hutus built up an anti-Tutsi sentiment based on the supposedly foreign nature of their ruling class. While creating independence movements in the 1950s, Hutu nationalism coalesced around the slogan 'Hutu Power', whilst the Tutsi leadership attempted to maintain their colonial position. Colonial borders did not help matters, since the Hutu/Tutsi split was not contained in the neat parcels of land the Europeans made into nation states. Neighbouring Burundi was also Tutsi-controlled and supported Tutsi incursions to gain power in Rwanda. After a raid on the capital Kigali in 1963, between 5,000 and 20,000 Tutsis were massacred and a Hutu republic was declared in 1964 that removed all Tutsis from political office. In Burundi, which had very similar dynamics, 200,000 of the Hutu majority population were slaughtered to quell unrest. The post-colonial Hutu (Bantu)/Tutsi (Hamite) division based on race and sealed in blood was complete.

The 1994 genocide came after a civil war sparked by the Tutsi Rwandan Patriotic Front (RPF) seizing land in Rwanda. By the time of the genocide the RPF had made substantial gains and one in seven Hutus from Rwanda were refugees who had fled from RPF-controlled areas. 'Hutu Power' made a strong comeback in Rwanda due to the war and fears of being dominated by the Tutsis again. A central part of this project was to restore the Hamitic myth and confirm that Tutsis were an alien race. By April 1994 a compromise sharing of power had been agreed and the Hutu republic had to concede to Tutsi representation. However, on 6 April a plane carrying the Hutu presidents Juvénal Habyarimana of Rwanda and Cyprien Ntaryamira Burundi was shot down. This act unleashed the anti-Tutsi sentiment that had been building up and when news spread the massacres began almost immediately. Given the scale of the violence, the genocide was well-planned, with the groundwork being prepared some time in advance. But the roots of the slaughter were planted almost a century earlier with the racialization and institutionalization of tribal difference by Europeans. This is not to excuse the actions of the murderers but to understand their behaviour in the context that produced it.

There are key similarities to the process of colonial genocide we have seen elsewhere. We have the idea of different racial groups pitted against one another and conflict that arises due to the clashes between the groups. When faced with defeat (in this case, power-sharing) the Hutu extremists did what all European forces in the colonies did, which was to exterminate the enemy to eliminate the threat. The history, logic, context and execution were not alien to the modern world: just as with the Holocaust, the Rwandan genocide was the product of the colonial logic of Western imperialism.

Genocide is an essential component of the current political and economic order. The West was founded upon genocide in the Americas and the Caribbean and was sustained with colonial slaughter around the globe. Western prosperity is propped on the countless bodies sacrificed for so-called development. Instead of engaging with the brutality of the system, the popular imagination pictures genocides as the product of evil-doers and savages committing atrocities contrary to Western values of reason and tolerance. But as we have seen, the roots of genocides such as the Holocaust and the horrors in Rwanda are a product of the West, which that could only have occurred in the house built on the violence of Enlightenment thought. To understand that genocide is a central pillar of the West is to begin to unpick the myths that sustain the illusions of progress. Just as genocide still echoes in the present day, so too does the next foundation stone of the West that we will explore: transatlantic slavery.

3

Slavery

On 9 February 2018 the Twitter account of Her Majesty's Treasury posted the following surprising #FridayFact:

> Did you know that in 1833, Britain used £20 million, 40% of its national budget, to buy freedom for all slaves in the Empire? The amount of money borrowed for the Slavery Abolition Act was so large that it wasn't paid off until 2015. Which means that living British citizens helped pay to end the slave trade.

Whoever sent out the post seemed to think that the public would be proud that 'millions of you' helped end the slave trade through your taxes. We have become so accustomed to historical inaccuracies in understanding transatlantic slavery that we can set aside the lack of any distinction between the slave trade, abolished in 1807, and slavery itself, which continued until 1838 and is the subject of the #Friday-Fact. But the idea that the public would be happy we have been paying taxes for the 'freedom' of the so-called slaves is so offensive that this tweet should only make sense as a macabre parody. The revelation that I and generations of family descended from those enslaved in the Caribbean effectively paid compensation to slave owners is sickening, not comforting.

Slavery was formally abolished in the British Empire by the Slavery Abolition Act passed in 1833, which became law in 1834. However, even though slavery was abolished, the enslaved were forced into what was called 'apprenticeship' for four further years. This meant having to spend three-quarters of their time working on the former slave plantations, for no wages. A funny sort of freedom. Perversely, the system was justified on the basis that the enslaved had to be trained into the ways of wage labour. The savages obviously could not be expected to understand how to be free. In defence of apprenticeship, Sir James Carmichael Smyth declared that the 'transition from the dejected and almost naked slave to the cheerful and decently clad labourer could only be believed by those who had recently revisited the colony after an absence of several years'.[1] In reality, apprenticeship did not have the welfare of the formerly enslaved in mind. The goal was to ensure that the slave owners should not 'lose . . . the benefit to which they were entitled to by contract' of slavery.[2] Therefore the enslaved had to pay for their own freedom by continuing to work for free, a key part of history oddly missing from the Treasury's fun #FridayFact. The other essential ingredient absent from their tweet was from who exactly the British taxpayer bought the freedom of the enslaved. Just as with apprenticeship, the money went to compensate slave owners for their loss of wealth.

In a shock development, the news that we have been paying slave owners with our tax money was not something the public widely celebrated. Especially considering that millions of us are descendants of the very enslaved who were not only never compensated but were also forced to work off their 'debt' to their masters. This incident speaks to the truth of slavery and Britain, but also the fantasy version of history that operates in the dominant historical narrative. Britain should, apparently, be proud of ending slavery but not feel guilty about profiting from it.

The reparation payment for slave owners is of an unprecedented scale in British history. Twenty million pounds represented 40 per cent of the entire expenditure of the British government in 1833. In today's money the payment would be the equivalent to £17 billion.[3] But £20 million represented around 5 per cent of GDP in 1833, which would be over £100 billion in 2020. Whichever number you prefer, it is clearly a massive transfer of wealth by the government. The only government pay-out in history that was larger was the one made to bail out the banks after the 2008 financial crisis, which cost £200 billion. However, that was a series of loans that have supposedly been paid back since. There simply is no other example of the equivalent of over £100 billion to compensate for private individual losses, an amount of money so overwhelming that the government had to take a loan from the Bank of England that was so large it took 182 years to pay back. The fact the government invested so much money in this bailout demonstrates just how essential the plantation system was to the economy.

Transatlantic slavery was the fuel that powered Western development. It was the massive wealth derived from the system that allowed the West to catch up with and then overtake the rest of the world. Slavery was not new: Europe developed on the back of the Arab slave trade that was hundreds of years old when Columbus sailed back from Hispaniola with indigenous Americans to sell into slavery. But the transatlantic trade was a unique development, reducing Africans to subhuman commodities who became the major currency for Western progress. By 1833, however, the system had begun to fray.

The Haitian revolution in 1804 had been a major factor in Britain abandoning the trade from Africa: the British were terrified of Africans who would revolt in the Caribbean. Between 1831 and 1832 the Christmas Rebellion of the enslaved in Jamaica led by Sam Sharpe also shook the British commitment to slavery.[4] Over 20,000 enslaved Africans took part and more than 300 were executed in the aftermath. Rebellion and resistance had made the system dangerous and less profitable. Sugar, which was the primary product in the British Caribbean, was also becoming cheaper and faced competition from new producers in places like India, who could pay close to slave-labour rates without the same risks. The plantation economies were in danger of collapse, which would have ruined the wider British economy.

Britain was not alone. The entire Western economic system depended on the wealth from slavery. That wealth remains with us to this day, as does the poverty created through the brutal system. We think of slavery as belonging to the distant past, but the world we live in remains created in its image.

LEGACIES OF SLAVERY

Britain was by no means the only country to engage in the slave system, nor to give reparations to its slave owners at abolition. Denmark, the Netherlands and Spain all paid out compensation, and as I will discuss in more depth later, France forced Haiti to pay over 150 million francs for having the audacity to successfully revolt against slavery. After claiming its independence from Britain, the United States rose to become one of the primary nations reliant on slavery. Lincoln authorized compensation for slave owners in order to achieve emancipation in Virginia in 1862. Every enslaved African freed merited a payment of $100, over $2,500 in today's money, and the largest individual pay-out was $18,000, the equivalent of almost $500,000.[5] Compensation was not widespread in the United States; in fact after the Civil War General Sherman confiscated slave owners' land and promised each emancipated African 40 acres and the use of a mule to tend the land, in reparation for their toil and suffering. But this order was reversed by President Andrew Johnson, who compensated the slave owners for their losses by returning the land taken from the defeated Confederacy.[6]

Britain is unique, however, in that it holds a comprehensive record of where the slave reparations went, thanks to the *Legacies of British Slave Ownership* project at University College London (UCL). The project has documented the 47,000 recipients of payments to try to establish where the money ended up.[7] What is abundantly clear from these records is just how widespread slave ownership was. The church, politicians, banks and thousands of individuals had personal stakes in slavery; and all were compensated at abolition. Among the notable people with links to slavery reparations are former prime minister David Cameron and his wife, who both have beneficiaries in their families. Samantha Cameron is descended from William Jolliffe, who received the equivalent of £3 million for his holding of 164 enslaved Africans. Slave-owning members of David Cameron's family include Sir James Duff, who also received the equivalent of £3 million for his 202 enslaved Africans in Jamaica. Cameron is not the only British prime minister with links to the slave trade. William Gladstone's father received £83 million in today's money to compensate for his loss of the labour of the 2,508 enslaved Africans he owned across a number of Caribbean plantations. The news of Cameron's links to slave-owner reparations was particularly egregious given that he famously told the Jamaican parliament in 2015 that their demands for reparations for being the victims of slavery were falling on deaf ears and that it was time to 'move on'.[8]

Researchers at UCL were also keen to follow this money into investments in British industry. They found that the money was invested across society, including in the railways, industry and philanthropy. Financial services were particularly implicated in slavery: the Bank of England has recently acknowledged that many of the Bank's directors in the eighteenth century were slave-owners or their descendants. The practice of banks using the enslaved as security for loans also 'permeated banking'.[9] Insurance brokers were central to the slave system, underwriting the hazardous journeys of slave ships and also the plantations in the Americas and Caribbean, and slave owners were constant features on the boards of insurance companies. Two of the first five presidents of what is now Royal Sun Alliance, one of the biggest insurance firms today, were slave owners, and the group grew by incorporating slave-owner dominated companies. Accounting was no different: two of the largest firms in the world today, Deloitte and Price Waterhouse Coopers, were founded by families enriched by profits from slavery. By accounting for the slave compensation money, the UCL project demonstrated just some of the afterlives of slavery. But the extent to which Britain, and the West as a whole, engorged itself on slavery cannot be captured solely in the money from slave-owner compensation.

As we have already seen, the 'discovery' of the Americas was the starting point of the West. Expansion across the Atlantic marked the shift from the limits of Europe to the endless possibilities of the so-called New World. Resources and labour were two of the elements that were essential to unlocking the wealth across the Atlantic, and slavery became central to both for over three centuries. Minerals such as gold, and other commodities that powered the industrial development of products like tobacco, sugar and cotton were all produced across the Atlantic, providing the fuel for Western expansion. In the first instance the natives were put to work, but genocide meant there were not enough workers to sustain production. European indentured labourers, conscripted as serfs to toil on the plantations for a limited number of years, were favoured by Britain into the seventeenth century. But when demand grew the nation enthusiastically embraced slave labour, in which the Spanish and Portuguese had been pre-eminent from the fifteenth century. Enslaving Africans to be put to work in the Americas and Caribbean became the basis of production in the Atlantic system, which was 'the first principle and foundation of all the rest, the mainspring of the machine which sets every wheel in motion' for the development of the West.[10]

Eric Williams' classic *Capitalism and Slavery,* first published in 1944, remains the go-to book for the case that slavery provided the fuel for British development. He painstakingly outlined how central slave labour and produce was to British industry and the development of capital. A chilling example is the case of Lloyd's of London, which is now one of Britain's largest companies, with assets in excess of £50 billion. In 2014 I remember watching an executive on BBC *Breakfast News* celebrating the company's 325th anniversary and being proud of their roots in 'insuring the merchant trade'. What she neglected to mention was that what Lloyd's cut their teeth on insuring was the slave trade. But Lloyd's commitment to slavery pre-dated its involvement in the trade, as Williams explains:

> In the early years, when Lloyd's was a coffee house and nothing more, many advertisements in the *London Gazette* about runaway slaves listed Lloyd's as the place where they should be returned.[11]

Following the global protests after the murder of George Floyd, Lloyd's apologized for its sordid past and committed to 'invest in positive programmes to attract, retain and develop black and minority ethnic talent' and offer 'financial support to charities and organizations promoting opportunity and inclusion for black and minority ethnic groups'.[12] The fact this stomach-churning PR move was dubbed 'reparations' in the press tells us how little we understand the centrality of slavery to today's conditions. There is nothing that a company that gorged on the flesh of enslaved Africans to amass its wealth could do to atone short of liquidating its assets and turning them over to Black communities.

Lloyd's was sued by the descendants of enslaved Africans, led by Deadria Farmer-Paellmann, in the United States in 2002 along with a slew of major companies and the US government. One of the US firms included in the suit was Aetna, among the nation's largest health insurance companies, founded in 1853. The company issued a public apology in 2000 for selling insurance policies for the enslaved on US plantations, after Farmer-Paellmann's activism had revealed their links to slavery. In 1853 Aetna New Orleans were selling policies for $17.53 per year, which would yield $600 if the enslaved African died. Such policies were not rare. There was a major industry of insuring the enslaved, with prices being cheaper for children than for those who were older.[13]

The involvement of insurance companies, accounting firms and banks is central to the argument that slavery fuelled development because of how important the finance sector was to Western industry. Credit and capital were absolute prerequisites for industrial development, and for the majority of the eighteenth century there were few better placed than slave owners or cotton brokers to invest in industry.

Plantations were hugely profitable, which is why so much money was paid out in reparations to slave owners to secure abolition. Barbados was Britain's richest slave colony in the seventeenth century, off the back of sugar production. The island had been producing tobacco by using White indentured labourers, but switched to sugar and primarily slave labour in 1640.[14] The transformation in the fortunes of the island were swift. Half a plot of 5,000 acres which had been purchased for £400 in 1640 was valued at £7,000 by 1648.[15] For an example of how much money could be made, Colonel Thomas Moyford emigrated to Barbados in 1647 and just three years later was boasting he had made a hundred times his initial £1,000 investment. James Parker, who found his fortune on the island, wrote a year earlier that 'a man with about 200 odd pounds . . . might quickly gaine an estate by sugar'.[16] Sugar became a highly profitable commodity as consumption ballooned in Britain and across Europe. Between 1650 and 1800 British sugar consumption increased 2,500 per cent, all of it produced by slave labour.[17] These profits from sugar and other slave-produced commodities were ploughed back into the nation, reaping untold collective dividends.

One of the many lies we like to tell about British development is that the Industrial Revolution was the product of scientific ingenuity and hard work. But what is often omitted from the story is how it also depended on the financing and resources from slavery and colonialism. James Watt and Matthew Boulton have for all intents and purposes been elevated to the status of saints in my hometown of Birmingham because of their input into the city. The story of the steam engine has an almost mythical quality, produced by the divine inspiration of our city's patrons. But Watt expressed eternal 'gratitude' to slave owners in the Caribbean because it was their finance that allowed him to realize his design and ambitions for the steam engine, and plantations were some of the first places to benefit from industrial mechanization, to refine sugar.[18] By 1808 the Spanish colony of Cuba already had twenty-five steam engines supplied by Fawcett and Preston, based in Liverpool.[19]

Cotton was also indispensable to the Industrial Revolution, both in terms of mechanization and development. Contrary to the misguided belief that industrial development replaced the need for slave labour, the relationship was the inverse. When Eli Whitney developed the cotton gin in 1793, he unleashed the potential for the fabric to be used in mass production. The separation of seeds from fibres in the plants is essential to make fabric but before the cotton gin this process was done manually and was extremely time-consuming. Prior to the cotton gin's invention slave labour was not generally applied to cotton because the time invested in the separation process made it unprofitable. But the invention gave a 'terrible second wind' to cotton produced on slave plantations and led to the major boom of the plantation economy, particularly in the United States.[20] So fundamental was this transformation that cotton plantations became the new centre of American slavery in the nineteenth century and cotton came to represent half of all US exports. Enslaved Africans were sold into the deep South, where cotton could be grown more easily than in the more northern plantations, to cash in on the cotton boom.

The boom in US cotton production also provided a major boost for the British economy. By the time of the abolition of slavery in the British colonies, cotton had become the dominant British industry. Between 1785 and 1830 cotton exports had grown from £1 million to £30 million in value. Between 1788 and just 1806 the amount of people employed in the cotton industry in Britain leapt from 350,000 to 800,000, and off the back of this production the population of

Manchester grew six-fold between 1773 and 1824. Cotton was king, but the enterprise was based on the import of raw cotton, which grew from £11 million to £283 million between 1784 and 1832.[21] Cotton does not grow in Britain, and at this point the majority of the raw material was being imported from the United States, procured, of course, by slave labour. After Britain abolished slavery in 1833, its imports of slave-produced cotton from the US South continued to grow, until the emancipation of the enslaved in America in 1865. From 1790 to 1860 the enslaved population of the United States grew from around 790,000 to over 4 million, and it was this growth that fed the cotton boom on both sides of the Atlantic. It is no exaggeration to say that slave labour built the north of England and that its beloved cotton mills, such a fixture in literary and historical imagination of the nation, are just as steeped in the history of slavery as the plantations in the Americas. The same is true for northern cities in the United States like Boston and New York, which were just as reliant on the wealth produced from the horrors of slavery.

THE TRIANGULAR TRADE

In the face of the insurmountable evidence of the importance of slavery to the development of Britain and the United States, various scholars have tried to downplay its significance for industrial development. A parade of academics in economics journals have apparently tested the idea that the slave trade was indispensable to British industry, their conclusion being to reassure everyone that Britain would have developed just fine without the horrendous trade in human flesh. Walter Rodney, the prominent Guyanese scholar, chided that 'this kind of argument is worth noting more as an example of the distortions of which White bourgeois scholarship is capable than as something requiring serious consideration'.[22] But this is not simply an academic debate that we can ignore, since these ideas frame how poorly society understands the centrality of slavery to the present day. My A-level teacher's, and the textbooks', off-hand dismissal of transatlantic slavery as a factor in the Industrial Revolution is a direct result of academic work. It is the same source which allows us to ignore massive global inequality today, since we believe the West deserves its riches and conveniently ignore the reality of oppression that produces them.

Not much surprises me any more about the lengths to which White scholarship (this includes a lot written by authors of colour) will go to try to minimize the centrality of racism to their current position of privilege. But even I raised an eyebrow when reading supposedly 'scientific' analyses diminishing the importance of slavery to the development of the British economy. It is worth exploring the acrobatic contortions such 'scholarship' has to go through to bend the abundance of evidence to support its dubious case. The principal device for doing this is by reducing the argument that the profits from slavery powered British industrial development, by counting solely the profits made from the voyages of slave ships.[23]

It has been widely recognized that the business of trading the enslaved was a dangerous task.[24] Voyages took months at sea, and from the time the ships landed on the African coast to when they left the Caribbean and Americas the crews had to deal with the resistance and revolt of their captured bounty. Conditions on slave ships were notoriously horrendous and the spread of disease was common. The death toll for those working on the ships was high, and was even higher for the enslaved Africans, a significant number of whom died in transit. Nations also tried to establish monopolies over the importation of the enslaved. Britain abandoned the approach of having one slave-trading Royal African Company for the logic of free trade in the 'market' in 1698.[25] But British companies were legally forbidden from trading with foreign-owned plantations, thereby limiting the trade. The profits from slave-trading voyages varied but it is not difficult to see how the trade itself would not be the most lucrative part of the system. However, it is absurd to overstate the case. Focusing on only the voyages from Africa also ignores the internal trade, where the enslaved were sold within the plantation system across the Americas often for huge profits. Given that the slave ships would often sell Africans to brokers in markets in the ports who would then trade with plantations, the trade was far larger than the voyages to Africa.

In a paper published in a peer-reviewed and respected academic journal it is argued that the 'direct participants in trade' did not profit 'because the price of a slave was too low'.[26] Reading this literature the focus and language of the research is as striking as it is disturbing. They reduced their scope of enquiry to 'logbooks', calculating expenses for transporting human cargo. This is like studying the Holocaust by a cost–benefit analysis of gas chambers.[27] Leaving aside the callous, inhuman way that these scholars discuss enslaved Africans, the basis of their conclusion is the definition of so-called 'voodoo' economics. They try to argue that African slave catchers were the greatest beneficiaries of the trade because they had more control over 'supply' and therefore the costs they could charge for Africans. This is done in a desperate attempt to minimize the importance of slavery to the economics of the West and at the same time to argue that Africa actually profited from it. These twisted arguments are used to reject the idea of reparations for slavery, by asserting that the West never actually made any money from it. You do not need to have more than a superficial understanding of the slave trade to see through this nonsense.

It is often called the triangular trade, because ships would leave from Europe, laden with goods to trade for the enslaved in Africa, then transport their human cargo to the Americas before returning to Europe with the products of slave labour from the plantations. There is no doubt that rewards on the African side of the transactions were far less valuable than the human capacity being traded away.

The goods that Europeans traded included guns and textiles produced in Europe. Wool was a key commodity that Africans desired, along with cotton fabrics. But these were finished products imported into Africa and not capital-producing, like the labour of the enslaved. The textiles and guns traded in Africa were a key outlet for exports that benefited Western economies. An argument could be made that guns were valuable in terms of acquiring land, but often these were purchased in order to defend against slave raiders or other groups who also had guns.[28] In return for millions of labourers who would produce untold wealth through commodity production, African enslavers received nothing that would stimulate any economic development. In addition, the risks to the enslavers on the continent were far greater than those for the Europeans involved. Journeys from the interior of the continent could take eight months, with up to 40 per cent of those enslaved dying on the way.[29] The risk of mutiny and attack was extremely high and the reward for all of this was relatively minimal. The truth is that slavery devastated the African political and economic system. To suggest that this is where the profits of the trade ended up goes beyond delusion into the realm of racist propaganda.

Reducing the impact of slavery to the profits of individual voyages is a fallacy, but so too is limiting the contribution of the slave trade only to its profit margin. Slaving voyages required a whole range of other industries to carry on the horrendous trade. Ships needed to be built and maintained, meaning a boom in the timber and shipbuilding trades. The ports involved also needed to develop, and these became focal points for commerce, labour and population. Bristol dominated the British slave trade in the early eighteenth century. Between 1721 and 1730 British ships in total carried 100,000 enslaved, but from 1728 to 1732 ships launched from Bristol alone carried the same number.[30] Bristol developed a trade that was bigger than the entire Dutch system and by 1790 40 per cent of the city's income came from the trade.[31] Slavery literally built Bristol. The hallmarks of this history remain across the city, most notably with the monuments and public commemoration of one of Bristol's famous sons, Edward Colston. His only notable accomplishment was profiting from the trade in human flesh. He is deified in the city because he used some of the money he earned to invest in local philanthropy. In the wave of Black Lives Matters protests a statue of him in the city was toppled after years of activism from #ColstonMustFall. But in a macabre way it is perfectly sensible to celebrate Colston, given that his trade is responsible for building the city, and Bristol is certainly not alone in owing its development to slavery.

By the late eighteenth century Liverpool had overtaken Bristol as the primary slave port in Britain, accounting for over 60 per cent of the nation's slave trafficking and more than 40 per cent of Europe's. Slave trading also sparked a population surge, with an increase from 5,000 inhabitants in 1700 to 34,000 by 1773. The rise in trade triggered an exponential growth in customs duties, from an average of £51,000 between 1750 and 1757, to £648,000 in 1785.[32] The slave trade brought money and people flooding into Liverpool, without which it could not have developed into the city it is today. None of this was lost on Liverpudlians at the time. There was fierce resistance to the abolition of the slave trade. James Penny, a principal owner of dozens of Liverpool slaving ventures, remarked in 1788,

> Should this trade be abolished, it would not only affect the Commercial Interest, but also the Landed Property of the County of Lancaster, and more particularly the Town of Liverpool, whose fall, in that case, would be as rapid as its Rise has been astounding.[33]

London similarly benefited from being a port for slave ships, and – in case you were worried this was solely an English endeavour – after the Act of Union in 1707 Glasgow became a major player in the slave trade, providing another Atlantic port. Tobacco and in particular sugar were essential to Glasgow's economy – as important as slave-produced sugar was to Bristol's economy. By the late eighteenth century Glasgow had eighty sugar refineries compared to Bristol's twenty, marking just how important the industry was to the city.[34] Make no mistake: this was a collective effort, and the trade impacted all corners of the nation.

Industrial cities away from the coast also saw an enormous boost to their income as a consequence of the development of the slave trade. To complete the trade triangle, the ships needed to be stocked with commodities to trade for human flesh. The wool industry boomed by providing the necessary currencies, and the same is true for cotton manufacturers, who turned the raw material from slave labour into fabrics that were used to purchase more of the enslaved. Manchester was a key beneficiary that depended heavily on the trade for its development. Liverpool becoming a centre for the trade led directly to the growth of Manchester through the cotton boom. In 1772 a canal was built linking the site of production with the port and it was this that led to the explosion of Manchester. By 1788 the city was exporting £200,000 worth of goods to Africa, the production of which employed 180,000 people.[35]

Even further inland the impacts of the trade were being felt. It was remarked that 'the price of a negro was one Birmingham gun', and the city was exporting between 100,000 and 150,000 guns a year by the nineteenth century, largely to support the trade.[36] Birmingham also produced the manacles and chains that were essential to enslave people. Unsurprisingly the city came out against the abolition of the trade, declaring that it 'was dependent on the slave trade to a considerable extent . . . Abolition would ruin the town and impoverish many of its inhabitants'.[37] In order to make these guns and shackles, huge quantities of iron were needed, boosting British ironworks in places like Merthyr Tydfil in Wales.

London's benefits from the trade extended beyond just being a port city. As we saw when tracing the legacies of slave ownership, insurance, accounting and banking all profited immensely from slavery. One of the factors that made the trade itself less profitable was its dangerous nature, and insurance took advantage of this by underwriting the voyages. While the cost of insurance premiums may have dented the profits of the ships, these were accrued by the insuring companies. The same is true for debt repayments for financing the loans. In fact, if you look at where all the money that reduced the profits of slave ship voyages went, the vast majority was dispersed throughout the British economy. To focus on solely the profit of individual slave voyages is to wilfully misrepresent how central slavery was to Britain as a whole. Untold sums of money were ploughed into the key industries that powered development, generated by the trade of enslaved Africans. But impact-of-slavery-deniers are correct about one thing: the trade itself was not the most significant aspect in terms of impacting Britain. It was the entire Atlantic system of production that could not have existed without the trade.

Another device to minimize the importance of slavery is to solely focus on the sugar produced by slave labour in the Caribbean, which although highly profitable was a consumer good that was popular but not strictly necessary. By isolating sugar, the idea is to claim that Britain could have done without it. Comparing the size of the sugar business to other contributors to the economy, the conclusion is drawn that industries like 'banking, insurance, horse-breeding, canals, hospitality, construction, wheat farming, fishing, and the manufacture of wooden implements' were equally, if not more, important to the British economy.[38] Hopefully, you can see through the distortions of this kind of thinking by this point in the book. The majority of the industries thought of as being separate from sugar were either dependent on or heavily involved in slavery. Banking and insurance were necessary to finance and underwrite the trade. Canals were essential to connect the ports to the manufacturing centres. Hospitality would have at least in part been built up around slave ports to serve their wealthy beneficiaries. Whole cities developed out of their role in slavery, thereby boosting construction. No doubt wheat, fishing and wooden implements supported either the system directly or along the supply chain. Elsewhere in this kind of supposed scholarship we see comparisons to cotton, wool and iron again ignoring the obvious links to slavery (though how this is possible with cotton is beyond me). If anything, these academic delusions are a reminder of just how important slavery was, because it permeated the majority of British industry at the time.

Yet all the evidence is distorted and misused to draw the conclusion (without any proof offered but their own certainty) that it was the Industrial Revolution itself that led to the increase in British industry. Apparently it is reasonable to believe that British ingenuity is so all-powerful that not only could it create the finance needed to bring about mass production, it could also create the markets necessary to sell its produce. This is the Immaculate Conception narrative of British industry, sparked into being by divine British genius. The truth is that the slave system produced the wealth, resources and markets that powered industrial progress.

The Atlantic system was the key to unlocking Western progress in general, and the British Industrial Revolution in particular. Commodities like tobacco, sugar and cotton generated wealth and commerce that fed back into the nation. Even impact-of-slavery-deniers recognize that the key advantage was that an abundance of 'suitable virgin land' was available in the Americas for free in order to cultivate the commodities necessary for industry.[39] What they fail to acknowledge is that this was because of the genocide of the indigenous people that I covered in the last chapter. Racism is the continuous underpinning logic of the West, and to solve the problem of labour in the Garden of Eden, Western powers enslaved millions of Africans. Without this labour the bounty of the Americas would have stayed locked away, unable to enrich Europe. That is the true value of the slave trade, which is impossible to calculate. You cannot isolate any one aspect because the enslavement of Africans made the whole system possible.

Even if the trade itself was less profitable its contribution to economic development was indispensable. So while it may be possible that British industry would have developed without slavery, that is speculation best left for a science-fiction novel about alternative realities. In the timeline that we are in, slavery cannot be untangled from the development of either capitalism or industry.

THE WESTERN SYSTEM

The Atlantic system represents the dawn of the West, the founding logic based on the interdependent exploitation of the rest of the world by those of European descent. Columbus, an Italian sailing under the banner of the Spanish, is the perfect symbol because his voyages represent the beginning of the new system of global conquest that came out of Europe.[40] Although there was fierce rivalry between European powers for domination of the system, it could not have prospered without their collaboration.

The Portuguese and the Dutch dominated the slave trade in the seventeenth century. Portugal had the benefit of the enormous colony of Brazil to supply with enslaved Africans. In fact, the largest number of enslaved Africans anywhere toiled on Brazilian plantations, accounting for between 38 per cent and half of all those stolen from Africa.[41] Between 1721 and 1730 alone, nearly 150,000 Africans were taken to Brazil.[42] Portugal's demand for slave labour was so high that the Portuguese held a near-monopoly of the slave trade in places like Angola, from where over 70 per cent of those enslaved ended up in Brazil.[43] Enslaved Africans in Brazil were forced to work mining for gold and diamonds as well as producing sugar, but the demand for labour was so great that it outstripped the Portuguese supply. Brazilian colonists relied on enslaved Africans from other slaving nations to make up the difference, particularly Holland in the seventeenth century.

The Dutch held their own colonies, most notably Surinam, but rose to prominence off the back of the slave trade rather than the plantations. Despite military losses in the region that meant ceding plantations, in the 1650s Amsterdam was the centre of the commercial world because it 'dominated the market' of enslaved Africans to the Caribbean.[44] The Dutch West India Company was founded in 1621 to hold a monopoly over the Dutch involvement and was extremely successful in its terrible trade. The Dutch did not possess a large number of colonies, which meant that the company was free to trade African flesh to other European empires because they were not in direct competition for labour. They used the small Caribbean island of Curaçao not as a plantation, but as a docking station for their human cargo. In just one example of the company's flexibility, when they were forced out of Brazil by a rebellion of Portuguese colonists, they took the opportunity to begin to trade with the British in Barbados.[45]

From the very beginning the Dutch West India Company was a model of collaboration between European powers. When it was set up in 1621, the Dutch proposed to the Danes and the French that they incorporate similar companies and embark on collective expeditions. The Dutch were central to Britain's early involvement in the slave system, not only supplying the enslaved but working together to break up Spain's monopoly in the Caribbean.[46] Without this facilitation and cooperation the system could not have fully developed in the seventeenth century. The same is true of the naval technological innovations which improved the speed and longevity of ships, which were essential in facilitating the trafficking of millions across the Atlantic. The Dutch developed the work of the Portuguese and Spanish, and ultimately Britain built on the advances of the Dutch and became pre-eminent.[47]

When Britain and France came to dominate the trade in the eighteenth century, we could view this period as one marked more by intense rivalry than collusion. Both nations were fierce enemies and their plantations were in direct competition. Nantes, Marseilles and Bordeaux at various times rivalled Bristol, Liverpool and Glasgow as slave ports. Nantes began trading in the enslaved in 1666 and by 1789 the city's merchants were investing 50 million francs annually into the Caribbean.[48] During the eighteenth century the Caribbean accounted for a fifth of France's external trade,[49] and the vast majority of French industries had links to either Africa or the Americas and the Caribbean.[50] Haiti was the jewel in the crown of French slavery. In 1759, 1,587 ships docked in Haiti, more than in Marseilles, a port that was used for more than the triangular trade. Haiti was a huge success for France – by the middle of the eighteenth century Bordeaux alone was refining 10,000 tons of raw sugar from the colony – and it was one shared across Europe. Bordeaux became a hub of Flemish, Dutch, Irish and even rival English traders keen to make money out of the booming industry. Haiti's produce was sold all across Europe, with profit being made across the region. In the early eighteenth century Hamburg was a major centre for refining sugar even though Germany was only a small player in the direct buying, selling and enslaving of Africans. The wealth from the Atlantic system created a new world order where Europe gorged on the fruits of empire, regardless of which nation state owned the various colonies.

Alongside France, Britain also fed this market, providing raw materials and produce for the networks of capital. British slaving interests depended on other nations both for markets to sell produce and also for the raw materials necessary for slavery. Timber for the ships needed to be sourced as did the steel needed for Birmingham to manufacture the guns and shackles. Sweden was a major supplier of iron for the slave trade and enriched itself greatly from the Atlantic system.[51] We often see Sweden and Scandinavia as some kind of bastion of equality, but the region is just as tied up with the history of slavery as anywhere else. Both Sweden and Denmark got their hands soaked in the blood of the trade. Denmark was more successful, having a foothold in Guinea for 200 years and trafficking as many as 4,000 enslaved Africans per year.[52] St Croix, now part of the US Virgin Islands, was a Danish colony from 1672 to 1917, prompting the Danish Foreign Minister Uffe Ellemann-Jensen to admit that the country had 'exploited the slaves in the West Indian Islands during 250 years and made good money on them', during a public commemoration of the 75th anniversary of passing the colony to the Americans in 1992.[53] No corner of Western Europe is untouched by the history of slavery.

As well as collaborating in the European economic network infused by their slave colonies, Britain and France also directly collaborated with each other in the trade. This seems counterintuitive, given that they were fierce rivals and both had to invest heavily in defence to ensure that their colonial treasures were not captured by the other power. Britain was jealous of Haiti and the revenues it was generating for its rival, but the reality was that Haiti, and all of French slavery, was only as successful as it was because of the British slave trade. By the start of the eighteenth century Britain had given up on the Dutch model of creating a monopoly company to run the British trade and had given into the logic of the free market. Although it was technically forbidden, traders made a fortune selling to whoever would buy. As a result, half of all the Africans trafficked onto French plantations came from the British slave trade.[54] So during the time that Britain and France were in direct competition and even conflict, French slavery was kept afloat by British merchants. This was particularly the case in Haiti, where around two-thirds of the enslaved were African born when the revolution broke out in 1791.

Conditions on Haitian plantations were so harsh that the enslaved were mostly worked to death like disposable beasts of burden, due to the cold calculation that it was cheaper to replace Africans than to raise them.[55] When William Pitt the Younger, prime minister of Britain, realized that the British trade was enabling the success of their bitter rival he enlisted a certain William Wilberforce to begin a campaign to end the slave trade in 1786.[56] The campaign was dressed up as a moral crusade but was driven by the calculation that British colonies had trafficked enough Africans to maintain the plantations for ever, whereas French plantations would be permanently damaged by losing their supply of enslaved Africans. This explains why a supposedly moral campaign did not attempt to end slavery itself and only focused on the trafficking of Africans. Even after the trade was officially abolished in the Empire, British merchants continued to supply those foreign colonies which continued to trade, and British companies carried on purchasing slave-produced commodities.

One of the hallmarks of Western economies is the domination of private interests over the state, and the Atlantic system is where we can see this emerge. Business interests colluded across national boundaries until they convinced the nation states to change their approach. Pitt's campaign is a reminder that whilst the state may well have wanted to maintain national supremacy and conflict, the market would not allow it. The abolition of the slave trade took over twenty years from his intervention and was mostly successful not because of the edicts of the nation state but because of resistance from the enslaved. After the trade ended the birth rate on the plantations plummeted as enslaved African women refused to breed the next batch of the enslaved.[57] Those invested in slavery were also terrified by the Haitian revolution. In 1804 the Haitians completed history's only recorded successful slave revolution, declaring their independence from France. The revolution took over a decade to complete, sparked by a Vodou ceremony at Bwa Kayiman in 1791 led by the enslaved Boukman Dutty and Cécile Fatiman. In a reminder of the collusion at the heart of the system, Boukman was originally enslaved in the British colony of Jamaica but sold to a Haitian plantation. The rebellion spread across the island, eventually uniting the enslaved and the far smaller number of free Black people, whose numbers included a class of 'Creoles' who were mixed heritage as a consequence of sexual abuse by plantation owners. Efforts were made by the French, Spanish and British to take back the island and break the revolt, but the revolutionaries stood firm. As already mentioned, one of the major causes of the revolution was that around two-thirds of the enslaved were African born. Not only were they born free, many were warriors sold into slavery as prisoners of a civil war in Congo. The direct linkages to Africa, and African traditions like Vodou, struck fear in the heart of the slave owners, and Britain decided it did not want to risk importing revolution into its plantations. Britain's firms calculated they had enough home-grown cattle to toil in their fields.

Spain was the empire that tried the hardest to maintain its national monopoly, to the detriment of its plantation holdings. In Cuba, the Spanish Crown refused to allow the importation of enslaved Africans by other nations until 1789. It was likely the British colonization of Cuba in 1762 that changed Spanish thinking on this issue. During their brief occupation the British opened the island to the full economic opportunities of the Atlantic trade. Prior to the British presence only six ships a year docked; eighteen years later the number had increased to over 200. The result was that plantation slavery also greatly increased. Between 1512 and 1761 around 60,000 enslaved Africans arrived in Cuba, but from 1762 to 1838 that number was over 400,000.[58] Although the Spanish Crown objected, its colonies had relied on foreign sales of the enslaved as far back as the seventeenth century from the Dutch. In fact, in 1692 Britain gave Jamaica and Barbados not only the freedom to trade the enslaved to the Spanish but also to provide protection to Spanish merchants during business. One of Spain's greatest losses in the Caribbean was Jamaica, which was captured by the British; but it may actually have proved beneficial in the long run because the presence of a large British slave colony meant there was a steady flow of enslaved Africans to purchase.[59]

In the Western imagination slavery often starts with the ships – the horrendous middle passage – and then follows on to plantation labour. It is this narrative that leads even contemporary Black scholars to mistakenly assume that a focus on slavery, or the 'middle passage epistemology',[60] excludes the experience of people in Africa. Slavery happened to Africa as much as it did to those who arrived in the Americas. It is as if we have forgotten that the people stolen in chains were African and left behind families, communities and societies. The loss of millions of people had a devastating impact from which Africa still has not recovered. If the population explosion in Europe is credited as a major factor leading to the Industrial Revolution then imagine the negative impact on economic development that the removal of millions of working or soon to be working-age people would have.

The lower end of estimates is that 12 million Africans arrived in chains in the Americas and the Caribbean. But this does not account for those who were smuggled illegally, nor for the loss of life that occurred during the process of enslavement. As noted earlier, up to 40 per cent of those captured and transported from the interior of Africa to the coast died, though it is impossible to fully account for the scale of human loss. When they arrived at the coast the European traders would often house the enslaved in forts like the notorious Elmina in Ghana. Conditions in these prisons were appalling, with the enslaved often imprisoned underground in what they called the 'slave hole', which was a 'massive airless cellar'.[61] After these became too risky, because of attacks from the natives and competitors, Europeans took to mooring their slave ships off the coast and as captives arrived, keeping them in the holds of the ships, potentially for months until the vessel was full. Death was not uncommon, mostly due to disease; those who perished were dumped on the shore.

I will not regale you with tales of just how harrowing the middle passage was. Rest assured, being kept cramped in the hold, bound together in chains and packed in so tightly that there was barely room to move, was not conducive to good health. So appalling were the conditions that some slave ships had a death rate of 50 per cent. It was not only disease that killed the enslaved: mutiny was common, as was suicide. So terrible was the situation that many would rather throw themselves overboard than continue to submit to the degradation. Given that the enslaved represented bounty and profits for the enslavers you might think that they would have had more concern for the health of those on board. But the price of an African was such that it was easier to pack them in as tightly as possible and anticipate that some of the niggers would die off. When all else failed there was always the option of an insurance write-off. The infamous case of the *Zong* slave ship is testament to how little African life was worth during slavery.

In 1781 the ship was in trouble due to running out of water. So the captain took the, at the time perfectly reasonable, step of throwing 132 of the Africans overboard so that the remaining water could be saved for the crew. There was nothing particularly notable about the act itself; the disposal of cargo in times of necessity was commonplace and covered by insurance. The case became prominent solely because of a dispute over whether the insurance claim made by the Liverpool-based Gregson Company should be paid out. Abolitionists later popularized the story by using it as an example of the inhumanity of the system, and the fact remains that it is probably the most infamous insurance case in history. In his ruling in favour of the insurers, Lord Chief Justice Mansfield made abundantly clear that the enslaved were 'property to be treated by the parties concerned as no different from any other animate chattel'.[62] It is not an exaggeration to say that the bottom of the Atlantic became a tomb, an unmarked grave for countless Africans who perished crossing the ocean in chains. Accounting for the entire loss of population to Africa due to slavery is impossible but the lower end of the estimates is at least 24 million.[63]

It was not only the loss of population that changed the continent. In order to procure millions of enslaved Africans for the Atlantic system an infrastructure had to be put in place: ports, slave castles and trafficking routes from the interior. African populations and communities were decimated and had to retreat from coastal areas and set up defensive mechanisms to avoid being stolen into the trade. The impact was the emergence of a way of life that dealt with the brutal reality of slavery. The changing state of African societies is the perfect example of the geopolitical shifts caused by the European trade. The historical record is somewhat cloudy as to the emergence of the Kingdom of Dahomey in West Africa. It conquered part of what is now Nigeria in the early eighteenth century, either to end the slave trade in the region or to gain access to the slave markets on the coast.[64] What is indisputable is that the Dahomey Empire grew out of the chaos that slavery brought to the region and gained prominence from its role in supplying Africans for the trade. The same can be said to differing extents of the Asante and Oyo empires in Ghana and Nigeria respectively. While slavery was outlawed within both nations, they colluded with the European traders to supply those from other ethnic groups, either through raids or by selling those defeated in wars. There is no doubt at all that slavery was facilitated by collaboration with Africans, but that does not mean it was not a Western system.

African collusion, and particularly the narrative that the involvement of Africans somehow mitigates the West's responsibility for the system, is nonsense for a number of reasons. Most simply, there were countless numbers of Jewish collaborators with Hitler's regime and this of course does not absolve the Nazis of responsibility. People respond to the situations that they find themselves in and slavery dominated the infrastructure of the continent. Make no mistake, this was a Western system from the outset: a range of European nations were involved in establishing the framework that some Africans collaborated in. By the end of the seventeenth century, Dutch, English, Danes and Germans were all present on the West African 'Gold Coast', creating the outposts to supply the Atlantic system.

Violence was the underpinning logic of the framework, with Western superiority being embedded by the barrel of the gun. In this system collusion and resistance often blurred together in the impossible situation that the barbaric trade created. For instance, people were given the opportunity to free their relatives from the trade by exchanging two other Africans they had captured. People were traded for guns, with the express purpose of the weapons being to defend their communities from the trade. One of the driving forces for the collaboration of kingdoms like Dahomey or Asante was that by colluding with the enslavers they would preserve their own people from being ravaged by slavery. There was also the obvious allure of making a living out of trading in human flesh. None of this mitigates the European involvement and we should never lose sight of the fact that slavery was not something that was beneficial to Africa. The loss of population and reorganization of social life, either to avoid or to collude in the trade, devastated the African political and economic system – and all for guns, textiles and trinkets produced in Europe.

In contrast to the Western system of slavery, we also need to recognize that Africans were not a unified political or economic entity at the time. There were different empires, nations and ethnic groups competing for land and commerce. The idea of African betrayal in this paradigm is clearly nonsensical because the disparate groups did not feel a particular affinity to each other. Europeans exploited these differences and rivalries to the fullest extent. To defend their own communities, Africans were enlisted to enslave others on the continent. Europeans used the lack of an organized African polity to exploit the continent, something that, as we will see, became a common tactic for Western domination of the globe.

Alongside African involvement in slavery being used to mitigate Western guilt, the existence of slavery on the continent prior to the European trade is also often mobilized. It is important to dismiss the notion of so-called African slavery from the start. What is often referred to as slavery in Africa is more like serfdom, where people were tied to a lord for a fixed period of time and enjoyed basic human rights. Africans in this position of servitude could rise from their position and eventually take full part in civic life. Given the differences between European and African 'slavery' (so stark it make no sense to use the same word), it is likely that Africans had little knowledge of what exactly they were selling people into. They would have witnessed the enslaved being transported to the coast and had some knowledge of the slave castles. But once on the slave ships, slavery was out of sight of those in Africa, and the abuses of the middle passage and on the plantation may as well have taken place in an alternate universe.

It is noteworthy that there were no plantations in Africa, although cotton and sugar could have been cultivated on the continent. Resistance from Africans is likely a major reason, given how much fortification Europeans had to invest in to prevent the natives rebelling. There were forts for a reason, because Africans would not tolerate plantation slavery on the continent, despite attempts to establish the system by Europeans. There was a stand-off in the sixteenth and seventeenth centuries when Europeans did not have the capacity to conquer the mainland but Africans were unable to reclaim the coast.[65] It took Europe time to develop enough military superiority to conquer and fully colonize Africa, with the devastation that the system of slavery left being a key contributing factor to that eventuality. European slavery decimated the continent but the West did not start the mass enslavement of African people. As with most ideas, the West did not originate the concept but took what existed before and developed it to new, unparalleled heights.

Long before Europe had the idea to turn to Africa for a slave labour force, Arabs who invaded North Africa in the seventh century had established a system of slavery on the continent. Over a span of more than 1,250 years around 6 to 7 million Africans were forcibly trafficked across the Sahara Desert.[66] It was, in fact, the Arab system that gave Europeans the idea and early access to African flesh. When Columbus enslaved the 500 indigenous Americans it was the Arab slave markets that he sold them into. Europe did not even invent the idea of Africans being inferior, as I explained in the last chapter. Ibn Khaldun, one of the most influential scholars in the fourteenth century (who is rarely recognized because he was Tunisian and not from the West), thought that Africans were submissive to slavery because 'they have little [that is essentially] human and have attributes that are quite similar to those of dumb animals'.[67] Even though Europe essentially plagiarized Arab racial thinking and Arab slavery lasted far longer, it is the Western system that had the most damaging impact on Africa and reaped the greatest rewards for the enslavers. Racial thinking was prevalent in the Arab world. But the West took those ideas and built them into the fabric of the political and economic system in order to exploit the globe and build the modern world.

Whilst racial constructs certainly informed the Arab trade, the role that Africans played in the system was not based solely on racism. Europeans were prominent features of slave markets. In fact, the word 'slave' derives from 'Slav' because of their prominence in the trade. Notwithstanding the diversity of those enslaved, there was an anti-Black hierarchy in the system. The Arabic work *mamluk* referred to a high-status slave of White European stock, whereas enslaved Africans called *abd* were cheaper and consigned to more menial tasks.[68] But, even so, the dehumanization that was an unremitting feature of European slavery was not always present. The story of Bilal ibn Rabah, at least in the Sunni view, is a case in point for the complexities of the relationship of the enslaved to society. An African born into slavery, Bilal was prevented from reaching the highest positions in Arab society, but he was one of the Prophet Mohammed's most trusted companions who was given the responsibility of leading the call to prayer.

We should not romanticize the Arab slave trade: it was a brutal system that killed countless Africans. The average life expectancy for the enslaved was only seven years and they were subject to savage mistreatment and abuse.[69] The slave caravans that took Africans from the interior and crossed the Sahara were deadly and those who could not make it were left to die where they fell. Just as with European slavery, the impact on African society was devastating. Major Dixon Denham, a British traveller to Sudan in 1823, witnessed how 'villages were raided, the young women and children enslaved, the surplus men who had not escaped massacred, and the old, the lame and the sick killed off or left to die on the roadside'.[70] We cannot overestimate the damage that this scene, reproduced on an industrial scale, had on the continent and we must acknowledge the central role that the Arab system had in creating the European trade that followed. But there is a major difference that distinguishes the Arab trade from the Atlantic system, which goes to the core argument presented in this book: African slavery was endemic in the Arab world but it was not essential to the political and economic development of that region.

The Atlantic system lasted for over 300 years, with a peak during the eighteenth century. The Arab trade existed over four times as long but enslaved around half the number of people. But it is not just the size of the trade that is important, we also have to look at the nature of the two systems. Around two-thirds of those captured in Arab slavery were women, and the two main employments of the enslaved were sexual labour and domestic work. The enslaved were luxuries of the elite, largely used for pleasure and as house servants. This is in complete contrast to the Atlantic system where around 80 per cent of those enslaved on British ships were men and the desire for slave labour was to produce commodities on plantations and to power the development of capitalism.[71] As we have seen, European slavery produced untold wealth which fired industrial development and formed the bedrock of European advancement. In contrast, the profits were in Arab trade, not in slave ownership. As profitable as the Arab slave trade was, there are tales of slave traders in the medieval period with nowhere to spend their fortunes.[72] The West is built in large part off the wealth of slavery, whereas the same cannot be said of the Arab world. This does not make Arab slavery less barbaric or objectionable but it is important to separate out the legacies of the two trades. The Atlantic slave trade is still with us, in both the wealth and poverty caused by the murderous industry.

REPARATIONS NOW

Photographs of slave markets in Libya, in 2017, sparked international protests against the treatment of Black Africans in the country. Under Colonial Gaddafi the African population was given protection and prominence, but after the US-led regime change in 2011 the forces of anti-Blackness were unleashed in the nation. We should not be at all surprised, given how central anti-Black racism has been in the region since the Arab invasion of North Africa in the seventh century. The crisis in Sudan that sparked the creation of the new state of South Sudan was also a reminder of the significant tensions that continue to exist. The Arab slave trade is the most obvious example of the history of conflict and brutality towards African people, and the scenes in Libya were a reminder of that painful legacy. It is clear that the practice has not ended, though it is now usually forced underground and called human trafficking. But as reprehensible as the events in Libya are, we must not fall into the trap of conflating Arab slavery with the European trade; that is perhaps the worst way to discuss the legacy of the system.

I have lost count of the number of times I have been at a Black History Month event and a discussion about Atlantic slavery has ended with a speaker talking about the need to end so-called 'modern-day slavery'. Google 'slavery' right now and you will find some video claiming the need to end modern-day slavery with a link to the history of the transatlantic trade. But not only is this completely nonsensical, it actually prevents us from looking at the work that actually needs to be done to repair the damage of the Atlantic system. Human trafficking is an outrage to human decency and must end, but it has no relation to the transatlantic slave trade, which was a perfectly legal system of chattel slavery that produced the modern world. It may make those in the West feel better to embrace a narrative that places Britain at the centre of abolishing the evils of slavery and at the forefront of trying to end modern-day practices in backward parts of the world. But the legacies of slavery are all around us, in the very same political and economic system from which we generate money for charity in order to combat the ills of human trafficking. Please do not just take it from me. Britain's favourite White supremacist, Winston Churchill, acknowledged as much when he explained

> Our possession of the West Indies, like that of India . . . gave us the strength, the support, but especially the capital . . . to come through the great struggles of the Napoleonic wars, the keen competition of commerce in the eighteenth and nineteenth centuries, and enabled us not only to acquire the appendage of possessions which we have, but also to lay the foundations of that commercial and financial leadership which . . . enabled us to make our great position in the world.[73]

As the wealth of Britain, and the wider Western world, was built on the back of slavery it therefore follows that a debt is owed to those descendants of the enslaved. I started this chapter by exploring the payment of reparations to slave owners, so large they created a debt so enormous that it was only paid off by the twenty-first century taxpayer. It is perverse that those who laboured and suffered received no restitution in any country.

There is plenty of legal precedent for reparations that are based solely on the experience of oppression. In 1995 New Zealand agreed to pay the Maoris for historic abuses committed under the British crown dating back to 1863.[74] Germany paid over $90 billion to Jewish victims of the Holocaust and their descendants, and the United States has made a number of payments and settlements with indigenous peoples, although these have been offensively small and little more than token gestures.[75] The horrors of the slave trade are such that a claim based solely on the torture and inhumanity of it would be worthy of restitution. But in this case we are also talking about centuries of unpaid labour that needs to be accounted for. If the slave owners were compensated at the end of slavery there can be no justifiable reason for denying reparations to those suffering the legacies of the system. There have been many campaigns for reparations across the diaspora.

The Nation of Islam and the Republic of New Afrika in the US in the 1960s both called for General Sherman's post-American Civil War promise of forty acres and a mule for each enslaved to be honoured by a parcel of land in the South being turned over to the Black population. The Black Lives Matter movement is currently campaigning for reparations for the damage caused and there is a Europe-wide movement for reparatory justice, the Pan-Afrikan Reparations Coalition in Europe (PARCOE). In Britain there is an annual Stop the Maangamizi march and calls for an all-party parliamentary commission into the subject. Africa also formed a reparations movement through the Organization of African Unity in 1990. The Caribbean nations have joined the reparations case through the Caribbean Community (CARICOM), demanding restitution for the impact of slavery. There are now widespread social movements that recognize that the West was enriched on the back of slavery and also that the poverty we see across the Black world today is the legacy of the system. Since the killing of George Floyd we have even seen companies jump on the reparations PR bandwagon. The problem with reparations, though, is whether they can ever account for just how important the system of slavery was to the development of the West.

Various calculations have been done based on damages and loss of earnings to arrive at an estimate of just how much the West owes. For the Caribbean alone, one estimate back in 2005 was $7.5 trillion.[76] In the United States the estimates range from $3 to $14 trillion.[77] What is clear from these figures is that if we were able to calculate a figure owed it would be so large that it would be impossible for the West to pay. The truth is that the figure is incalculable because of how steeped the West remains in the wealth from the Atlantic system. It touches every part of the West's society and economy and has also impoverished the Black world to a degree that cannot be overestimated. The West remains built on these foundations and to transfer the wealth necessary to repair the damage would destroy the West, not only because of the money involved, but also because if the Black world had freedom that would mean the end of the Western project. Reparations are due, and tearing down Western capitalism is an utter necessity if we are serious about ending racism. But to realize the revolutionary politics necessary for this transformation we first need to recognize that the West can never pay full reparations for slavery without destroying itself.

Slavery may have ended, but the next phase in Western supremacy was colonialism, built on the same principles of racial hierarchy and exploitation. The West simply cannot end racism through reparations because racial hierarchy is the fuel that feeds the system. The end of slavery dissolved into the colonial era of racial exploitation, which is still very much alive and well today.

4

Colonialism

If you want to see colonialism at work today, take a visit to Cadbury World in Birmingham. The site is still a working factory, the home of the Cadbury empire, one of Britain's leading brands with annual revenues exceeding $3 billion.[1] From its humble start as a grocery shop in 1824 the company has become a global juggernaut, selling over 350 million of its signature Dairy Milk bars every year. Cadbury's employs more than 45,000 people worldwide and, including its supply chain, is responsible for keeping thousands of people in work in the city of Birmingham. Neither the city nor the company is shy of boasting about the tremendous success of the business and in 1990 Cadbury World opened on the site of its Bournville factory, attracting visitors to learn about the history and future plans of the company. They have added different attractions over the years but the central structure of the place has remained the same. A tour through Cadbury World takes you from the first European encounter with chocolate right through to its present-day production. While the aim is to celebrate the success of the company, walking through the space is the perfect tour of neo-colonialism, providing all the ingredients to explain why the West remains just as built on racism today as it ever was.

Aztec civilization greets you when you first step into the exhibition. Well, a plastic replica of jungle replete with smiling cocoa beans and wax figures. There is at least a recognition here that Europeans did not invent or 'discover' chocolate, which was introduced to the continent when the Spanish brought it back from South America. In fairness to the curators, they give a nod to some of the violence committed by the Spanish, and reference the Aztec ruler Montezuma being killed by the forces of Cortés in the sixteenth century. But, typical of how this period is remembered, the genocide we have already explored is breezily skipped over. I suppose recounting the murder of tens of millions in a children's attraction would be bad for business.

After you learn about the origins of chocolate the story moves to Birmingham, and the founding of the original shop by John Cadbury in 1824. We hear about his ingenuity and hard work, and how he came up with the magic formula for the incredibly popular Dairy Milk. In these foundation stories we are told about cocoa and milk, but conspicuous in its absence is any reference to the other main ingredient, which is of course sugar. As we saw in the last chapter, sugar was one of the main slave-produced commodities. When Cadbury's began as a small shop, slavery was still fully functioning in the British Empire, and slave-produced sugar would have made it into the country until at least 1888, when Brazil abolished the system. Cadbury's became a huge commercial success in the latter part of the nineteenth century after building the Bournville factory in 1878, so is often not seen as having ties to slavery. But this misses the point for two main reasons. Firstly, Cadbury's was able to open Bournville due to the wealth it had generated from using slave-produced sugar. As we have already seen, wealth produced from slavery was used after abolition to continue development. More importantly, the ending of slavery did not stop the exploitative relationship between the Caribbean (or the rest of the Empire) and Britain. Caribbean colonies continued to produce sugar, often in dire conditions and certainly for pay that was not too far removed from the realities of enslavement. Sugar production was a system created by slavery, with a workforce descended from those stolen in chains and indentured labourers from other parts of the Empire. There was nothing clean about the sugar that went into building Cadbury's.

Instead of focusing on the exploitation at the heart of Cadbury's, the exhibition is a celebration of the entrepreneurial and philanthropic spirit of the Cadbury family. Not only did the family build the factory, they also secured a 120-acre site and on it created the village of Bournville. We are told that George Cadbury 'was a housing reformer interested in improving the living conditions of working people in addition to advancing working practices'.[2] Bournville was a model village for workers in the factory, with swimming pools and parks. Workers also received far better treatment than was usual in Victorian times, with the Cadburys seen as 'pioneering employee welfare'.[3] In fact, the housing and development of Bournville was so attractive that it is now one of the most expensive places to live in the city. The irony of celebrating the success of Cadbury's in supporting the working classes when they have long since been priced out of the area seems entirely lost. Being serenaded with tales of how wonderful an employer the Cadburys were in Birmingham is also telling for what, or more particularly who, is absent in the story.

Only once, and very briefly, do we see the workers in Ghana picking the key ingredient for Cadbury's product: cocoa. I wish I were joking, but sadly not. In a grainy black-and-white film narrated by an exceedingly posh gentleman, who is actually wearing the white pith helmet we associate with colonialism, we see the smiling natives happily chopping down the cocoa and loading it into vans for export to Britain. There is no mention of the conditions they faced either historically or in the present day. But when the president of the World Cocoa Foundation declared in 2018 that 'our first and most important target is to raise farmers above the extreme poverty line' of $1.90 a day,[4] you can imagine just how appalling the situation is still for those harvesting the base ingredient for a multibillion dollar empire. The complete lack of care by the Cadburys, or consideration by Cadbury World, for workers outside Britain is the perfect demonstration of how gains for workers in the West are built on the back of exploitation of those in the global South.

By the end of the tour we are introduced to the innovations in advertising and the array of different products that Cadbury's now produces. The impression given is very much that the company is a local and national success: the best of British as it were. But Cadbury World were honest, the tour would end with the singing of 'The Star-Spangled Banner' as staff pledge allegiance to the Stars and Stripes. Cadbury's has not been a British company for over a decade now, having been bought by American giant Kraft Foods in a hostile takeover in 2010. As testament to just how successful Cadbury's neo-colonial business model is, the company cost them $18.9 billion. The US takeover also tells us much about what colonialism looks like in the present day. The old colonial regimes are no longer leading the charge. America is now setting the tone for Western imperialism.

NO SUCH THING AS FAIR TRADE

To understand the continued exploitation of the developing world by the West, we can start by undoing the fallacy of the idea of fair trade. Cadbury World again provides a good starting point for this discussion. In their exhibition they quite openly describe the process of raw cocoa leaving Ghana and being shipped to a processing plant in Britain before ending up in the Bournville factory. As part of the tour you get to witness the production process and see the finished commercial products (they are even nice enough to give you a discount at the gift shop). There is no recognition of the exploitation at the heart of this relationship. A resource from Africa is taken out of the continent at an extremely low cost, processed into a luxury good in Europe and sold for a huge profit, often back into Africa. It is the European company that makes all the money off an African resource. Kwame Nkrumah, the first president of Ghana, said this reality had an '*Alice in Wonderland* craziness' about it.[5]

In the context of trade relationships like this, companies like Cadbury's partnering with the Fairtrade Partnership may mean that farmers get a few more pennies a day, but the notion that there can ever be *fair* trade is as offensive as it is absurd. Cocoa farmers receive only 6 per cent of the money made from the product they labour over.[6] The nations which produce raw materials like cocoa receive a pittance for their resources, while Western corporations make a fortune exploiting resources that they otherwise would have no access to. As we saw in the first two chapters, the expansion of the West was necessary for both the resources and the labour needed for modern industrial progress.

The thread that unites Western development since 1492 is the exploitation by those of European descent of the rest of the world. We incorrectly think of the horrors of Western empire as separate, disconnected historical events. First, genocide in the Americas, then transatlantic slavery and finally colonialism. But in reality they are

overlapping manifestations of White supremacy that cannot be separated from each other and which bleed into the current forms of
colonial domination. In the Caribbean, for instance, colonialism did
not follow on after slavery. The islands were slave colonies, taken
by deadly force from the natives who were wiped out in a genocide.
Colonialism is often understood in its dictionary definition of direct
rule over a subject people by a foreign power, but this is an inadequate
way to view the process.

Africa provides the perfect example of the far more widespread
talons of colonialism. Most of the continent was under direct rule by
European powers for a period less than a hundred years. But it would
be wrong to think that a colonial relationship only existed for that
short period of time. Ever since the West dug its claws into Africa
it has been building and then sustaining its exploitative hold over
the continent. As we saw in Chapter 2, the transatlantic slave trade
fundamentally transformed the politics, economies and organization
of the continent. As well as looting the continent for slave labour,
Europe also plundered resources like gold from it. Before formally
taking control of any part of the continent, Europe had already begun
to 'underdevelop' Africa.[7]

In Walter Rodney's classic *How Europe Underdeveloped Africa* he
lays out with supreme clarity the damage done to the continent. The
book explains the global economic contradiction that 'many parts of
the world that are naturally rich are actually poor and parts that are
not so well off in wealth of soil and sub-soil are enjoying the highest
standards of living'.[8] Slavery powered Western development to the
point that one of the main problems since the late ninetieth century
has been finding the resources to feed into its industrial machine. The
wealth from the Atlantic system enabled European powers to colonize
large parts of Asia and replace slave labour with the inhumane wages
we still see in the world. So the focus on Africa shifted from seeing
it as a source of cheap labour to the rush to milk the continent for its
resources. Centuries of slavery enabled this by devastating both the
political and economic system of Africa and its ability to resist.

By the end of the nineteenth century almost the entire continent was
under colonial rule. 'Underdevelopment' is used to describe Europe's
involvement because when Europeans took control of the continent

they halted any African progress in order to enrich their respective mother countries.

At a time when Africa needed to be developing industrial farming techniques to provide food and resources for the continent, precisely the opposite was occurring. From the nineteenth century to the present day many African economies have depended on cash crops from small-scale farmers. It is these barely-above-subsistence-level farmers who provide much of the cocoa for Cadbury's factories. Individual farmers selling their wares to a trader are extremely easy for large corporations to exploit financially, which is one of the main reasons why the price of most commodities is so low. This method of procuring crops has been doubly cheap for the West, which did not have to invest in heavy machinery or even worry about transporting the crops to the depot. Under colonial rule, infrastructure was only ever developed to the extent it was necessary to take commodities out of Africa, with 'all roads and railways leading to the sea'.[9] One result of this underdevelopment was that people, mostly women, were forced to trek miles on foot to deliver the cash crops to the depots.[10] Cotton, rubber, oil palm, cocoa, coffee and more were procured to be exploited away from Africa, with huge profits going to European companies.

Under formal colonial rule Africans were often forced to work cultivating particular crops for their colonial masters and accept whatever price they were given. Conditions were particularly harsh during economic crises like the Depression, or the World Wars, when the colonies were expected to support the war effort. One of the most extreme examples of forced labour was the building of the Brazzaville to Pointe-Noire railway in Congo from 1921 to 1933. Every year 100,000 Africans were forced to work at the site in conditions so appalling that '25% died annually from starvation and disease'.[11]

In 1938 Britain established the West African Produce Control Board to regulate prices for commodities. As evidence of just how lucrative this system was for European companies, in 1946 the control board paid £16.15 to African suppliers for a ton of oil palm, and this same ton then sold for £95 in Britain. For groundnuts the purchase price was £15 and the sale price £110. This does not even consider what the British company then received after processing the product and selling it on.[12] Whilst Africa may no longer be under colonial rule, and subject to direct physical oppression, it is abundantly clear that this economic relationship remains unchanged.

One of Britain's largest companies is so successful that its £44.68 billion turnover for 2018 represented a 'dip' in its performance due to 'challenging market conditions'.[13] Spare a thought for its shareholders who had to take a dividend of merely £8.6 billion for the year. Unilever is a global giant that makes all manner of soaps meant to clean everything from your skin to your floor. Much like Cadbury's, the company has its roots in nineteenth-century Britain when the Lever brothers began manufacturing and selling soap. Like the Cadburys they procured the main ingredient for their product from Africa, in this case oil palm. Lever Brothers sourced this from Nigeria, Sierra Leone and Liberia, forming the United African Company to manage its procurement. Oil palm has a lot of uses, and the company expanded into foods, making margarines and oils, eventually merging with a Dutch company, Margarine Uni, in 1929. The growth of the company was based on its success in European markets but Unilever acknowledged the source of its prosperity. In 1920 the Information Division of the company recognized that

> Unilever's centre of gravity is Europe, but far and away its largest member (the UAC) is almost wholly dependent for its livelihood (represented by a turnover of £300 million) on the well-being of Africa.[14]

In a pattern we see repeated again and again, a Western corporation grew extraordinarily rich by exploiting the resources of a colony. Nothing has changed today, except that the countries are now formally free. Unilever still depends on oil palm for its success, a crop that is becoming increasingly important as an alternative fuel source. It is no coincidence that the same crops that were so important to development during colonialism are powering the global economy today. From 2000 to 2013 the space that sugar-cane plantations took up across the globe grew from 19 to 26 million hectares; rubber from 7 to 10 million; and oil palm from 10 to 18 million.[15]

It is realities like this that make a nonsense of the Western navel-gazing concern with the apparent 'rise of the robots', which I will cover in more depth in Chapter 7. Millions of poor people in the underdeveloped world find themselves trapped in work and working conditions similar to those under colonial rule. Most oil palm production is now located outside Africa, with Indonesia and Malaysia producing over 80 per cent of the global market.[16] Sadly, this is not a sign of progress, just a continuation of the same neo-colonial relations that mark the African story.

Indonesia accounts for the bulk of oil palm production and farming in Malaysia is often done by Indonesian migrant workers. Dutch colonization of Indonesia goes back to 1602, with the Portuguese involved in the region prior to that. By 1823 the Netherlands East India Association, the successor to the much-reviled Dutch East India Company, was reliant on coffee produced in Java for 77 per cent of its export revenue. Forced labour was the norm in the colony and it is estimated that in 1840 30 per cent of Indonesian families were toiling against their will.[17] Thousands of people were forced into what were effectively work camps in the nineteenth century because they would not voluntarily accept the low wages on offer.

Oil palm did not develop as a crop in the region until 1930, and in a nod to just how global the colonial network was, the first workers were indentured labours from China. These workers had been in Indonesia before oil palm was, working under inhuman conditions. Known as 'contract Coolies' they were ruled by a set of ordinances which meant they were subject to whippings, prison and execution if they did not show enough deference to their masters, put in enough effort, or if they tried to escape their plight.[18]

Today, such conditions no longer exist. However, there is a reason that most oil palm is produced in Indonesia, or by Indonesian labourers, and it is because Indonesians are cheap to employ. The majority of workers are not employed on a permanent basis, making them even more insecure. There has been much hand-wringing over the need to improve the wages and conditions of oil palm workers but Wilmar International, one of the largest global oil palm corporations, openly admits that on some of its plantations only 5 to 10 per cent of the workers are on permanent contracts.[19]

CORRUPT 'DEVELOPMENT'

Africa became less attractive as a producer of cash crops like oil palm for a number of reasons. Demographics is the simplest explanation. Labour is cheaper in East Asia because there is an abundance of workers. India and China both have more inhabitants than the entire African continent. Slavery is the most important reason behind the lack of population in Africa, the only underpopulated part of the world. But after slavery ended, the logic of underdevelopment ensured that Africa's population would remain low. The genocidal tendencies of the West spread into Africa. Leopold's murder of 10 million in Congo stands out, but countless Africans were killed across the continent to exert colonial control by all the major European powers. But it was not only direct slaughter that culled the African population. Under colonial rule the continent was only developed to the extent that it benefited the European powers, and this did not include supporting the welfare of the native population.

On taking over as president of Ghana in 1957, Kwame Nkrumah inherited a state that had only thirty-seven hospitals for 4 million Ghanaians.[20] This was no different to the rest of the continent. In neighbouring Nigeria in the 1930s under colonialism, the 4,000 British immigrants (let's not dignify them by the term 'ex-pats') had the use of two modern hospitals while the 40 million Nigerians had to share fifty-two.[21] Facilities like medical care or sanitation were reserved mainly for the White population, meaning that when so-called independence came, African countries were sorely lacking in the infrastructure they needed to take good care of their populations. Europe had not only stolen their wealth but had also prevented the development necessary for them to prosper. This put African governments in an almost impossible position because their economies needed mass investment but remained under economic oppression from the West. Taking over the government offices did not mean removing the claws of the West, which dug so deep and extracted so much.

Under colonial rule Europe made huge profits, with investments making 25 per cent more in the colonies than in Britain. Profits being leached from Benin by French investors represented half of the colony's GDP.[22] The US-based Firestone Company, which extracted rubber from Liberia, made so much money that in 1951, even after it had paid tax to the Liberian government the company still made three times the amount of the total income of the state.[23] By 1955 Africa was contributing £1.446 billion annually to British gold and dollar reserves – over half of the total. Belgium and France extracted so much wealth from their colonies that they did not need to take out loans to pay for their war efforts.[24] The West literally drained the financial, human and mineral resources out of Africa and continues to exploit the continent using the same economic tools.

France continues to use hard power, a 'coercive neo-colonialism'[25] that locks its African colonies into a currency union based around the West African CFA franc. As part of the West African Economic and Monetary Union, which covers Benin, Burkina Faso, Côte d'Ivoire, Guinea-Bissau, Mali, Niger, Senegal and Togo, France can still veto monetary policy. This currency dependency also encourages the nations to remain over-reliant on French imports of goods manufactured from the former colonies' raw materials. Britain and other Western powers take a more indirect approach, through international trade and bodies such as the International Monetary Fund and the World Bank, but the result is the same.

There were varying models for running colonies in Africa. In places like Zimbabwe, then Rhodesia, there was a far larger presence of British citizens than in countries like Nigeria. Even when indirect rule was chosen as the model, a very limited native elite was trained to administer colonialism. This meant there was a strong presence of European civil servants across Africa who worked above the native administrators. For example in 1930s Ghana, European civil servants were paid £40 per month, while Africans received only £4 for the same hours of work. There was no need to educate the locals because they were deemed unworthy of rising into the intellectual ranks that could lead the country. In 1959 Britain 'spent £11 per African pupil, £38 per Indian and £186 per European' in Uganda for their schooling.[26] On independence Kenya had only thirty-five schools for 5.5 million young people.[27] In 1950 the student body of the University of Sakar, established for all those in the West African French colonies, was 50 per cent White.[28] This lack of educational provision was not only meant to convey the idea that Africans could not think, but created a reality where the native population did not have the skills (particularly in literacy) to administer their countries. The select few who were given the opportunity for education received the most Eurocentric indoctrination imaginable, having to travel to the mother country to be taught in the ways of Whiteness.

The purpose of educating Africans was to create a class who could administer European colonialism as a proxy for Europeans. It brings to mind Malcolm X's description of the Uncle Tom figure from the slave plantation:

> The slavemaster took Tom and dressed him well, and fed him well, and even gave him a little education – a little education; gave him a long coat and a top hat and made all the other slaves look up to him. Then he used Tom to control them. The same strategy that was used in those days is used today. He takes a Negro, a so-called Negro, and makes him prominent, builds him up, publicizes him, makes him a celebrity. And then he becomes a spokesman for Negroes.[29]

Replace 'Negro' with 'African', and 'celebrity' with 'administrator' and you have the exact relationship of the colonial period. On independence it was these anointed ones who were trusted to 'lead' their countries. Given that all the leaders who emerged from the continent went through different varieties of this process, the surprise is that so many of them rejected their masters' ideas. The movement to unite and liberate the continent from European control emerged in Britain and America and was spearheaded by Africans educated by their respective mother countries. It is also true that ultimately too many of the leaders betrayed the radical promise of continental unity in favour of the individual status and wealth gained from leading their nations further into the bowels of the West. But revolutionary leaders like Kwame Nkrumah in Ghana, Amílcar Cabral in Guinea and Patrice Lumumba in Congo were also educated in the West. The problem is that they were never given the chance to implement their revolutionary programmes because the West made sure to dispose of them and support puppets in their place who had taken to the Western training they had received.

Patrice Lumumba's assassination is the perfect case study in the corruption the West embedded into Africa, post-independence. Lumumba was the first prime minister of independent Congo, who sought to Africanize the government and administer state-led economic development, using the resources of the nation for the benefit of its people. Congo was (and remains) far too important to the West to allow this to happen, being one of the most mineral-rich parts of the world. Rather than allow the people of Congo to decide their destiny the West, including the Belgians and the CIA, supported his rival, the reactionary Moise Tshombe. Malcom X devoted a lot of time speaking about the situation in Congo, condemning the United States' role in supporting Tshombe, the 'Uncle Tom' leader who was a puppet for Western interests. In 1961 the Lumumba problem was taken care of when he was killed in what has been dubbed the 'most important assassination of the twentieth century'.[30]

Tshombe's leadership led to the dictatorial reign of Mobuto Sese Seko, which lasted from 1965 to 1997, and which devastated Congo, opening up the nation to Western interests and impoverishing it further. He also personally looted billions of dollars. The civil wars sparked after his departure claimed more lives than any other conflict since the Second World War. Congo is just one example of what has happened across Africa and the rest of the underdeveloped world when leaders threaten the interests of the West: regimes are changed to install pro-Western governments. It is the political and economic system that is corrupt in Africa, and the puppet 'Uncle Tom' leaders who syphon off money into Western bank accounts are a by-product of that central problem. Just as there is no such thing as free trade, so-called good governance is a nonsense in this system.

THE DE-INDUSTRIALIZATION OF INDIA

The British Empire was vast, by 1900 covering a quarter of the globe and ruling over 372 million subjects. This scene from Queen Victoria's Diamond Jubilee in 1897 demonstrates the extent of her dominions:

> 50,000 troops from every corner of the empire – Camel Corps and Gurkhas, Canadian hussars and Jamaicans in white gaiters, the procession led by the loftiest officer in the army, 6-foot-8 Captain Ames

of the Horse Guards – had marched or trotted through London to celebrate.[31]

India was Britain's largest colony and Britain did not just under-develop India, it actively de-industrialized the region. When Britain colonized India in the late eighteenth century, it was a rich nation that accounted for 25 per cent of the world's trade. By the time Britain's rule collapsed in 1947, India only held a 3 per cent share. Before British colonialism the standard of living in India was on a par with what would become the mother country. Afterwards, levels of absolute poverty no longer seen in Britain plagued the nation.[32] During the initial eastern expansion of their Empire the British did not seize what they wanted at the barrel of a gun. Europeans used gifts and signed treaties to gain access to societies in the East. It was only in the eighteenth century that attitudes towards India began to change, and rather than being seen as people worthy of trade, Indians were viewed as brutes to be dominated.[33]

That is not to say that in the beginning there was none of the underlying White supremacy we saw at work in the Atlantic system. Although the westward expansion of empire was important, the move into the East was just as indispensable to the emergence of the West, and equally brutal. Vasco da Gama is less celebrated than his Italian counterpart Columbus, but his opening up of India to the Portuguese in 1497–9 was as pivotal as Columbus's so-called discovery, and he wrought a similar campaign of terror. The year 1492 marked the expulsion of the Muslim conquerors from Spain, but they maintained power in the East. Europeans set about destroying ports and strongholds in the Muslim world on their travels eastward, and da Gama showed no mercy, as this tale of how he dealt with a ship full of Muslim pilgrims returning to India shows:

> he ordered the ship to be set on fire . . . Women held up their jewellery to beg for mercy from the flames or from the water, while others held up their infants to try to protect them. Da Gama watched impassively, 'cruelly and without pity' as every last passenger and crew member drowned before his eyes.[34]

Dehumanizing ideas about those from the 'East' have a long history in the European imagination. The battle of East versus West has been played out in the Greek and Roman Empires, in the Crusades from the eleventh century, the battles against the occupation of Spain by the Moors, wars with the Ottoman Empire, and into the present day with the supposed 'clash of civilizations' between the West and the Islamic world that is shaping much of the West's policy agenda.[35]

The long history of the West viewing the East through a lens of the exotic and inferior is dubbed 'Orientalism' by scholar Edward Said, who defines the idea as a 'Western style for dominating, restructuring, and having authority over the Orient'.[36] Importantly, he argues that European culture gained strength and identity by setting itself 'against the Orient as a sort of surrogate and even underground self'.[37] In other words, the West's self-belief in its superiority, given supposedly scientific legitimacy in the Enlightenment, was in part bolstered by the supposed inferiority of the people and cultures it encountered in the East. But for all of Europe's aggrandizing ideas, the reality was that Westerners were not superior to those they encountered in the East, and they had no choice but to ingratiate themselves in order to trade.

In the fifteenth century Europe was emerging from its Dark Age and lagged behind the East. It wasn't until the eighteenth century that the West was able to begin to assert its dominance. In fact, the same was true in Africa, where, although the first instinct may have been to conquer, Europeans found this impossible given the strength of the societies they encountered. There is a reason that Europe never directly colonized Africa until much later, and kept its forts and presence for the most part limited to the coast. White supremacy had to be established. It was not a divine right.

Britain had to wait for its opportunity to fulfil its ambition to conquer India, which came with the decline of the Mughal Empire in the mid eighteenth century. The Mughals ruled a vast area in India from the sixteenth to well into the seventeenth century – a centralized power that the British could not displace. But the death of Emperor Aurangzeb in 1707 tipped the Empire into a series of wars to decide who would succeed as ruler. Within fifty years the Mughal regime had collapsed in on itself, unable to keep control of its sprawling dominions. Britain seized on the chaos caused by the fall of the Mughals, and through the East India Company (EIC) embarked on colonization. By 1857 the EIC had an army of 260,000 troops and dominion over 200 million subjects.[38] Echoing present-day US imperialism driven by private corporations, the EIC was a business, set up with a monopoly over British interests in India.

The British government provided loans and support to establish the company and individuals made massive profits from its endeavours. There was no surer investment in the eighteenth and nineteenth centuries than EIC stock, and its directors amassed fortunes from exploiting the people and resources of India. Between 1765 and 1815 Indians paid over £18 million a year to the EIC in taxes alone. The word 'loot' comes from Hindi, and directly from the pillaging of India, incorporated into English by the same people who robbed it. Robert Clive 'of India', military general, first governor of Bengal and director of the EIC, amassed a personal fortune in excess of £40 million in today's money. The seizure of Calcutta in 1757 was a large source of this wealth. After claiming the region, the employees of the EIC shared the tax take of £2 million – billions in current money – between themselves. As the EIC was gorging itself on the locals' taxes, the first Bengal famine struck, killing millions of people – up to a third of the region's population – but the British 'had thought only of enriching themselves as the local population starved to death'.[39] Such callous disregard for lives that are not White in the face of profit has been the defining feature of Western development.

The abuses by the EIC were such that eventually even the British government had to step in. It took a rebellion of the Indian population in 1857 to spur the government into action and to disband the EIC. The last thing the country needed was restless natives in one of its most important colonies. India was hugely important for British trade and industry, particularly after the end of the transatlantic slave system. In fact the price of labour there was so cheap that it rivalled the economy of slavery even when the system was ongoing.[40] Commodities like cotton and sugar were increasingly derived from cheap labour on Indian plantations and therefore Britain had to maintain order over the colony. But, in the same way as when Belgium took over Congo from Leopold, when the British government ruled India as a colony the relationship established by the private corporation did not change. Through violent subjugation India continued to be milked of its resources by Britain.

In 1901, the salary for the Secretary of State of India brought in the same amount of income that 90,000 Indians survived on. By the 1920s 7,500 British civil servants in India were taking a total of £20 million annually in pensions. The British Indian army was also paid for out of Indian taxes, sustaining a standing army of over 325,000 troops by the late nineteenth century.[41] But robbing India through taxation was not the only way that Britain de-industrialized the nation.

In keeping with the logic of Western imperialism, the sheer brutality of British colonialism did major demographic damage to India. This included the kind of genocide to conquer the natives we have seen in other parts of the world. Disease was also a major killer, where outbreaks such as cholera epidemics claimed the lives of millions. Cholera had existed in India before the arrival of the British but troop invasions into India were associated with outbreaks, as they carried the disease across the region. Cholera was also a massive killer during famines, intersecting with starvation to deadly effect.[42] It was these famines in India that accounted for the majority of those killed by British colonialism. I have already briefly discussed the first famine in the nation in 1770, but these tragedies continued to beset colonial India even after the British government had taken the reins from the EIC. As Shashi Tharoor explains in his book *Inglorious Empire*,

> in the entire 107 years from 1793 to 1900, only an estimated 5 million people had died in all the wars around the world combined, whereas in just ten years 1891–1900, 19 million had died in India in famines alone.[43]

In total over 35 million Indians died in famines under British colonial rule. The most infamous is perhaps the second Bengal famine in 1943 which took the lives of 3 million people before Britain mobilized an appropriate response. This particular famine has had more public attention because of the involvement of British wartime hero Winston Churchill.

Prime minister at the time, Churchill took the decision to divert grain away from India and actually import grain from the famine-hit country into Britain, so that it could be stockpiled for the war effort. He did so with full knowledge of the scale of the crisis. Worse still, Britain prohibited Indian ships from sailing to get food, or using their currency reserves to buy it. Churchill's defence was to blame the Indians for 'breeding like rabbits'; in any case they would soon replenish their number. He had such a total disregard for the Indian people that the Secretary of India at the time Leo Amery (hardly an avowed anti-racist) once told him that in terms of his views of Indians, he could not see 'much difference between his outlook and Hitler's'.[44] This ghastly episode is a reminder of the disposability of Indian life in the Empire, but Churchill was just carrying on a well-established tradition. Viceroy Lord Lytton had banned any price reductions during famines in the nineteenth century and when colonial administrators imported rice to feed the hungry during the Orissa famine in 1866, *The Economist* magazine chastised them for sending the message to the Indians that it was 'the duty of the Government to keep them alive'.[45]

Such disregard for life was even seen when Britain left India. Labour's Attlee government wanted a quick exit from the colony after the War, and Britain hastily drew up plans to leave. Divisions between the Hindu majority and Muslim minority had been stoked by Britain, divide and rule being one of the best forms of maintaining control. The Muslim League, under the leadership of Muhammad Ali Jinnah, was campaigning for a separate state for the large Muslim population. Lord Mountbatten was put in charge of the process and came up with the plan to partition India, creating the new state of Pakistan. You may know him as 'Uncle Dickie' in the Netflix series *The Crown*, although in keeping with the idealization of such figures you are much less likely to have heard about the significant amount of blood on his hands from the catastrophe of Indian Partition.

Despite warnings of the carnage and upheaval that would be unleashed by creating a religious national divide overnight, the British went ahead and, following colonial tradition, arbitrarily drew a new boundary. On Independence the result was as expected: more than 14 million people became refugees, fleeing for the safety of their appointed homelands. During the ethnic violence that was then unleashed, over 1 million people lost their lives. British hands may not have been directly involved in the slaughter, but they were by no means clean: they had callously created the conditions that allowed India to become a bloodbath.

Under British rule India went from being one of the richest places on earth to one of the most underdeveloped. The textile industry was purposely prevented from competing with Britain. Cities shrank as work disappeared. Indian shipping and steel production were also destroyed by the Empire to create British supremacy. By the time the British left in 1947 poverty and illiteracy had become the norm. It was only after Independence that the country began to grow and prosper, and today India is one of the fastest-growing economies on the planet and expected to be in the top three in terms of size in the coming years.

Extreme poverty has been slashed in India: according to the World Bank only 5 per cent of the population lived on less than $1.90 a day in 2018, compared to a quarter in 2011. On Independence the literacy rate in the country was only 18 per cent, which improved to 80 per cent by 2017, the same year that Union Human Resource Development Minister Prakash Javadekar announced a 'guarantee that within next five years, it will be 100 per cent'.[46] In a seeming reversal of the economics of empire, India once again manufactures the clothes for Britain and much of the world. Even the steel sector is booming: in a sign of the apparently post-colonial times an Indian company, Tata, in 2007 took over what once was British Steel. Part of the pitch of those pushing for Britain to leave the EU was so that they could forge independent trade deals with countries like India. You could be mistaken for looking at India and claiming a success story; empire happened, but that is all in the past. That would be to mistake a mirage for a waterhole.

Of all these prosperous figures, GDP is the most misleading. India is the second largest country by population, by some distance. Only China also has more than a billion inhabitants, and the third largest country is the United States with over 300 million people. GDP measures the product of the population and more people should lead to a higher output; India is *supposed* to have a large economy. Britain has a comparable GDP to India but a population of only 66 million. If we look at GDP per capita (person), India only ranks 139th in the world. In other words, poverty is still rife. Extreme poverty may well have declined in recent years, but hundreds of millions of Indians live in conditions unimaginable in the West. Wealth is not being equally distributed across the country. While claiming back textile production sounds like a success, it is actually the opposite. Manufacturing jobs moved to places like India *because* poverty made it cheaper to pay workers in the underdeveloped world a pittance in sweatshops, rather than pay a decent minimum wage in the West. Indian labour is being exploited by multinationals in exactly the same relationship as we saw under colonialism. We can celebrate the boom in the service sector in India, but just consider the economics of having people thousands of miles away working in call centres for Western countries. It is only cheaper to offshore this kind of work because the standard of living in India is so much lower than the West. If conditions improved and wages rose enough to provide the Western lifestyle that we are so comfortable with, then the jobs that are underpinning the so-called success of India would quickly be moved to a poorer part of the world. It is a strange sort of prosperity that depends on millions of your people being poor.

Such poverty has dire consequences. Neo-colonial India may have dealt with the problem of famines, which were so widespread under British rule, but in 2018 almost a million children died in India before their fifth birthday because they were poor.[47] India is making as much progress as any nation of a billion Brown people can in a racist world order. We only accept the poverty and appalling conditions because they are imposed on those who are not White. Doing the dirty work so that we in the West do not have to is exactly what they are worth, these disposable bodies propping up the West.

AMERICAN EMPIRE

The updated system of Western imperialism needs to be understood in the context of supposedly post-colonial nations like India, but also in the shift of the centre of power from Europe to the United States. One of the main lies America tells itself is that it was a victim of colonial oppression which freed itself from the tyranny of the British. While it is true that the original thirteen states were colonies of the British Empire, the Pilgrims were the first ex-pats, pioneers bravely taking their religion and so-called civilization to the New World. Opening the American frontier was the essential first step to building the West. American settlers are not just implicated in but directly benefited from the founding genocide. The nation was then built on the back of slave labour from Africa. The United States is a settler colony where we can see the logic of the West play out in its clearest, most undiluted form.

When the newly United States broke away from their British over-lords, this did not mark a break in the progress of the West but a necessary evolution. Losing the colony ended up being of benefit to Britain. Trade with the United States increased after independence in 1783. After the abolition of slavery in Britain, when the country was basking in its moral superiority to the United States, it was perfectly happy to import the products of US slave plantations. During the US Civil War in the early 1860s, when the North blockaded Southern ships, there was a cotton famine in Britain that led to a steep decline in the industry, with many factories closing down and people out of work. The impact was to raise pro-slavery sentiment and support for the South in Britain, particularly in places dependent on slave-produced cotton.

During the war Liverpool was a stronghold of Confederacy support, with three out of the four local papers on the side of the South. The city even held a Confederate Bazaar in 1864 to raise money for Southern prisoners of war. The bazaar was held in the grand St George's Hall and was attended by prominent businesspeople, aristocrats and the local member of parliament. The *Liverpool Daily Courier* called the event a 'triumphant success' as it raised £20,000 (more than £2.5 million today) and was attended by thousands of people.[48]

By 1850, 40 per cent of British exports were finished cotton goods and at least three-quarters, and in some years 95 per cent, of the raw material imported into the Liverpool docks was from US planta-tions.[49] New Orleans hosted the biggest market in enslaved Africans because of its centrality in connecting US cotton plantations to fact-ories in the north of England. The United States was also a key market for British industry, and a destination for capital finance, making it more important than any part of Britain's actual empire. In the long term Britain has maintained a special relationship with its former colony, basking in the reflected glory of the new centre of Western imperialism.

As well as being a settler colony, the United States has been and remains a colonial force in the classic sense of the word. At different times Puerto Rico, the Philippines, Hawaii, Haiti, the Dominican Republic, Guam and Samoa have been US colonies. Hawaii has since been incorporated into the nation, Puerto Rico has a unique status as not quite colony or state, and the US Virgin Islands remain a colony to this very day. The United States even took the very European step of establishing a colony in Africa.

Liberia was founded in 1847 with the intention of solving the supposed race problem that would result from having millions of formerly enslaved people running free in the United States. The idea was to repatriate the Black population to Liberia, thereby cleansing the nation.[50] Liberia was formally a free state led by African Americans who, with support from the US military, subjugated the natives of the area in order to establish their new homeland. In reality, Liberia was a colony of the United States, entirely dependent on the mother country for resources, military support and trade. In keeping with the pattern across the rest of the continent, Liberia was developed only insofar as this benefited the mother country and was set up to strip the new nation of its resources. US companies flocked to Liberia to make their fortunes and underdevelopment was an essential element of this process. If Liberia had industrialized it would have challenged Western dominance on the continent.[51] As well as using the colony to enrich the mother country, Liberia was also a tool in wider US interests in the region.

One of the main reasons that a more revolutionary approach to African unity never occurred after most countries gained their independence was that a group of them, including Nigeria, Ethiopia and most of francophone Africa, were fundamentally opposed to truly unifying the continent. Instead they sought the trappings of nation-state sovereignty and maintaining close links to their paymasters in the West. It is no coincidence that this group were dubbed the 'Monrovia bloc', after the capital of Liberia, holding their first meeting there in 1961.[52] Given the importance of Africa in terms of resources, the United States and the rest of the West were terrified of a radical vision of African political unity. Liberian president William Tubman spearheaded the successful efforts to block radical proposals for change, and the country went much further in doing its colonial master's bidding.

In 1975 President William Tolbert ignored the ban imposed by the Organization of African Unity and hosted South African apartheid prime minister John Vorster. The meeting of the leaders of two of America's client states in Africa was more than just symbolic. Liberia was also used as a base for CIA operations in Chad in support of warlord Hissène Habré in 1982, and more recently for US efforts to oust Gaddafi in Libya.[53]

America's use of Liberia as a military outpost is just part of a much larger aspect of US colonial foreign policy. To solidify its power across the globe the US has over 800 military bases in more than seventy countries. Africa is no exception: there are at least thirty-four US bases on the continent.[54] In 2007 the United States announced its intentions in Africa by launching its Africa Command, known as Africom. President George W. Bush explained that the aim was to 'enhance our efforts to bring peace and security to the people of Africa and promote our common goals of development, health, education, democracy, and economic growth in Africa'.[55] The neo-colonial intent of the operation is embedded in the quote, from the paternalism of wanting to 'bring peace and security' to the continent, to the list of aspirations that the mission wants to fulfil. Africom stands out from other US commands because of its largely non-military objectives. The official rhetoric makes it sound more like an aid agency than an army. The fact that the United States believes it needs the might of its military power to 'bring' prosperity to the continent should be no surprise.

Colonial civilizing missions were always done at the barrel of a gun. We should also be sceptical of these noble intentions. Africa is a key resource for oil and other minerals and Africom's presence appears aimed at securing the safety of the extraction of these rather than promoting authentic continental supremacy. It should also be noted that even the reactionary African leaders that run the continent today are wary of Africom. No country has accepted US overtures to host the headquarters of the command, which runs out of Stuttgart in Germany. A US military command for Africa, run from Germany, should give all the symbolic clues to its nature that we need.

A major part of US imperialism is the power it wields as the dedicated police force of the world. The establishment of Africom is meant to further those networks and allow the US to strike across the globe. We have already seen the use of US hard power, with Africom leading the coalition of Western forces to topple Gaddafi, military action that went expressly against the wishes of the African Union (which replaced the Organization of African Unity).

The invasion of Iraq in 2003 was the most blatant neo-colonial expression of hard power of the twenty-first century. A key source of oil and a strategic defence against Iran, Iraq has been a major piece in Western dominance of the Middle East. Saddam Hussein was once a key ally of the West; in fact, I grew up driving past the Saddam Hussein Mosque in Birmingham, built in the dictator's honour. Not long after the Second Gulf War the name of the mosque was changed as Britain tried to create a new narrative around its involvement in the region. Whether we view the war as legal or moral are important questions, but what is indisputable is that it reflected the entitlement of the West, led by the United States, to enforce its will on other parts of the world. There was no global mandate for invasion – there was not even agreement across the West – but it occurred, nonetheless. The result was the destabilization of Iraq and the rise of the Islamic State, which quickly became the new bogeyman for the West. In the same way that the United States had not tried to create al-Qaeda as a terrorist group that would kill thousands of people in New York, neither was it a conscious act to create its descendants. But as damaging as both groups have been in the West, they have perversely served the expansion of the militarist US-led empire.

Before the Iraq War the invasion of Afghanistan was supported by the Western world in order to bring down the Taliban regime that harboured al-Qaeda. Iraq was never implicated in 9/11 and therefore a different pretext was needed to expand the mission. But without the initial presence in Afghanistan it is very unlikely that the Iraq invasion would have happened, no matter how many weapons of mass destruction the United States imagined Saddam Hussein was stockpiling. Al-Qaeda provided the pretext for a reshaping of relations in the Middle East, one of the most important regions for the US Empire, which invested heavily in its neo-colonial adventure. The United States may have spent as much as $3 trillion on Iraq alone,[56] not to mention the vast sums of money allies like Britain ploughed into the invasion. Part of this gigantic outlay was because of neo-colonial arrogance – the idea that these puny countries in the desert would quickly bow to Western military might.

The sight of George Bush the younger landing in a fighter jet on the USS *Abraham Lincoln* aircraft carrier on 1 May 2003, to unveil a 'mission accomplished' banner is the most obvious symbol of the hubris of the US Empire. The war would not actually end for more than eight years and there is still chaos in the region. As has been true for anywhere there has been colonialism, there was also resistance, and the United States and its allies were trapped for years in conflict that claimed the lives of thousands of Western troops. But the blood and treasure were worth it. The invasion renewed Western control over resources in the region and solidified a new frontier in the US Empire.

The bombing of the World Trade Center led directly to the signing of the Patriot Act in October 2001, which has been much criticized for trampling on domestic civil liberties. But the Patriot Act, and other laws passed in the aftermath of 9/11, allowed the United States to make more gains for its global empire. Following the attacks the US government froze the assets of any group suspected of funding terror abroad. Sanctions were imposed without the need for trial or much evidence. The ban was widespread and covered all 'aspects of financial support including food and medical aid'.[57] As a result the assets of a number of Islamic charities were frozen, irrespective of whether they were actually funding terrorism. The impact of these decisions was felt not only by those in need of aid but may also have contributed directly to financial crisis in Somalia.

As many underdeveloped countries do, Somalia relies on remittances from its diaspora. A large proportion of these were handled by Al-Barakaat, a Muslim money-transfer company which the United States financially ruined 'despite lack of evidence, trial or conviction'.[58] The collapse of the company sent Somalia into an economic tailspin. The economic attacks of the US Empire were the softer side of the wider offensive.

Alongside massive military operations in Iraq and Afghanistan, the United States also increased its militarization of the entire region, and beyond. Extraordinary rendition of subjects to black sites, beyond the jurisdiction of international law, where they were subsequently tortured, became the norm. Almost 800 people were imprisoned in Guantánamo Bay, including British citizens. The majority were eventually released without charge. Despite President Obama's promise to close Guantánamo Bay within a year of his coming to office in 2009, at the time of writing there are still people imprisoned in the camp. The CIA has ramped up its activity around the world and legitimized the use of drone strikes to kill terror suspects without the need for anything like arrest and trial. The US security apparatus has extended across the globe and set precedents for the use of force that are reminiscent of old colonial days. It has been estimated that since the start of the 'War on Terror' between 244,124 and 266,427 civilians have been killed in Afghanistan, Iraq and Pakistan, the three main targets of the US mission. In addition, over 100,000 members of the local armies and police forces have lost their lives.[59] Not all of these deaths were the direct consequence of US armed forces pulling the trigger or dropping a bomb, but they are a consequence of their neo-colonial agenda in the region. The callous disregard for life that is not White can be seen in the drone strikes targeting 'terror' suspects in Afghanistan, Pakistan, Yemen and Somalia. Between 8,858 and 16,901 people have been killed by remote control from the sky, including up to 2,200 civilians, of which as many as 454 have been children.[60] US imperialism has industrialized and legitimated the killing of Brown civilians, including children, in pursuit of its goals.

A key feature of the expansion of the US Empire is one reminiscent from older forms of colonialism: of the fortune that the United States spent on the invasion of Iraq, a third was spent employing private military contractors, often ex-soldiers paid by a private company to wage war. As such, there is far less scrutiny of and accountability for their actions. The biggest force in Iraq apart from the US army was the private militia, paid for by US tax dollars. Iraq is just one example of the global trend. Private militias operate in more than ninety countries, amassing budgets of over $100 billion.[61] Not only did they make a financial killing from the conflict in Iraq, they also profited mightily in the reconstruction effort. Contracts worth at least $138 billion were handed out to private firms to rebuild the damage caused by the US-inflicted war. Most controversially, a company previously run by the then Vice President Dick Cheney was the most rewarded from this privatization of state rebuilding, receiving contracts worth $39.5 billion.[62] Capitalism, from Columbus's voyages to slave-owning companies, to outsourced colonial corporations, to hedge-fund managers today, has been based on the state setting the table for private interests to fill their bellies.

Western empires have facilitated the ransacking of various parts of the world, underdeveloping supposedly backward nations so that the West can continue to profit. The myth of the risk-taking entrepreneur is central to justifying the staggering inequality the system produces, but it is also rooted in colonial logic. In fact, the notion is central to Enlightenment ideals of progress, which identify the rational, individual White man as he who ploughs the way for capitalist progress. Ignored in this is the role various states have played in tilting the playing field so far in their favour that you would be forgiven for believing that it is natural for wealth to fall into the hands of the West. The current version of the US Empire is simply the latest, most efficient way of delivering Western imperialism.

5

Dawn of a New Age

After the Second World War the initial version of Western imperialism could no longer continue to function in the same way it had during the previous centuries. Competition between European nation states vying to dominate the globe led to the loss of millions of lives and bankrupted these seats of empire. The great European powers simply no longer had the resources to directly control and maintain their colonies. Worse still, both World Wars were truly global and the natives who had fought in their millions for the mother countries were restless. They demanded freedom and had the experience of armed warfare to achieve it. The fifth Pan-African Congress, which brought together leaders of resistance movements across Africa and the diaspora took place in Manchester in 1945. For the first time in the movement's forty-five year history the delegates from Africa, the Caribbean and the Americas proclaimed their demands for the full independence of Africa from European rule.

The writing was on the wall, and the empires that had defined the world were in danger of collapse. In fact, in the popular imagination this is exactly what is thought to have happened. Europe had to, either in response to armed resistance by the natives or through a supposedly benevolent process, eventually grant independence to its colonies. The old logic of racial domination melted away, leading to the globalized world we inhabit today.

Unfortunately, that version of history is an utter myth. Rather than marking the beginning of the end of Western imperialism, the Second World War instead led to a system update that changed the delivery of a racist, unjust social order, but maintained all of its logic. By rebooting the system it was able to continue, in many ways more successfully than in the first, outdated version. In the deluded world-view of historians like Niall Ferguson, the brutal forms of colonial oppression in the earlier version of Western imperialism did more good than harm, representing a sort of 'liberal imperialism' that brought light to the backward parts of the world.[1] These arguments are distorted, dangerous and wrong-headed, as any reader of the previous chapters will understand. Inadvertently, however, Ferguson stumbles upon the perfect phrase to capture the updated form of the system that emerged after the Second World War: liberal imperialism. The current incarnation of Western empire is one that presents itself as working for the good of humanity, while maintaining the colonial logic upon which it was founded.

Before the Second World War had even ended, plans were being made to update the imperial system. After the carnage of the First World War and the subsequent Great Depression it was becoming clear that the system was unstable even prior to the rise of Nazi Germany. In order to move to a more sustainable system of imperialism the West realized that it had to go beyond the nation state-led format that had until this point been its dominant feature. Collaboration between Western powers was *always* a central feature of the emergence of the current racial order. European nation states simply could not have dominated the globe without cooperation and systematic coordination. But this was still done under the banner of nation statehood, with competition and wars an unrelenting reality. Given this history, the outbreak of neither the First nor the Second World War came as a great surprise.

After the Germans lost in 1918 their colonies were divided up between the Allies, and this became a key source of national frustration that contributed to the rise of such a virulent, racist nationalism in the form of Nazism. Western nation states at war with each other was bad for the business of exploiting the world and therefore a more substantive form of unity was necessary. The League of Nations, founded in 1920, was the first attempt. It was ultimately doomed to failure because, although President Woodrow Wilson was a key proponent of the League, the United States never joined due to opposition in Congress. The fact that the United States was essential to making the alliance work also marks a key shift in the centre of Western imperialism. By 1920, although Europe still controlled most of the world, the stage was set for the United States to become the heart of the Western empire. The wealth and power of the United States were the definition of colonial logic and European collaboration. It was a nation formed in genocide, built by slave labour to offer a new frontier for peoples from across Europe. The US was engorged by wealth accrued from the first stage of Western imperialism and was ready to lead the transition into the new world order.

When the United States decided to end its isolationist stance and take its place on the world stage, it did so on the basis of the same grand vision that remains largely intact today. While the Japanese bombing of Pearl Harbor was the act of aggression that ultimately tipped the United States into the Second World War, the stage had been set earlier. In August 1941 Churchill and Roosevelt signed the Atlantic Charter, which was not a treaty or binding document but rather a pledge of the principles that would govern world affairs after the Nazis had been defeated. The eight principles of the Charter were designed to create lasting peace and even included the 'abandonment of the use of force', which, given the empire that Britain ruled over at the time, would have been a remarkable new principle, had they ever intended it to apply to the colonies.[2] In fact the entire Charter reads like an anti-colonial manifesto, promising that 'countries seek no aggrandizement, territorial or other'; 'no territorial changes that do not accord with the freely expressed wishes of the peoples concerned'; and 'the right of all peoples to choose the form of government under which they will live'. Whether Britain liked it or not, once professed, the principles enshrined in these documents became used by decolonial freedom movements in both the colonies and the mother countries. When Malcolm X founded the Organization of Afro-American Unity in 1964 he explained that they were partly 'inspired by' the Atlantic Charter in their quest for self-determination.[3]

As well as inspiring liberation movements, the Charter became the foundation of the United Nations (UN), created in 1945 in order to meet the aims of national cooperation, global peace and security. By maintaining the nation-state framework the UN has been able to convince countries to sign up and agree to general principles of collaboration. As each member has one vote the UN has been seen as a site where the global majority, i.e. those countries not in the West, can have its say. As an organization the UN has certainly done some good in the underdeveloped world, spearheading development programmes and working to reduce ills like infant mortality. But don't be fooled by the façade of internationalism. It is no coincidence that the UN was originally conceived by the British and Americans, nor that its headquarters are in New York. The principal function of the UN has always been to aid the transition from the old system of imperialism to the new. Nothing could be stronger evidence of this than the make-up of the real decision-making body in the UN.

The General Assembly, with its one-country-one-vote, may well be a perfect space for grand speeches denouncing colonialism, but all the real power lies with the Security Council, which is made up of five permanent members: France, the Russian Federation, the United Kingdom, the United States and China; plus a further ten nations elected to two-year terms. At the time that the UN was founded, Russia was technically not in the West; at that point it was the major state in the Soviet Union and the foundation of the Communist bloc. The USSR was undoubtedly a major power, and since the Soviets had been pivotal in defeating the Nazis, they could not be excluded. And, of course, Communism's difference to the West on the fundamental issue of the global racial order is a matter only of degree. China stands out as the only non-White country on the council, but it was also a key ally in the War and has been entirely complicit in racial capitalism in order to develop itself. Not being White has never automatically meant being opposed to the colonial logic of White supremacy.

Permanent Security Council members have the right of veto over substantive resolutions, which is why the Iraq War was never declared illegal by the UN. That ultimate power means that the five permanent members shape the decision-making of the organization. As neither Russia nor China remain Communist in any meaningful sense, the domination of Western interests in the UN is now indisputable. The UN is the global institution with the best reputation in the world but it is inextricably bound up with the International Monetary Fund (IMF) and the World Bank, whose names evoke fear across the underdeveloped world. In fact, article five of the Atlantic Charter speaks of the 'desire to bring about the fullest collaboration between all nations in the economic field', which became the most important frontier for the updated global system of Western imperialism.

In 1944 the seeds were planted for the IMF, World Bank and World Trade Organization at the Bretton Woods Conference in New Hampshire. They were later dubbed an 'unholy trinity' that developed a 'regime' of financial control over the world.[4] Just as with the UN, Britain and the United States took the lead in establishing both the meeting and the ensuing global institutions. Bretton Woods' express purpose was to reshape the global order after the War. In keeping with tradition, the headquarters of the IMF and the World Bank are in the United States, both in Washington, DC. The special relationship across the Atlantic was more than just symbolic. It represented a passing of the torch from the former centre of Western imperialism to the new one. Britain and the United States spent two years designing the framework of the new world order prior to Bretton Woods, and the purpose of the meeting was simply to ratify this. To maintain the appearance of a global agreement, forty-four countries attended; but only fifteen sent their finance ministers. Demonstrating just how central their role in the process was, Guatemala sent a postgraduate economics student. In testament to the attitudes of the architects of the new system, John Maynard Keynes, the British economist who was instrumental in Bretton Woods, had made an effort to restrict the participation of countries other than the United States and Britain 'fearing that a "great monkey house" would result if all of the wartime allies were invited'.[5] The financial regime ratified at Bretton Woods therefore represented US economic priorities, slightly steered by Britain, rather than any unified global alliance.[6]

American dominance should not come as a shock given the context. Europe was bankrupt and depleted after years of war, whereas the United States' economy was buoyant. The US used the opportunity to establish its place at the head of the table in the post-war period, notably giving the equivalent of $100 billion in aid to Western European countries impacted by the War, in the Marshall Plan of 1948. As well as providing aid directly to Europe, the US also supplied the bulk of funding to establish the new global economic institutions.

The IMF began operating in 1947 and its principal initial purpose was to provide loans to stabilize Western economies and promote collaboration between countries. France was the first country to borrow from the IMF and between 1947 and 1971 Britain drew down $7.25 billion.[7] There were five original shareholders: the United States, Britain, France, Germany and Japan. Voting rights depended on the amount of money a nation put in, and the size of the United States' share in 1947 meant that it had an effective veto over the fund. The United States was willing to invest so much money in stabilizing the Western powers because it was in its economic interests to do so and shifted the centre of the global economy across the Atlantic. It was also in its economic and political interests to fight the spread of Communism. If Europe had become infected by the Red menace, the economic system that the United States had inherited leadership of could have come to an end.

After 1971 the role of the IMF changed significantly. At this point Western economies had largely recovered from the War but there was a new problem. The West has always depended on the exploitation of the underdeveloped world, but by the seventies most of the former colonies were ruling themselves. There was a major fear that they would turn to Communism, which would also have ended Western economic dominance, given its dependence on the logic of empire. We should not pretend that the old forms of coercion were not attempted in this more liberal period of imperialism. Many countries had to win their freedom through armed struggle, and in places like Mozambique and Angola the death throes of direct colonization were brutal for the natives. Radical leaders were assassinated in order to install corrupt puppet regimes. The United States also began violent campaigns to prevent the spread of Communism, taking colonial-era violence to places like Vietnam and Korea. But for the most part the methods of control in the new age of empire were financial, and the IMF played a pivotal role.

Colonialism had left the newly independent countries underdeveloped. They lacked basic infrastructure and were impoverished by colonial exploitation. After so-called independence neo-colonial trade practices ensured that even if they were rich in resources, like most African countries, their wealth was in the hands of foreign multinationals. Independence was gained by individual nation states that were too small to wield any influence on the world stage. Most of the underdeveloped nations found themselves in steep debt not long after the mirage of their liberation, and the IMF was only too willing to oblige them with loans. Unlike lending to Western countries, in the underdeveloped world these loans had strong conditions; they came with strings attached. The prevailing assumption was that the nations had got themselves in debt by acting economically inappropriately. For their economies to prosper and therefore pay back the loans they would have to make structural adjustments to their economic life. The orthodoxy of what apparently makes for a successful economy includes abolishing controls on imports, imposing austerity to reduce the size of the state, devaluing the currency and opening the doors to foreign private investors.[8] Countries in desperate need of support continue to voluntarily submit to these conditions because they have no place else to turn.

What on the surface was an economic bailout was in reality direct interference in the political decision-making of underdeveloped countries. Reducing public spending is a euphemism for cutting jobs and privatizing services, making them more expensive, in the poorest countries in the world. Consequently, IMF policies have caused strikes and riots across the underdeveloped world. In 1976 protests erupted in Argentina after government wages were frozen. A 1981 general strike occurred in Mexico after government subsidies on food were removed. The removal of subsidies on petrol brought unrest to Nigeria in 1988. Riots broke out in Egypt in 1997 and Indonesia in 1998 after food subsidies were removed or reduced. Decisions to make the poor even poorer are made with the coldness that only a global bureaucracy could produce.

The evidence shows that IMF involvement in underdeveloped countries is a net negative. A study of 135 recipient countries found that accepting money from the IMF significantly increased income inequality.[9] Structural adjustment has a negative effect on women's employment.[10] IMF loans lead to higher suicide rates in countries that accept them.[11] IMF policies also reduce human rights in a recipient country, specifically increasing the incidence of torture and extra-judicial killings.[12] The whole purpose of IMF intervention is meant to be to save struggling economies, but financial crises are a continuing feature for IMF recipients.[13]

'Structural adjustment' is a term often associated with Latin America, where a debt crisis in the eighties sparked an economic shock across the continent. The root of the problem was that, particularly due to a steep rise in oil prices, in order to balance their budgets Latin American countries had been borrowing money from Western banks and governments, and were unable to service their foreign debts. For instance, by 1982 Bolivia was spending 15 per cent of its gross national product (GNP) on debt repayments, a clearly unsustainable position to be in. But Bolivia was not treated as harshly by the IMF for reasons that reveal the true motives for Western financial intervention.

Although Bolivia had one of the worst debt ratios of any country, because it was a small and poor country its absolute debt was relatively low: it owed only $44 million to Western banks. Argentina, on the other hand, was spending 4.5 per cent of its GNP on debt repayments, but as a richer and larger country had a total debt of $45 billion.[14] It seems obvious that the two economies were vastly different and would not require the same prescription, but the IMF mercilessly and harshly imposed structural adjustment on Argentina in any case. The purpose of these policies was not to solve the problems of the recipient economies but to secure Western interests. Argentina owed vastly more money to the West and needed to be squeezed to ensure this was paid back.

Another reason for the blanket application of the IMF prescriptions is that by devaluing the currency, privatizing utilities and opening up the economy to foreign direct investment, structural adjustment makes the receiving nations ripe for takeover by Western interests. Global capital has been aided in its expansion across the world, looting whole economies to fill the coffers of Western financial capitals.[15] The eighties are referred to as the 'lost decade' in Latin America for a reason: triple-digit inflation, enforced austerity and poverty had a devastating impact on the region. Mexico was one of the countries hardest hit by the debt crisis and the international financial regime: the impact was so severe that the economy had not fully recovered two decades later, remaining 30 per cent below where it should have been.[16]

The idea that organizations like the IMF act solely on the basis of sound economic principles is a fairytale. The organization is based in Washington and funded by Western governments, on whose say the amount of money to be invested depends. Bolivia's more favourable treatment by the IMF exposes the political incentives behind the actions of the Western financial regime. The United States is the dominant source of funding, and the priorities of the IMF align with the holders of the purse strings. In the 1980s the US pursued a 'war on drugs' in Central and South America, even though attacking the coca-leaf producers decimated the lives of the quarter of a million farmers and their families who depended on the crop.[17] Bolivia was a key ally in this war, and as a reward for its fealty to American interests, received a somewhat more lenient ride with the IMF. This was also the case with the monstrous Pinochet regime in Chile, which received preferential treatment in negotiations with the IMF, after taking power following a CIA-backed coup d'état against socialist leader Salvador Allende in 1973.[18] It is always worth remembering the dictators and despots whose politics have aligned so well with the West.

The history of the IMF as a political tool is by no means restricted to Latin America: preferential negotiations were used to try and prevent Pakistan from arming itself with nuclear weapons as well as to induce Turkey's support for the Gulf War.[19] Countries in the underdeveloped world who vote more often with the United States in the UN also get a better deal from the IMF.[20] The new age of empire functions on the basis of this financial intervention regime, one that plunders the economies of the underdeveloped world to support the interests of the West.

It might be tempting to argue that the IMF takes its actions in good, but ill-conceived, faith. That the countries are in debt because their economies are badly run and they need support to make the correct adjustments on their way to becoming highly developed capitalist utopias. But the West is not rich because of its genius, democracy and capitalism. It is affluent because it has expropriated wealth from the underdeveloped word: the Rest is poor *because* the West is rich. Newly independent nations were always going to end up struggling and having to take loans from Western interests, who only had the resources to lend because they were plundered from the Rest. Third World debt is obscene at every level. It's as if I stole your money and then, when you failed to make ends meet, offered you a payday loan at extortionate interest rates, all the while berating you for being bad at running your personal finances, and then forcing you to spend the money in the way that benefited me the most. The West can never be the solution to global poverty because it is *the* cause of it. The places in the underdeveloped world that have made the biggest strides forward since the dawn of the new age of empire are those that have had the least support from the West.

Prior to the late nineties, East Asia was seen as a miracle of economic development. Korea, Thailand, Malaysia, the Philippines and Indonesia had experienced three decades of economic growth and poverty reduction. Contrary to Western economic wisdom, this had not been achieved because they followed the dictates of the Washington consensus but because they had not.[21] In particular, in these countries the state had been heavily involved in their economic transformation, and economic liberalization and privatization were happening only slowly.

At the end of the Korean War in 1953 South Korea was poorer than India, but by 1990 it was so 'successful' it was a member of the Organization for Economic Cooperation and Development (OECD), a pool of largely Western countries tasked with stimulating economic trade and so-called global progress. All of this was done with little foreign direct investment, although it did rely on loans from Western banks. We should never forget that the so-called progress of nations like South Korea is built on their integration into the mechanism of Western imperialism. Alongside including steep inequalities within their borders, this also means feeding off the bounty of global White supremacy. Dealing with the devil has its consequences, as many of the nations in East Asia found out at the end of the nineties.

In 1997 currency speculators drove down the value of the Thai baht, which caused an economic crisis that spread across the region. In stepped the saviour, in the form of the IMF, who managed to only make the problem worse. The IMF provided $95 billion in loans, which was in effect a bailout for the Western banks the nations were having difficulty repaying. As always, the money had strings attached that included austerity, tax increases on the poor and neoliberal structural reforms. The results were disastrous. GDP collapsed across the region and unemployment increased four-fold in Korea and three-fold in Indonesia. In Korean cities a quarter of the population fell into poverty. Austerity made the situation far worse than it could have been, and reductions in food and fuel subsidies for the poor led to riots in Indonesia. The IMF may not have started the crisis but their actions deepened it, and placed a heavy burden on the poor. As economist Joseph Stiglitz explains, the impact was so negative in the region that 'history is dated "before" and "after" the IMF, just as countries that are devastated by an earthquake or some other natural disaster date events "before" or "after" the earthquake'.[22]

As an example of the absurdity of IMF orthodoxy, Stiglitz offers Ethiopia in 1997. The IMF refused to loan Ethiopia money in the midst of an economic crisis because they argued that foreign aid was too big a proportion of the country's economy. They genuinely suggested that Ethiopia would be better served by paying foreign aid into the nation's reserves, rather than spending the money on schools and hospitals. Stiglitz uses this example to make the case that the World Bank was a more benevolent organization, since it had workers on the ground trying to engage with and support the poor. But the World Bank was created by the same people and for the same purpose as the IMF. As a former director and chief economist of the World Bank, we should take Stiglitz's pronouncements about the organization as little more than company PR.

THE 'WHITE MAN'S BURDEN'

Unlike the IMF, the World Bank sees itself as a development agency. It aims to end extreme poverty and it was primarily set up to provide support for the underdeveloped world so that countries would not fall for the charms of the Soviets. Just as with the IMF, the organization is financed largely by Western governments and the United States is the biggest donor. Also like the IMF, the World Bank is used as a political tool, so it should be no surprise that its programme benefits wealthier nations, whilst supposedly supporting the underdeveloped world.[23] While Stiglitz has been more critical of the economic orthodoxy of Western financial intervention, the World Bank generally has not. It has embraced the same conditionality to its loans as the IMF, and the two names are often used interchangeably because of the collective destruction they have wrought on underdeveloped economies. John Williamson, whose tenure at the World Bank spanned over a decade, said in 2004, 'we argue the desirability of completing rather than reversing the liberalizing reforms of the Washington Consensus.'[24]

Rather than challenging the cartel of Western intervention, the World Bank has been happy to enforce neoliberalism on the nations it is supposed to be helping. When the World Bank was considering the impact of charging people for healthcare in Peru in order to shrink public debt they came to the conclusion that 'the introduction of user fees at public health facilities will have only a small effect on the rural poor because they tend not to visit health facilities.'[25] The fact that the poor do not have access to healthcare somehow became a reason to introduce charges. The callous disregard for life outside the West is one of the key features that has been maintained in the updated system of racial oppression. To borrow from Stiglitz, 'from one's luxury hotel, one can callously impose policies about which one would think twice if one knew the people whose lives one was destroying.'[26]

The intentions of the World Bank may genuinely be positive. They are a resource of information on global poverty and invest billions of dollars in the underdeveloped world. But the road to neo-colonialism is paved with good intentions. Believing that you are doing good while inflicting damage is not a new feature of Western imperialism. Even during the horrific violence of its first iteration, colonialists imagined that they were doing the savages good by dragging them into civilization. Kipling said it was the 'White man's burden' to lift the world out of its state of nature. We can see this rhetoric at work in the new centre of empire when in 1901 Vice President Theodore Roosevelt declared the need to annex the Philippines, explaining that 'it is our duty toward the people living in barbarism to see that they are freed from their chains.'[27] In the development agenda weapons are not used to save the savages. Instead aid is sent, and expertise is granted, to help pull up the underdeveloped world.

In exactly the same way that the notion the underdeveloped world should be indebted to the developed world is absurd, so is the idea that aid could be of any serious benefit. We are trapped in a similar paradox to the reparations debate, where the wealth necessary to repair the damage would destroy the entire Western economic system. The West enriches itself off the Rest, and therefore donating an extremely small amount of that money back through aid is clearly not going to solve the problem. While the absolute numbers in terms of aid sound high, they are actually relatively small. By the early 2000s the West had spent $2.3 trillion on foreign aid.[28] But when you consider that Britain's GDP in 2017 alone was $2.6 trillion you can begin to understand the scale of the problem. It should be no surprise then that the record of foreign aid is not encouraging. For instance, $2 billion has been invested in Tanzania's roads, but they show little improvement.[29] There have been strides made in the underdeveloped world but most of the countries that have done well received relatively little development aid.

In 2000 the United Nations committed to a series of Millennium Development Goals that it hoped the world could achieve by 2015. Progress was made in most areas and many of the targets were hit, including more than halving the number of people living in extreme poverty across the globe to 14 per cent.[30] The proportion of under-nourished children also fell by almost half, more children were in education, including girls, and the number of people in the global working middle class grew significantly. All this apparent progress is accompanied by a host of cheerleaders promising us that we are well on the path to a better world.

Psychologist Steven Pinker assures us not only that the Enlightenment has 'worked' but that its ideals are 'stirring, inspiring, noble' and nothing short of a 'reason to live'.[31] Bill Gates, perhaps the embodiment of the White saviour complex, called Pinker's ode to the Enlightenment his 'favourite book of all time'. Sam Harris, self-described neuroscientist (but in reality pop psychologist), is so convinced of the power of so-called science he believes it will ultimately determine correct moral values.[32] Having endured an undergraduate degree in psychology, it is no shock to me that authors steeped in the subject have so fully drunk the progress-narrative Kool-Aid. Psychology is trying to make its presence known, having been promoted to the premier league of pseudo-sciences, vying for position with stalwarts such as economics, politics and some versions of sociology. But wherever you look you can find plenty of academics waving pom-poms in support of progress. Development studies was basically designed to lead the PR campaign for Enlightenment ideals, and Hans Rosling, with his captivating TED talks, colourful charts and accessible books, is the leader of the cheer squad.[33] But before we get lured by the allure of the future dead White men we only need to take a closer look at all these so-called gains to see through the mirage.

In terms of the poverty indicators, China accounted for the vast majority of improvements. This is the same China that received very little aid and has a planned economy run by its central Communist Party machinery. Though the numbers of people living in extreme poverty fell in Africa, this did not happen to anything like the same extent. In fact, by 2015, 36 per cent of people *in work* in Africa lived in extreme poverty. The World Bank figures report that half of people living in extreme poverty are in so-called sub-Saharan Africa, and that figure will be nine in ten by 2030.[34] As we have already explored, anti-Blackness is a feature of Western empire, so we should have been prepared for the news that progress is far slower in Africa. But we should not get carried away by how much life has changed for most of the world's poor.

The UN Millennium Development Goals report admits that 'almost half of global workers are still working in vulnerable conditions, rarely enjoying the benefits associated with decent work',[35] while the World Bank estimates that half the world lives on less than $5.50 a day. To qualify for the working middle class you only need to earn more than $4 a day, and over 80 per cent of people in the world live on less than $13 daily. The development agenda has never been about equality, but has been tailored to remove the harshest edges of suffering from the global system of oppression. In a 1977 speech to the World Bank, Robert McNamara, its fifth president, gave the game away when he explained that

> closing the gap [between the developed and underdeveloped worlds] was never a realistic objective in the first place. Given the immense

differences in the capital and technological base of the industrialized nations as compared with that of the developing countries, it was simply not a feasible goal. Nor is it one today.[36]

The same is true now. The UN goals are all worthy. Reducing extreme poverty, educating children and tackling health emergencies like HIV are imperative to alleviate human suffering. But this is not the same as addressing global inequality. The fact that people earning $4 a day are labelled 'working middle class' should be proof of the obscenity of this paradigm. Conditions that we would never accept in the West are marked as progress in the Rest. Whereas we may have accepted that killing and enslaving the natives is wrong, we have normalized poverty for the Black and Brown because in the new world order our lives matter, just a lot less. In many ways this is the fulfilment of Kant's universal reason, rooted in his 'moral geography'. We have a supranational body (the UN) working to ensure that the savages are not murdered or deposed by colonial troops, but are given just enough to subsist on so that the West is free to carry on exploiting them through colonial logic, with no twinges of its conscience.

The UN's complete ignorance of race can only be understood in the context of Enlightenment reason, which imagines civilization rebooted in Europe in the eighteenth century (after a long hiatus following the fall of the Romans). Cheerleaders like Pinker and Rosling point to the data supporting the idea that progress is being made in areas like infant mortality and absolute poverty around the world. This is the world-view that allows the UN to claim victory in its millennium goals. Conveniently ignored is that we are measuring progress since the destruction wrought by Western imperialism. It is perverse to celebrate marginal gains in the underdeveloped world after genocide, slavery and colonialism produced the racially unjust social order. The number one cause of global poverty is racism, with nations so desperate to improve their condition because of the lived reality of White supremacy.

It would be charitable to see this foreign-aid industrial complex as a benevolent form of imperialism, where at least people's hearts are in the right place. In just one example, a UN-funded Millennium Villages project in Uganda trained farmers in techniques to provide a higher crop yield. The result was a bumper harvest, but there was no market for the goods and they ended up rotting, with the famers losing out even further because of their increased costs of production.[37] Maybe we should forgive such misguided errors and the well-to-do bumbling of do-gooders. But when we look at how the money is spent it is very hard not to see a purposeful campaign to maintain the dispossession of the underdeveloped world. It is even more difficult to avoid this conclusion when the British Minister for International Development openly declares that she wants to use her budget to 'tear down the barriers to free trade', as Priti Patel did in 2017.[38]

The Conservatives are not typically seen as a party that supports foreign aid. In both classical and neoliberal versions of Western economics the idea of giving handouts is a terrible distortion of the sanctity of the market. There is a whole body of economic thought, typified by Milton Friedman, that believes global inequality is caused in part because the underdeveloped world is 'receiving unwarranted assistance'.[39] But since gaining power in 2010 the Conservatives have been keen to champion their foreign aid credentials. On his last day in office, after crashing his premiership on the rocks of Brexit, David Cameron claimed that his government's commitment to spending 0.7 per cent of GDP on foreign aid was one of his 'proudest achievements'.[40] The aid spending was particularly significant for a government that pursued the severest austerity agenda in British history, and they weren't forced into it by the IMF either. The Department for International Development saw its budget increase by 24 per cent from 2010/11 to 2015/16 at a time when cuts to other departments were 28 per cent.[41]

Given how the aid budget is actually being spent, however, it becomes far less surprising that the Conservatives have been so keen to invest. Before the Cameron government came to power, in 2009, the Tories published a Green Paper extolling the virtues of 'capitalism and development' as 'Britain's gift to the world'.[42] Once in power the Conservatives set about changing the law so that they could use the aid budget to support the interests of global capitalism and British business in particular.[43] A perfect example of such worthwhile spending was to grant £450 million to Adam Smith International (ASI), a free-market London-based consultancy – more than the government spent in total on human rights and women's equality, and double the amount given to combat the spread of HIV and AIDS.[44] One of the roles of the ASI is to advise countries to liberalize (meaning privatize) whatever they can. Since 2005 the ASI has led a £99 million project to advise Nigeria's government on reforming infrastructure in order to benefit the poorest. Its main achievement has been the privatization of the electricity sector, which is seen as a success because it is so total it would be almost impossible to reverse. The result of this 'progress' is that electricity prices have been hiked by up to 45 per cent; over half the country remains without any power; and the service cuts out so regularly that even those with electricity have to rely on back-up generators. The only beneficiaries of the UK aid were the ASI and the private companies feasting on Nigeria.

Another form of creative accounting in the UK aid budget is the dispersal of £1.5 billion over five years into the university sector. Announced as part of the comprehensive spending review of the coalition government in 2015, the Global Challenges Research Fund aims to 'harness the expertise of the UK's world-leading researchers' in the cause of saving the underdeveloped world.[45] I work in the sector so I do not want to totally undermine the validity of my profession, but the idea of transferring £1.5 billion of a budget meant to save lives to academics is obscene. This is even more so the case when we dig into how this money is being allocated.

I first found out about it in a meeting at work where it was re-vealed that as part of our core research funding the university had been given a slice of the development budget without even having to request it. The university higher-ups then managed to retroactively find some activity that we could pass off as 'development' focused. In this meeting we were discussing how we could find projects to justify keeping our grant from the fund. Not all the money has just been dished out to UK universities. For most of it there are rigorous controls, and applications have to be sent through funding bodies. UK Research and Innovation has a website where you can see the various countries and research projects that have been funded.[46] The sheer volume tells you just how much money is being invested in the scheme. Some very interesting projects on issues ranging from social policy to health and violence prevention have been funded. But identifying Western universities as a conduit for development creates the paradox of offering a 'new White Man's Burden to clean up the mess left behind by the old White Man's Burden'.[47]

The Eurocentric knowledge that is vitally important to maintaining the unjust racial order was produced in universities. That is no different today, with the dreaded Washington consensus, the name given to the economic policies supported by the IMF and World Bank, and by a wealth of academics. In fact, the workforce of the Western financial intervention regime is an army of graduates trained in development orthodoxy. It is through the façade of pseudo-scientific technical expertise presented by the World Bank and the IMF that their looting of economies in the underdeveloped world is justified. If we accept that the development industry is just another mechanism to continue Western imperialism, then universities are one of the foundation stones of that agenda. One of the key mechanisms of neo-colonialism is the training of thousands of students from the underdeveloped world who are sent back home with all the tools to continue letting the West ransack their economies. Giving development aid to universities only makes sense if the purpose is to continue to produce knowledge that entrenches global racial inequality.

Syphoning money from the aid budget in order to support British private enterprise is a longstanding problem and so it makes perfect sense that funding is now being diverted to universities. Since the reforms of 2017 British universities have almost fully completed their transition into private companies. We charge fees, operate in a marketplace and treat students as customers. Pumping in £300 million of the aid budget each year for half a decade is essentially a public investment in the private sector. As is the same with any non-governmental aid agency, the majority of costs go on employing staff in the West. It would be revealing to see just how much of the money ended up paying staff, overheads, travel and catering expenses in British universities. We are essentially using foreign aid to pay the elite (academics) to take on the burden of pulling the underdeveloped world out of its barbarism. The difference between sending administrators to the colonies, the Adam Smith International consultants, and universities producing expert solutions is one of degree.

Britain is not alone in using its foreign aid budget to support its own companies or national interest. USAID (the United States Agency for International Development) is as much a brand that bolsters the progressive credentials of the United States as it is a development agency. In the recent past the United States has been guilty of the most brazen forms of using foreign aid to further its agenda. The 2003 invasion of Iraq was the perfect example of how, when necessary, the United States has embraced 'the violence, brutality, and barbarity befitting any European imperialist power'.[48] After the carnage and devastation of Iraq, the rebuilding of the country provided an opportunity for USAID to loot an underdeveloped economy through 'aid'. The United States prosecuted the war under the guise of 'advancing freedom' in the Middle East.

Almost two years after the invasion President Bush delivered a live prime-time speech at the military base of Fort Bragg in North Carolina where he uttered the word 'freedom' twenty-one times to emphasize the civilizing mission of America.[49] The freedom he was referring to was not what most would understand by the word. Rather than freedom from tyranny, want or fear, Bush really meant unleashing the forces of the free market in Iraq. Once President Saddam was toppled, the US-led Coalition set about regime change, installing the fundamental principles of Western financial intervention. The Coalition's first acts, through USAID, included making half a million soldiers and public officials unemployed, removing barriers to foreign direct investment and privatizing 200 state industries. To put icing on the neoliberal cake they also contracted an affiliate of the leading international services firm KPMG to construct a free market from the ground zero the invasion had created.[50] Iraq became a breeding ground for profiteering from nation-building.

To truly understand the problematic nature of the foreign-aid industrial complex we need to look no further than the recipient of the highest amount of US aid dollars. Rather than pouring money into one of the poorest countries in the world, one in terrible need of infrastructure spending, the United States has donated around a fifth of its aid to Israel, a relatively rich country not considered a developing nation.[51] In 2016 the United States signed a military aid package for Israel worth $38 billion over ten years.[52] Not only does Israel receive the most aid from the United States, it does so under the most favourable conditions: it does not have to account for where the money is spent like other recipient countries.

The United States has company in using its aid budget to support Israel and its armed forces. In 2017 Priti Patel had to step down as Minister for International Development in Britain when it was revealed that she was having secret meetings with the Israelis and attempting to use her department's budget to fund Israel's military activity.[53] Although this somehow did not prevent her from being appointed Home Secretary less than two years later. Israel's subsidy through foreign aid is important not just because it exposes the contradictions in funding. It also highlights another fundamental change in the updated version of empire that marked the new age of empire that emerged after the Second World War.

POST-RACIAL IMPERIALISM

A visceral and overt form of racism underpinned the first iteration of Western empire. A racial hierarchy was clearly coded and enforced with racial science, providing the pseudo-intellectual backing for White supremacy. If the Second World War brought an end to violent competition between Western powers, as well as ending direct control of their colonies, it also reframed the racial logic necessary to dominate the world. The slaughter of 6 million Jewish people in Nazi Germany brought racial logic home, disturbing the otherwise largely settled consensus. The horror of the concentration camps upset the social order and it was decided that 'race' had to be abandoned to the dustbin of history. A 1950 statement brought together by the United Nations Educational, Scientific and Cultural Organization (UNESCO) declared that

> National, religious, geographic, linguistic and cultural groups do not
> necessarily coincide with racial groups: and the cultural traits of such

groups have no demonstrated genetic connection with racial traits. Because serious errors of this kind are habitually committed when the term 'race' is used in popular parlance, it would be better when speaking of human races to drop the term 'race' altogether and speak of ethnic groups.[54]

In other words, the West had used the concept of race to slaughter people and dominate the globe, and when the horror of that system was brought home they decided to terminate the idea. On the face of it, abandoning such a flawed concept of race seems like a noble pursuit. Embracing ethnicity retains the idea of difference but allows for more complexity. But over sixty years after the UNESCO statement the world remains ordered around the logic of race, so this change has clearly only been semantic. This is largely because ethnicity merely became a stand-in for race, so all the hierarchies were retained, just with cultural justifications rather than biological ones. Africans were inferior not because of their genetics but because of their tribal affiliations and backward way of life.

The main problem with this shift in discourse was that in erasing race it becomes almost impossible to talk about racism. Black people remain oppressed because of our race; we just talk about the problem in relation to ethnicity and then wonder why the inequalities persisted. There is a reason that the UN makes no mention of racism in its goals: it simply does not have the language to talk about race. This post-racialism is important to the system update of Western imperialism because it helps to maintain the façade of progressivism that is so important when it comes to justifying the continuing oppression. We tumble into a deluded view of the world where the West cannot possibly be racist, because they abandoned race and are investing trillions of dollars in aid.

It is ironic then that one of the responses to the Holocaust was to reify race and racism, and to engage in older forms of colonial violence. Israel was founded in 1948 after a longer struggle of Zionism that sought to return Jewish people to their biblical homeland. Zionism had some support before the Second World War but it was the Holocaust that spurred action from Western powers, who became certain of the need for a Jewish homeland. The only problem of course was that the land where Israel was created had an established population. With a mindset reminiscent of those who created the settler colonies that cleared the way for the West, German rabbi Isaac Rolf declared before the War that

> In our land there is only room for us. We will say to the Arabs: move, and if they disagree, if they resist by force – we will force them to move, we will hit them on their heads and force them to move.[55]

Before 1948 Palestine was a British-held colonial territory and therefore directly subject to the logic of empire. Zionists did not appeal to the Arabs living there but to the British who ruled the territory. Britain had been on the fence about Zionism but embraced the idea of a Jewish homeland in 1917 when Lord Balfour declared, 'His Majesty's Government view with favour the establishment in Palestine of a national home for the Jewish people, and will use their best endeavours to facilitate the achievement of this object.'[56]

Britain had its own reasons for supporting Zionism. The Balfour Declaration was in part used to legitimize the British invasion of the territory earlier in the year in an effort to further extend the Empire. Coming out for Zionism was not an easy decision and was also predicated on the belief that the global Jewish citizenry were vital to the First World War effort. There was a genuine belief in the British government that if they won over American Jews they in turn would use their influence to get the United States involved in the War. It was also felt that after the Bolshevik Revolution, Russian Jews would move to take Russia, a key ally, out of the War and therefore needed to be appeased. In large part it was the fear of the power of the influence of a global Jewish cabal, a deeply racist trope at the heart of anti-Semitism, that sparked the Balfour Declaration. Activists were well aware of this reality. Edgar Suares, a leader in the important Alexandrian Jewish community, wrote to the Foreign Office in 1916 that 'England could assure to herself the active support of the Jews all over the neutral world if only the Jews knew that British policy accorded with their aspirations in Palestine.'[57] The Zionist campaign depended on anti-Semitic ideas about the power and coordination of Jews worldwide for it to succeed. Theodor Herzl, a central figure in the early Zionist movement who died before the Balfour Declaration, argued that anti-Semitism was the 'chief asset' of the movement.[58]

When the UN recommended the partition to create the Jewish state of Israel in 1947, they did so as an apparently anti-racist act. Supporting the Jewish people who had been racialized and slaughtered as an ethnic/national group in need of a homeland perfectly suited the new post-racial order. But to establish the new nation the West would have to support the kind of racist colonial acts it had supposedly left behind. For a start, the very notion that a state of White settlers could be built with a complete disregard of the native Brown population is the epitome of colonial logic. In order to clear the land of the natives, large-scale violence reminiscent of the previous colonial era was necessary.

At Deir Yassin on 9 April 1948, 250 unarmed people were slaughtered, a number that included 100 women and children, by 120 militiamen from the Zionist paramilitary groups Irgun and Lehi.[59] Menachem Begin, the leader of Irgun, praised his troops, declaring 'as in Deir Yassin, so everywhere . . . Oh Lord, Oh Lord you have chosen us for conflict.'[60] This kind of violence was not uncommon and it was meant to terrorize the Palestinians into fleeing their land. It had the desired effect, with over 700,000 Palestinians becoming refugees by the time Israel was established in 1948. So traumatic was this period in history that Palestinians named it the *Nakba*, which literally translates as 'the catastrophe'.

The violence enacted to clear the ground for the Israeli state is eerily reminiscent of the genocidal frontier campaigns to establish the United States. This was not lost on Israel's greatest ally. With the Jewish state facing threats from Arabs on all sides, in 1967 White House aide John Roche drew the perfect analogy, explaining, 'I confess, I look on the Israelis as Texans', drawing parallels with those who braved the United States' frontiers and tamed the threat from Mexicans.[61] The United States' dogged support for Israel could be in no small part down to recognizing the plight of a fellow settler colony that needed to rally the wagons in order to defend itself from the existential threat of the hordes of natives.

The United States' support for Israel has been questioned on the strategic front. The sheer amount of financial assistance means there is an economic burden, but there are other ways that Israel is detrimental to the interests of the United States. For one, Israel's actions undoubtedly adversely impact on the United States' global image. As a settler colony Israel is one of the few examples left of the unrestrained brutality of the previous colonial era. For all the pretence of ethnicity, Israel is a Jewish state with citizenship based on blood rights.[62] Minorities are brutally oppressed and locked out of full participation in the state: to establish itself, Israel has serially abused the rights of the Palestinians. It continuously flouts both international law and United States' advice by attacking civilians and building illegal settlements on the West Bank. The situation is so dire that comparisons to apartheid South Africa are not only common but appropriate. The United States' embrace of Israel means that it regularly defends abhorrent actions to protect its ally, particularly blocking the international community in the UN from taking any action against what is in many ways a rogue state. Reputational damage is not just about PR but has consequences for the United States. Israel's treatment of the Palestinians has long been a motivating factor for Islamic extremism, and by being an extension of Israel, the United States is a prime target for terrorists.

Israel has a dire relationship not only with Palestinians but also with its neighbouring Arab states, being involved in multiple wars and having annexed territory from Syria, Jordan and Lebanon. Israel's military policy frequently consists of 'unilateral aggressive actions' that destabilize the region and could jeopardize the United States' access to its most valuable commodity, oil.[63] Not to mention Israel is the nuclear power that may be the likeliest nation to unleash Armageddon. Israel's existential crisis is rooted in its precarious position as a settler colony unable to fulfil its genocidal logic. European settlement into the Americas and Australia was secured by the almost complete erasure of the native threat. Israel will never achieve that security surrounded by hostile Arab states, which is why its reaction to threats is so extreme and disproportionate. It is certainly not too difficult to imagine Israel pressing the nuclear button in a pique of settler colonial genocide. Such murderous brutality would fit perfectly into the logic of Western imperialism. It is because of this existential dread that Israel is prone to bite the hand that feeds it, frequently spying on the United States, passing on information and colluding with its benefactor's enemies.[64]

To understand America's steadfast support for Israel we need to put it in the context of the new age of empire. Whilst the West rallied to Zionism after the Second World War, the United States only began the journey towards wholeheartedly embracing Israel in 1956, and this transition was not complete until 1967. It was then that the fledgling nation was seen as an essential strategic interest to block the Soviets from influence in the Middle East.[65] Israel was able to embarrass Egypt's Soviet-backed President Nasser with swift victory in the Six Day War in 1967 and has since served as the battering ram for the United States' soft power in the region.

Oil was the key commodity underpinning the transition into the new age of empire and the United States needed to control the area that produced most of it. Israel is the reminder that, as much as things have changed, they have stayed the same within this iteration of empire. Aid may be the carrot, but the stick can be wielded at any time. By offshoring its violence to Israel, the United States can maintain the pretence of benevolence in world affairs. Islamic extremism is the new bogeyman raised to justify Israel's role in the Middle East. It is the counterweight to Iran and the last bastion preventing an Islamic caliphate being established. Of course this is nonsense: for all its protestations about the clash of civilizations between Christianity and Islam, and moralizing about human rights in the region, the United States' other major partner in the region is Saudi Arabia. That nation *is* an Islamic state that harshly imposes its reading of Sharia law. Israel is useful to the United States because it can trample on the rights of the Brown natives to maintain Western imperialism.

Israel is unique because it allows the old forms of imperial brutality to be continued in plain sight in the new age of empire. Because we have abandoned race, the Jewish state is defended as a mechanism of ethnic self-determination and therefore Israel has the 'right to exist', regardless of the consequences for the region or the Palestinians. In fact, because of the horrors of the Holocaust, to question Israel, Zionism or its steps to defend itself is to run the risk of being labelled anti-Semitic. Under the widely adopted International

Holocaust Remembrance Alliance definition of anti-Semitism it is forbidden to claim that the 'existence of a State of Israel is a racist endeavour'. But what other conclusion could we draw from looking at the historical record? And this has nothing to do with being anti-Semitic: the United States, Australia, Argentina, Brazil and any other settler colony are all 'racist endeavours'. More to the point, we could say the same about the existence of every country in Africa, with their boundaries drawn by colonial administrators; or India and Pakistan after the horrors of Partition. But in the new post-racial order we exempt Israel from proper scrutiny and in doing so legitimize the continuation of Western imperialism, and the key, brutal role that Israel plays.

Western imperialism did not end after the Second World War, it merely evolved. The horrors of the Holocaust did away with the notion of race, which was simply replaced by a version of ethnicity that allowed colonial logic to continue. Israel is a reminder of the brutality of the older order that underpins the new. The UN, IMF and World Bank pose as friends to the underdeveloped world, all whilst creating a framework that continues to allow the West to leach from the Rest. We live in a time defined by the dreams of the Enlightenment, universal values that set in stone the unjust racial order. Aid is offered as the solution to absolve the West of its sins, whilst it actually works to further oppress the underdeveloped world and enrich Western interests. But we are so keen to believe we are making progress that we ignore the uncomfortable truth before us. The starving children beamed in haunting images onto our TV screens are in dire poverty *because* of our excessive wealth. No matter how big your direct debit is to whichever charity tugged your heart strings, it cannot change the fact the reason you can afford to donate is because those children have no food. But we can all comfort ourselves with delusions that we are moving towards a better, more enlightened world.

So complete and perverse is the new age of empire that it has allowed the face of Western domination to become increasingly diverse. In order to maintain the façade it is essential that the only diners at the trough of empire are no longer just White people. There have always been those in the underdeveloped world who colluded with the oppressive system to enrich themselves. One of the more dispiriting features of the new age is that there is a growing class of Black and Brown faces profiting off the logic of racial oppression who are, knowingly or not, being used to market the fairness of the system.

6

The Non-White West

In 2018 US president Donald Trump launched a trade war against China, railing against the 'billions of dollars' lost to the country each year in unbalanced trading on his favourite medium, Twitter. In a particularly alarming social media rant, even for Trump, on 23 August 2019 he declared that

> The vast amounts of money made and stolen by China from the United States, year after year, for decades, will and must STOP. Our great American companies are hereby ordered to immediately start looking for an alternative to China, including bringing your companies HOME and making your products in the USA.

Trying to reassert American economic protectionism is one thing, but believing that he had the power to order private corporations around displayed a spectacular misunderstanding of both global capital and his own role. Trump's concern over China was the substantial trade deficit between the two countries. In 2018 the United States exported $120 billion worth of goods but *imported* over $539 billion worth, making an almost $420 billion loss in terms of trade.[1] To counter this, the substance of Trump's trade war was to increase tariffs on Chinese imports so that companies are disincentivized from doing business in the country. China retaliated, imposing its own tariffs on American imports, with both countries using their actions as leverage for a new trade agreement.

Trump's trade war was sparked by wider fears that globalization is disadvantaging the West, and in particular working-class communities that have seen their jobs disappear overseas. The reason for the trade imbalance is that China is now the workshop of the world, leading the way in manufacturing goods for sale in the West including the United States. Nations across the West have experienced the kind of de-industrialization that has seen factories relocate to the under-developed world and large swathes of people lose their jobs. Trump was elected in large part because he won in the American 'rust belt', the Midwestern states whose populations lost out when manufac-turing moved overseas. The trade war was a key part of his 'Make America Great Again' appeal, taking on foreign nations who are attacking United States power, and reasserting economic nationalism. In this version of the new world order the real victims of the new age are the White formerly working class, left behind by a global system that now privileges foreign nations.

It is undeniable that the post-war settlement has led to some inter-esting, and likely unintended, consequences in the operation of Western imperialism. Manufacturing was previously the domain of the West. Producing the goods to sell into newly found markets around the world was one of the main goals of empire. India's textile industry was purposely destroyed so that Britain could lead the way in manu-facturing. This situation has now been completely reversed. Along with China, India is one of the fastest growing economies and there is a real sense that centres of power are shifting to the underdeveloped world. China is now seen as the main threat to the West and there are projections that it will eventually become the largest economy in the world. It has positive trade deficits with every major nation and trillions of dollars in foreign exchange reserves.[2] The new economic and political order created after the Second World War has paved the way for the rise of China and other underdeveloped nations. But if we imagine that the development of non-Western, non-White countries proves that the racial logic of empire has changed in any substantive way we are sorely mistaken. China's rise is instructive, considering its predicted global dominance has been due to the logic of Western imperialism, not in spite of it.

After the declaration of the People's Republic of China in 1949, the nation was a key part of the Communist challenge to the capitalist status quo. China's support was central to the defeat of United States forces in Korea and Vietnam, and China also backed several Afri-can liberation struggles that threatened Western dominance on that continent.[3] But the China that has emerged today is not the revolutionary Communist state that sought to reshape the economic order. In truth, it is quite the opposite. To achieve its current status China had to realize that the 'Western order is hard to overturn and easy to join'.[4]

China's economic rise only began after the death of Mao Zedong in 1976 and the subsequent repudiation of his policies. At that point China was an extremely poor country which had undergone one of the worst famines in human history a decade earlier. From 1978 the nation embraced capitalism, undergoing a series of market reforms, welcoming foreign direct investment and making exports the basis of its economy.[5] This meant opening up China to the rest of the world and fully engaging with global finance, and it was an extremely successful approach: the nation pulled 600 million of its citizens out of extreme poverty between 1978 and 2010. China's success could be mistaken as evidence that the new economic system is not inherently racist, if an underdeveloped country can make such strides. But, as always, we should not get ahead of ourselves.

China's emergence has been due to the very reason that Trump started his trade war: its domination of global manufacturing. 'Made in China' has become so commonplace it is almost a surprise when an item is produced elsewhere. But this occurred because the cost of labour in China is so low relative to the West. It is the same problem I discussed in relation to India's economic miracle. While there is lots of wealth in China, and many newly minted billionaires, there is also an abundance of poverty. China may have the second largest economy in the world, but the important measure is GDP per capita: the amount of wealth produced per person. By this measure China is 65th, demonstrating that many people are not feeling the benefits of the growing economy. China is extremely unequal and government statistics class anyone earning $295 a month as middle-income, despite the complaints from those living on that amount that they cannot make ends meet.[6] Because China's position depends on being the world's primary exporter, mass poverty is necessary in order to sustain its economic growth. Just like India, if the standard of living rises so too do the wages and manufacturing costs. Soon enough China would find itself in the same position as the West, offshoring its factory labour to a poorer country. What Trump has seriously misunderstood in his trade war is that even if increased costs through tariffs on Chinese goods incentivized manufacturers to move, they would simply relocate to a different Black or Brown country with inhumanly low labour costs. There is only one source in the West that can compete with the wages in the underdeveloped world and that is prison labour, which no doubt explains why Trump is a supporter of increased privatization of the sector.

In order to establish itself China has relied on hundreds of millions of its own citizens living in conditions and taking wages that would be unacceptable in the West. It's one of the key principles of Western imperialism: Black and Brown life is worth less and it is therefore legitimate to exploit it. But it is not only in exploiting its own citizens that China has embraced the logic of empire. White supremacy is based on a hierarchy from White down to Black, with anti-Blackness a specific feature of the system. In order to establish a secure footing, or to move up the ladder of supremacy, there is a long history of other racialized groups using Black populations as a stepping stone. China is no different, as an examination of the nation's increasing role in Africa demonstrates.

THE CHINESE SCRAMBLE FOR AFRICA

China's links to Africa go back centuries, at least as far as the Han dynasty in 202 BC. (The idea that Europe initiated global trade and connectedness is one of the many fictions of Whitewashed intellectual history.) The Communist People's Republic of China had strong ties to Africa and the liberation movements to end colonialism. In the global fight against capital, Mao was keen to support the armed struggle in places like Mozambique and Angola. China was a key player in the 1955 Afro-Asian Bandung Conference, which sought to create a united non-aligned front to combat the global power of both the West and the Soviet bloc. China's credentials in Africa were well forged and included building a railway line connecting Zambia to Tanzania in the early 1970s. In return for its support, African nations backed UN recognition of revolutionary China and supported the nation's rise to prominence on the world stage.[7]

China was influential in the Black radical imagination and was seen by many 'as the land where true freedom might be had'.[8] The Black Panther Party initially started fundraising by selling copies of Mao's 'Little Red Book' to college students,[9] and co-founder Huey P. Newton invoked Mao in his book *Revolutionary Suicide* when he argued that their revolutionary commitment was the Panthers' 'great leap forward'.[10] Numerous Panthers visited China, including Elaine Brown who would become the party's chairperson. Given China's progressive history with Africa and Black politics, its increasing influence on the African continent has been welcomed by many. Indeed, China plays off its historical relationship, painting itself as an underdeveloped country aiming for a mutually beneficial relationship with a friend in need.

Although China's links to Africa are not new, its economic role in the continent has drastically changed since the start of the new millennium. From 2000 to 2012 trade between China and Africa grew twenty-fold to $200 billion.[11] Between 2001 and 2010 China's Export–Import Bank provided $67.2 billion in loans to so-called sub-Saharan African countries, $12.5 billion more than the World Bank.[12] The West is wary of China's rapid expansion in Africa due to the increased competition for resources in the region and also because Chinese money provides an alternative to the conditional loans enforcing the dreaded Washington consensus.[13] China does not attach structural adjustment strings to its loans, preferring to stay out of matters of state and stick to finance. Chinese aid has empowered African countries to say no to the devilish pacts with the IMF and the World Bank.

While the West has looted resources and meddled in political and economic systems, China has been busy building the roads, dams, buildings and railways that Africa so sorely needs. Not only that, but China has also invested in the manufacturing sector, to the tune of over $3 billion by the end of 2012.[14] With its history of comradeship, its massive investment, and the fact it represents an alternative to the hated IMF and World Bank, it is easy to see why there is some optimism and a view that 'the Chinese are our friends' among many on the continent.[15] But we must remember that the China that holds the revolutionary link to Africa is an historical artefact. Since China's economic reforms, the country has embraced the same political and economic order that oppresses Africa, and in many ways has legit-imized neo-colonialism by posing as a friend.[16]

To understand China's neo-colonial role in Africa we need look no further than the reason for its increased involvement in the first place. After China embraced the capitalist global order, and its econ-omy grew on the basis of production, it needed to find fresh sources of raw materials. You cannot make the goods for the world without their ingredients. China's entry into Africa has been driven by the need to acquire resources such as oil and minerals to secure its place in the global economy. China's expansion in Africa also occurred mostly after it joined the World Trade Organization in 2001 and it therefore operates firmly within the global economic consensus that is a major part of the continued underdevelopment of Africa. While Chinese money may not come with the requirement for structural adjustment, it is a lie to say there are no strings attached. For China finance is tied to natural resource extraction rather than political control. China's interest rates are typically higher than those from Western financial institutions and it generally takes payment in the form of mining rights rather than cash. Therefore the vast majority of Chinese assis-tance goes to mineral-rich African countries.

In places like Congo, Angola and Zambia, China is providing money to build infrastructure while stripping the natural resources of the countries. A classic example of this arrangement, in what was dubbed the 'deal of the century' when it was signed between China and the Democratic Republic of Congo (DRC) in 2007, is a $9 billion loan that meant China would commit to building roads, hospitals and other vital infrastructure projects in return for almost monopolistic control over the mining of cobalt and copper.[17] It may sound like a good deal for Congo, but consider that the minerals in question are worth an estimated $87 billion and it is quickly apparent that China is extracting the materials from Congo for a fraction of what they are worth.[18] The IMF were against the loan because they wanted to offer their own finance package with the usual conditions. But by avoiding the Western institutions the DRC has jumped out of the frying pan and into the fire.

Across the African continent, countries are making the same deals with China, selling off their most valuable resources on the cheap to get at least some infrastructure built. It is not hard to see why, when Africa is in dire need of such spending, with estimates that it requires well over $22 billion spent annually to address its infrastructure problems.[19] But these resources are precious to the future of Africa, which by rights should be the richest place on earth thanks to its abundance of natural wealth. By cashing in, the continent is destroying its future. Natural resources are finite and for Africa to prosper it should be maximizing the wealth produced from them to truly transform the continent. Green technology will become the next boom industry and Africa holds a bounty of the minerals necessary for the shift to sustainable energy. China, on the other hand, has only accelerated the exploitation of Africa's resources.

Worse still, the model used to build this infrastructure is of more benefit to China than Africa. When signing agreements such as the 'deal of the century' China insists that it provides the majority of the equipment and labour (usually 70 per cent).[20] In effect the vast majority of the 'aid' that is given to a country is spent buying goods from China and paying Chinese companies and workers to rebuild Africa. China is basically providing a stimulus to its own economy, dressed up as foreign aid. Not only does the recipient country have to pay this loan back with interest but China also reaps massive profits from its preferential access to precious mineral resources. This model has all of the *'Alice in Wonderland* craziness' about it that Kwame Nkrumah described in Western neo-colonialism.[21] Even China's support for infrastructure spending is not as benevolent as it can appear.

European colonizers spent massive sums on roads, railways and the like because they were necessary to extract the wealth out of the continent. When the Chinese offer to build roads that connect an untapped mine to the sea, they are not doing so out of their wish to better the economic circumstances of Africa. China has also built forty-four sports stadiums in Africa, raising serious questions about the nature and utility of its infrastructure spending.[22] These projects routinely end up as white elephants, something the rulers can use to show off but which have no long-term beneficial impact on the economy.

It is abundantly clear that China's involvement in infrastructure is not a break with the logic of Western empire. It may be a different model, but it is one that supports the principles and functioning of the current system. After all, the Chinese are extracting these resources to make products to be sold, in large part, to the West. China's presence in Africa is also not always at odds with Western interests. There are a number of direct collaborations between Chinese and Western companies in Africa, who are after all in the region for the same reasons. The French company Total partnered with a Chinese oil company to extract oil from the Nigerian seabed,[23] and Chinese companies also enrich themselves by bidding for contracts funded by Western agencies like the World Bank. Bamako International Airport in Mali underwent a $181 million upgrade between 2007 and 2012 funded by the Millennium Challenge Corporation, a US aid agency. Regardless of the fact that China and the United States may be in a struggle for global dominance, this United States government contract was carried out by Chinese workers.[24]

Migrant workers being imported into Africa to rebuild the continent has created a specific form of tension. It is estimated that there are now over 1 million Chinese people living in Africa, attracted to the continent by the opportunities there. It should be no surprise that the natives of the poorest continent in the world are wary. Chinese migrant workers enjoy better pay and working conditions. This marks a reversal of Chinese people being used as a cheap and discriminated-against labour force to build the original version of Western empire. China is now providing the frontier folk, seeking new opportunities. It is also not difficult to find attitudes reminiscent of the old European colonizers who went to Africa to make their fortunes. In journalist Howard French's book *China's Second Continent* he explains how commonplace colonial-era racism was with the Chinese migrants he spoke to across Africa. His discussion with Hao, a migrant to Mozambique, stands out. Hao had migrated with little, had not learned a local language, and yet managed to acquire 5,000 acres of land, much to the displeasure of the locals, and planned to grow cash crops to sell to Western countries. He explained his decision to try his luck in Mozambique as follows:

> Can you imagine if I had gone to America or to Germany first? The people in those fucking places are too smart. I wouldn't have gotten

anywhere. I don't think I could have beaten them. So we had to find backward countries, poor countries that we can lead.[25]

Colonial-era attitudes could also be found among those delivering aid projects. Li Jinjun, head of the Central Agricultural Research Institute in Liberia, explained that the Chinese would only run the project for a limited time in order that the locals 'learn to support themselves'. In classic civilizing mission language, the Institute was proud that 'little by little . . . can change them in this way.'[26] Of course, we cannot generalize these attitudes to the whole of the Chinese migrant population in Africa but we also should not be surprised if they are prevalent. They are only important insofar as they speak to the wider power dynamics of the Chinese neo-colonial relationship with Africa.

Objections to Chinese migration are not solely down to their colonial attitudes or denying locals the opportunity to work on infrastructure projects, but tie into the other major area where China has continued the work of Western imperialism on the continent. As heralded as the increased trade between China and Africa has been, it represents the classic relationship between colonizer and colony. China's imports from Africa are comprised of well over 90 per cent oil and other natural resources. At the same time, Africa's imports from China are 90 per cent finished manufactured products. Africa exports its resources well below the value that they are worth to China, which manufactures goods and sells them back into Africa, collecting all the profit. As a result China is able to produce cheap goods and flood African markets at prices that local producers have no way of competing with. The result has been a de-industrialization of Africa as local manufacturers are forced out of business.

In 2008 manufacturing made up 12.8 per cent of GDP in Africa, and just eight years later that figure had fallen to 10.5 per cent. Between 1980 and 2008 Africa's share of global manufacturing was down from 1.2 per cent to 0.9 per cent.[27] In Nigeria the impact of Chinese textile imports has been devastating to local manufacturing. In the 1980s there were 175 textile factories in the country, but within twenty-five years that number had declined to only twenty-five. Even though imported textiles are illegal they account for over

85 per cent of the market and are valued at $2.2 billion annually, versus only $40 million for locally produced products.[28] The impact on jobs has been catastrophic, with the number of those working in Nigeria's textile industry in 2015 declining to 20,000 from 600,000 in the 1990s.[29] The result has been tension and even strikes in Senegal over the presence of the Chinese in local markets: they have become a feature as imports have flooded in. There is no doubt that the Chinese who are trading into Africa are profiting from the underdeveloped state of Africa and taking advantage of the situation created by Western imperialism. This kind of opportunism from those whose skin is not White is also nothing new for Africa. Lebanese traders were dominant as middlemen between the French and their African colonies and there was a similar relationship between South Asian communities in East Africa and the British.

The only real difference with the Chinese is that they are not playing the role of middlemen to European colonizers; instead they represent one of the strongest emerging neo-colonial forces. China is certainly not a colonial power in the same way as Britain, France or any of the other European nations were. There is no invasion, violence and domination of political affairs. But, as we already know, that is not how the new age of empire works. Although the former colonial masters may have links and historical advantages in particular countries (particularly in relation to language), underdeveloped economies are open to exploitation from any nation or corporation that has the capital. There is no metropolis, no mother country, just a racialized political and economic system that allows for such exploitation.

BUILDING BRICS OF EMPIRE

China is not alone in following Western colonial logic to build its wealth. The new scramble for Africa features a whole host of underdeveloped countries vying to make the most of the devastating position that the continent has been placed in. As underdeveloped nations begin to acquire more wealth there is celebration of the progress being made. None more so than in recent years with the rise of the so-called 'BRICS': Brazil, Russia, India, China and South

Africa, whose rapid levels of growth have marked them out as new economic forces in a supposed reshaping of the global order. In reality, talk of BRICS is disingenuous because South Africa is in a very, very different situation to the rest of the perceived bloc. If we remove South Africa, then the BRIC countries increased their foreign direct investment from less than $10 billion in the 1990s to $147 billion by 2008.[30] Much of this 'investment' went to Africa in the same exploitative relationship as China's investments.

For all the Cold War tension between the capitalists and the Soviets, the USSR no longer exists and Russia has returned firmly to its historical place as part of the Western bloc. Putin's Russia may seem like a menace, but remember there has always been discord between the various Western powers. On the fundamental issue of the economic world order Russia is firmly in step with the West. We should not be shocked to find the logic of empire alive and well in Mother Russia. But Brazil and India have taken the same approach as China to fuel their economic growth, using Africa as a stepping stone.

Along with China, India was one of the main players in the Bandung Conference in 1955, which pledged allegiance to Afro-Asian solidarity. India also has a common experience of colonialism with Africa, having been part of the same British Empire that large chunks of the continent were occupied by. This shared history means that India has a presence in Africa, with around a tenth of the Indian diaspora living there, and it has tried to build on these links to make partnerships. Like China, India needs resources, and trade with Africa almost trebled between 2007 and 2013.[31] India has also been involved in infrastructure projects, and exports finished products to Africa, but its economy is based more on services than Chinese-style manufacturing.

A good example of how India offers aid to Africa is the telemedicine project that was piloted in Ethiopia and then rolled out in fifty-three countries. India provided finance for Africans to be able to access Indian doctors through video conferencing software to combat the shortage of doctors on the continent. Considering that Ethiopia has 0.1 doctors per 1,000 people compared to India's 0.9 and Britain's 2.8, the shortage of doctors is a serious problem.[32] Providing access to Indian healthcare on a short-term basis may be essential, but it does not solve the problem long term. Africa needs more doctors, and exporting medical care to places like India only makes the shortage more acute. In typical colonial fashion there is a built-in dependency, where Africans come to rely on the care provided over the internet instead of building up their own resources. In Britain we raise hell when our calls to the bank are diverted to India, and I can only imagine the outrage if our GP appointments were diverted to a teleconference with a doctor in Mumbai. But this is seen as acceptable for Africa because Africans are less valued. Teleconferencing projects are also seen as aid, and India is following the example of the West by spending development money on projects that benefit itself.

Indian doctors and technicians are paid out of development funding, in the same way that a significant proportion of the aid from China is spent on Chinese labour. In many ways these projects are tools to provide employment opportunities for the two largest workforces in the world. It is also necessary to build the infrastructure to support teleconferencing, which is an area that Indian businesses excel in. Across Africa Indian companies are building (and owning) the telecommunications that are so vital to the twenty-first century. On the plus side this has meant that Africa is connected to the globe, with over 80 per cent of people in 'Africa proper' owning a mobile phone (most likely imported cheaply from China).[33] But the necessary infrastructure and access are foreign-owned, making Africa not only dependent on outside interests but also locked out of the wealth created by these industries.

Brazil has a complicated relationship with Africa. At least 38 per cent of the enslaved people stolen from Africa were taken to Brazil and the nation has the largest population of African descent of any country other than Nigeria. Under the more progressive presidency of Luiz Inácio Lula da Silva (Lula) between 2003 and 2010, Brazil rhetorically embraced its African roots and made overtures to the continent, increasing trade with Africa from $4 billion in 2002 to $27 billion in 2012.[34] But Brazil is also the perfect case study in how wrong-headed our understanding of the racial nature of global capital is. In reality, there is no reason whatsoever to assume that Brazil would have any affinity with Africa, other than the colonial logic that built the country. Brazil is more like the United States than it is any African country. It was a European settler colony where the indigenous people were all but wiped out and enslaved African labour was used to build the economy. There may be a very large population of those of African descent but Brazil is one of the most racially unequal countries in the world, in which its Black population is subject to intense discrimination. In a country where half the population is Black, President Lula's appointment of four cabinet members of African descent was seen as a watershed moment, but this only happened in 2009. Lula's government was the exception, not the rule, and the current fascist president, Jair Bolsonaro, is far more representative of the racial politics of the nation.

After independence in 1825 Brazil was happy to continue enslaving Africans legally until 1888, over fifty years after Britain implemented its so-called abolition, and more than twenty years later than the United States outlawed the inhumanity. Brazil was also the only underdeveloped nation that voted against UN resolutions condemning Portugal's barbaric colonial regimes in Africa, and for good measure continued to trade with apartheid South Africa during the embargo.[35] Brazil is representative of Latin America, which is a collection of European settler colony ethno-states where White supremacy exists in its most virulent form. It is only due to the poverty of Western political philosophy that we imagine Latin America as a bastion of 'people of colour' who can challenge the Western order.

Make no mistake: there are millions of Black and Brown colonial subjects in the region, but they are victims of their various states rather than being represented by them. Latin America features poverty and conditions that we would not accept in the West, and Western financial institutions, particularly the IMF, devastated their emerging economies through structural adjustment. The colonial dependency relationship we have discussed in relation to Africa also applies to much of Latin America. So the region is definitely not (yet) *in* the West, but it is *of* it and far up the ladder of global White supremacy in general, which is why a nation like Brazil has the finances to be investing in Africa. But just as many people *in* the West are not *of* it, the same applies in Latin America and its millions of neo-colonial subjects. This is not really much different than during slavery, when Brazil's population included millions of enslaved

Africans, overseen by a European settler elite. Brazil was technically a colony, so not *in* the West, whilst the Portuguese settlers were *of* the West and the enslaved and indigenous were the system's victims. That same relationship continues in the stark inequalities that exist today.

Brazil may have some of the poorest people in the entire world, but tens of thousands of Portuguese migrated to Brazil following the global financial crisis to take advantage of its growing economy.[36] As demonstrated by the hordes of almost exclusively White crowds at the 2014 football World Cup hosted in Brazil, the descendants of White settlers inhabit a different nation to those at the bottom of the racial hierarchy. It makes perfect sense that Brazil's relationship to Africa follows the same exploitative logic of Western imperialism.

Brazilian corporation Companhia Vale do Rio Doce (Vale) is one of the largest mining companies in the world and has a presence in Guinea, Zambia, Congo, Angola, Gabon and South Africa. Extracting a range of resources, it is also involved in the classic colonial relationship of funding infrastructure projects. To put the size of the company in perspective, its $34 billion revenue would make it the fifteenth biggest economy in Africa, with a larger GDP than almost all the countries it extracts resources from. Brazilian companies have also entered into partnerships similar to those of China across Africa, and have a tendency to use migrant labour. An area where Brazil is a world leader is in the production of biofuels and it has seen the potential for Africa to be a source for the necessary crops. Alongside mineral wealth Africa holds 60 per cent of the uncultivated arable farmland on the planet.[37] In the new scramble for Africa this abundance of fertile farmland is one of the key commodities.

The race for farmland is not only taking place in Africa. By 2020 it is estimated that investors had spent more than 'one hundred billion dollars for over 40 million hectares . . . from Ethiopia to Indonesia' in order to acquire land.[38] As the Brazil example demonstrates, this is driven by the rising demand for food for an increasing population, and also for other commodities like biofuels. Oil palm is a key crop, used in a range of products from soap to plastics. It has become so popular that by 2040 an additional area the size of Germany may be necessary to cultivate enough of it to meet the demand.[39] The fires spread in the Amazon rainforest in 2019 are an example of the lengths that people will go to create additional farmland. With its vast acres of uncultivated land, Africa is a centre of global land acquisition.

Alongside the West, Saudi Arabia, South Korea, Qatar and China have all been key players in the land grab in Africa. It is estimated that between 2004 and 2009 2.5 million hectares of choice land had been allocated to foreign entities in Ethiopia, Ghana, Madagascar, Mali and Sudan.[40] In 2007, China acquired rights to 2.7 million hectares in the Democratic Republic of Congo alone.[41] As with all the other examples, we could welcome the investment that comes with foreign capital, but it is surely obvious how damaging it is to sell off every commodity that the continent has to foreign interests for far less than it is worth. The insanity of the land grab is demonstrated in the reality that the nations suffering the most from hunger are also those selling off their farmland.[42] Burundi, Chad, Ethiopia and Congo are some of the countries where this contradiction is the sharpest. Africa is once again being carved up by foreign actors to feed the updated version of Western imperialism. The only difference now is that many of the nations leading the way are not led by White people. But throughout the book I have highlighted non-White collusion in building Western imperialism.

Without the Arab slave trade, which lasted far longer than the Atlantic system, it is not clear that the enslavement of Africans would have occurred. It was Muslim scholars who first codified anti-Black racism, something later picked up by Europeans, and created the slave-trading networks that Europe tapped into. To gain access to the riches of the East, the West used the wealth gained from enslaving Africans. When the Portuguese and Spanish began mining precious metals in the so-called New World the wealth generated dispersed across Europe, with countries like France, Britain and Holland using the commodities to enrich themselves. At this point the West was not particularly advanced, but access to gold and silver in the Americas allowed the 'relatively backward' European merchants to tap into Asian markets and eventually monopolize them, creating conditions under which the West would come to rule.[43] It was demand from China for silver that made the early slave plantations in the Americas profitable. The Taj Mahal was built with gold mined from slave labour, since empires in the East were more than happy to accept the wealth produced by racism. In the new age of empire it is this same relationship that survives today, with the economies of Asia and Latin America being boosted by the looting of Africa. There is nothing truly new in this system, just updated manifestations of the old order.

As an indicator of how embedded India, China and Brazil are in the new global order, in addition to Africa's resources, farmland and markets, they are also keen to gain the continent's influence in the United Nations. China achieved its UN recognition largely through African votes. Brazil and India are both seeking permanent seats on the Security Council, and the continent with the most countries is not a bad place to garner influence.

If the idea that the emergence of the BRIC countries represents systemic change is an illusion, then the idea that Africa, led by South Africa, is achieving some kind of renaissance is a mirage. Whilst there certainly have been some improvements in terms of health, literacy, poverty and economic growth rates, Africa remains firmly at the bottom of the global racial hierarchy.

The illusion of the African renaissance is based on its levels of GDP growth, which from 2000 until 2015 ranged between 3 and 6 per cent annually, although they have tapered off since.[44] South Africa was seen as the leader of the continent in growth and economic development, hence its inclusion in the BRICS. South Africa's economic boom in the 2000s was also accompanied by a steady fall in its unemployment rate. After rising to 33 per cent by 2000 the percentage of those out of work fell to 22 per cent by 2008. In a reminder of how connected African economies are to the West, the financial crisis caused by sub-prime lending in Europe and the United States had a devastating effect on the continent. Since 2008, the joblessness rate has been increasing and in 2019 stood at 28.5 per cent.[45] After the end of apartheid there was optimism about the future of the nation but South Africa remains one of the most unequal societies in the world, and while the economy has grown in the last twenty years, so has the poverty rate.[46] This same pattern is replicated across the continent. In Nigeria between 2005 and 2011 the economy grew by 5 per cent a year but unemployment rose from 15 to 20 per cent, with 60 per cent of young people out of work.[47] None of these figures should be a shock given everything that we have learnt so far about African so-called development.

Economic growth is entirely the wrong focus if we want to understand progress. African GDP figures are inflated by the increase in foreign investment and trade with the formerly underdeveloped world that has accelerated the stripping of the continent's resources. All those cut-price sales of minerals boost GDP but harm progress in Africa. Billions of dollars in loans from the Chinese to pay Chinese companies and workers to build infrastructure may inflate the economic balance sheet but offer little work and few skills for African people. A large part of the supposed growth in Africa is really just an indication of increased wealth extraction.

The other fallacy of growth is that it is inevitable that African economies will grow because the population is rising rapidly. In the next thirty years it is estimated that the majority of the world's population growth will occur in Africa, with the number of people living on the continent doubling by 2050.[48] By 2100 it is possible that the population will have trebled to 3.5 billion and there will be more people in Africa than in India and China combined.[49] As the population grows, so too does the economy, but since 2015 GDP growth has been smaller than it should be, given the rise in population.[50] In other words, economies that are already struggling to provide for the people they have are falling further behind their rising populations. To put the growth figures in context, California has a larger GDP than the *whole* of Africa, and yet somehow we are supposed to be celebrating the rise of the continent.

It is truly terrifying to imagine Africa with treble its current population, given the track of underdevelopment it remains firmly planted on. By 2100 the majority of its natural resources will have been depleted by foreign interests and its farmland either overused or in the hands of offshore investors. On its current trajectory it is impossible to imagine a future that does not involve the same kind of colonial dependency that has been the hallmark of Africa's relationship to Western empire. The fact that some countries which are not predominantly White will have firmly joined that system makes no difference.

A CORRUPT SYSTEM

Up to this point I have painted a very bleak picture of life in Africa, but we should avoid falling into the trap of seeing the continent through the eyes of Live Aid. Many people have been able to find success, build businesses and prosper. It is not uncommon to hear about those living in the West migrating back to Africa to invest in and pursue opportunities that are a distant dream to Black people living in their former mother countries. There are also many affluent Africans who travel frequently, settle and are educated in the West, who have the kind of wealth that is mythical to the majority of White people in the world. But just as we should not let the images from charity appeals distort our understanding of life in Africa, we should not allow the people who have acquired wealth make us fall for the lie that progress is being achieved.

The proportion of those in the middle class in Africa has actually declined since 1980 to only 13.4 per cent.[51] The reality is that the majority of Africans are not pot-bellied and covered in flies, but nor do they have the money to send their children to British private schools. There is a huge scale of inequality, and unfortunately most people in Africa are towards the wrong end of it. As with all features of the new order, there is nothing new about a scale of Black inequality. There have always been those who have been somewhat better off in the system.

Studying the plight of Africa, it is clear that not all of its problems are to be located in the foreign interests which have ravaged the continent. Nothing that we have discussed to this point would be possible without systemic collaboration in Western imperialism by those who are empowered to run the continent. In Western development parlance, one of the main problems in Africa is the lack of 'good governance', which is a more polite way of saying that the disease of corruption is killing the continent. Many of the conditions tied to Western development aid are related to building greater transparency in political affairs, with the hope that by shedding the light of democracy through Africa this will end corrupt practices and allow the continent to succeed. We can again see the influence of Enlightenment ideals – that if only the savage parts of the world would embrace Western values they could be lifted out of their barbarism. Furthermore, billions of dollars have been spent on so-called good governance initiatives and there is even a 'corruption perception index', which ranks countries.[52] Needless to say, African countries fare poorly, as does most of the underdeveloped world.

On the Transparency International website, the German-based company that runs the index represents corruption on a world map with countries allocated a colour based on where they rank. The deeper the red, the more corrupt, the lighter the yellow, the less. It may as well be a map of the West versus the Rest, as the only areas in yellow are Western Europe, North America, Australia and Japan. The top two most corrupt countries by this measure are Somalia (in at number one) followed by South Sudan. The message is abundantly clear that the problem of corruption is something the West has dealt with and that it is holding the rest of the world back.

There is clearly a problem with corruption across the underdeveloped world and certainly in Africa. Between 1970 and 2015, thirty African countries lost $1.8 trillion to capital flight – i.e., the money left those economies – a figure dwarfing the $497 billion these nations owed in foreign debt, and representing 65 per cent of their collective GDP in 2015.[53] Over $148 billion in capital flight occurs on the continent every year, with at least 60 per cent of this down to 'mispricing of resources', or in other words, fraud.[54] There is no term to describe what many of the elites are doing in Africa other than looting.

Consider the case of Angola, where between 2007 and 2010 $32 billion disappeared from the country's account, which was at the time a figure larger than the GDP of forty-three African countries.[55] Isabel dos Santos is celebrated as Africa's richest woman, with a net worth of over $2 billion, but given that she is the daughter of Angola's former president José Eduardo dos Santos we should not be impressed by this wealth. Dos Santos ran the country for thirty-eight years, during which time he took a personal stake in the nation's resources and presided over the looting of billions of dollars. After 700,000 documents were leaked about how Isabel built her business empire she now finds herself subject to criminal investigation in Angola. The documents were damning, showing how numerous Western interests had enabled her to embezzle a fortune from her ownership stake in

the state-run oil company Sonangol.[56] Angola is the perfect model for
how corruption functions in Africa. As well as personally enriching
themselves, dictators like dos Santos use money from foreign investors to prop up their regimes. One of the poorest countries in the
world, Angola 'spent 1.4 times as much on defence as it did on health
and schools combined' in 2013.[57] Having access to vast amounts of
money also helps to win elections when they are called.

Angola is hardly alone. There is undoubtedly a political elite who
are participating in Africa's continued underdevelopment so that
they can plunder its resources to fund their own personal wealth. In
return they open up their countries to be exploited by foreign interests with extraordinarily favourable terms and tax requirements.
The result is stark: for instance, the public purses of Zambia and
Congo received only 2.4 and 2.5 per cent of revenues from their raw
materials exported during the commodity price boom in the early
2000s.[58] So it may seem relatively simple: African corruption is the
problem that needs to be solved. But there is nothing African about
this corruption.

Even the slightest glance at this situation demonstrates that it is
a problem created from the outside. Of cross-border corruption,
between '1995 and 2014, virtually all (99.5 per cent) involved non-
African firms' and all of this money, which is being used to buy off
African leaders, is flowing in from foreign interests.[59] In a frankly
astounding corruption case in the Italian courts, oil companies Shell
and Eni stand accused of a $1.1 billion bribe for President Goodluck
Jonathan of Nigeria and other government officials in return for access
to oil-drilling rights.[60] Worse still, this money was not a gift from the
companies but came out of Nigeria's share of the future oil take. When
this $1.1 billion was taken offshore the leaders were stealing money
directly from the nation. Western companies like Shell have had to
admit, or been found guilty of, a range of bribery schemes, with some
being so ridiculous they would be funny if not for the consequences.
An instalment of a $5 million kickback in Nigeria from Kellogg,
Brown and Root (KBR) took up so much space when converted into
Nigerian nairas that it had to be delivered in trucks.[61] African leaders
are being corrupted by foreign investment and showered with money
so that the global system can continue to bleed the continent.

Colonialism was a form of corruption, and what we are seeing today is just an updated version. When the European powers departed they left behind a local elite who took the place of colonial administrators but whose power remained limited.[62] As long as the remaining elite followed the rules laid down by the departing powers they could survive, otherwise they would be deposed.

When leaders like Patrice Lumumba emerged in Congo, pledging to overturn Western domination of Africa's resources, they were dealt with. As already mentioned, Lumumba, the first elected prime minster after independence, was assassinated in 1961 with the help of the Belgians and the CIA in order to make way for a more pliable regime.[63] The West were happy to support the brutal military dictatorship of Mobutu Sese Seko from 1965 until 1997. During his reign Mobutu amassed a personal fortune of over $5 billion which he used, in part, to build a $400 million palace where he hosted such luminaries as the Pope, the King of Belgium and the director of the CIA.[64] Like other African kleptocrats he spent lavishly in European department stores and had a penchant for flying Concorde. After Mobutu was chased out of office he was replaced by the equally Western-compliant Laurent Kabila, whose son, Joseph, inherited the presidency when Kabila senior was assassinated. In case you thought the Kabilas might have turned away from the colonial methods of running the country, it is estimated that Kabila Jr was taking $4 million a week from mining companies during his presidency. He also brutally put down a rebellion in Kilwa, killing over 100 peaceful protestors in 2004.[65] But he received full support from the West until he threatened to ignore his nation's time limits on the presidency and illegally stand for re-election after his term expired in 2016.

The framework established by the new age of empire is clear. Leaders who comply with the prevailing order are supported and lavished with money to keep them in power and build staggering personal wealth. If you are still questioning the complicity of the West in this system then just examine where all this wealth that is fleeing from Africa goes. It is offshored into the same banks used by hedge-fund managers and corporations who are seeking to avoid paying taxes at home. It is lavished in Western department stores and invested in property in places like London. None of this so-called African corruption would be possible were it not facilitated by Western interests. As former leader of opposition party UNITA in Angola, Isaías Samakuva, explained of corrupt African rulers, 'the only explanation we can find is that they have the blessing of the international community'.[66]

Underdeveloped countries jumping on the foreign direct investment bandwagon have, if anything, made the problem more acute. While, largely through pressure from media and activism, Western governments and agencies have become more wary of supporting abusive regimes, China has avoided moral judgements. During the crisis in Darfur the UN Secretary General warned of the risks of genocide and the West wanted to isolate the regime, but China increased its investment, reaching $5.6 billion in 2006.[67] The West deserted Guinean military dictator Captain Moussa Dadis Camara after his troops slaughtered 156 protestors and gang-raped dozens of women in public in 2009. China, however, continued with a $7 billion investment package and Dadis used part of the money to buy arms to solidify his power. It was only his betrayal by his right-hand man, who shot him in the head, that ended Dadis's reign of terror.[68]

Empowering elites in the former colonies is also a continuation of older colonial logic. To control Africa, Europeans ruled through a system of tribal chiefs. Where none existed, Europeans created them to rule the people.[69] Each chief had only one superior and that was the European advising him.[70] The chiefs collected taxes and enforced labour, doing the bidding of their colonial masters. The uncomfortable truth is that Europeans simply could not have run their colonies without the use of indigenous collaborators. Across their various empires Europeans established systems of indirect rule to administer colonialism. For example, by 1893 out of the 4,849 officials running India only 898 were British, and in 1885 the 78,000 British troops in the colony were outnumbered more than two to one by 154,000 Indians.[71] Those leaders today who are selling out Africa to the interests of global capital are simply picking up the baton from their predecessors.

Consider Omar Bongo Ondimba, who ruled Gabon from 1967 until 2009 (his son took over after him and is currently carrying on the family dynasty). Bongo served in the French army during colonialism and the French engineered his rise in Gabon following independence.

He admired de Gaulle so much that he wept during the former French president's funeral and is on record for declaring 'his gratitude to the French for their assistance in the development of his country'.[72] Despite being oil and mineral rich there is widespread poverty in the nation. Gabon actually has one of the highest GDPs per capita in Africa but a third of the population live below the poverty line and 20 per cent of people are unemployed, including 35 per cent of young people.[73] Bongo's administration facilitated foreign control of Gabon's economy and resources in exactly the same way you would expect a native chief doing the bidding of a European colonial agent. It is the system that is corrupt in Africa. The only difference now is that there are more Black people getting incredibly wealthy from the exploitation.

Nowhere is this more apparent than in the economic darling of the continent, South Africa. The end of apartheid was meant to herald the birth of a non-racial democracy that could provide justice and equality for all of the nation's citizens. Free and fair elections have been held since 1994, with South Africa not being beset by the kind of blatant abuses of power at the ballot box that we have seen in other nations. In terms of transparency, South African democracy was meant to lead the way for the future of the continent. But for all the promise of the fledgling state, since the advent of so-called democracy a Black elite has been created but a number of corruption scandals have shaken people's faith in the new politicians. So rampant has the corruption been that even the former president Jacob Zuma is set to stand trial for taking bribes related to an arms sale whilst in office, and no one believes this to be his only offence.

Given how deeply rooted corruption has become in South Africa, it is now common to talk about the 'state capture' by corrupt forces. There is even an official Judicial Commission of Inquiry into Allegations of State Capture that started holding public hearings in August 2018. Much of this corruption is linked to the noble desire to boost so-called Black economic empowerment by ensuring that Black South Africans get access to lucrative contracts. The system has been open to abuse and has blurred the lines between politics, business and corruption. The case of the Watson brothers, two White anti-apartheid heroes, demonstrates that it is not just Black Africans who have managed to cheat the system. Bosasa, the company they ran, was supposedly a Black majority-owned company that received government contracts to run a range of privatized state operations, including prison catering and IT, worth up to $140 million between 2000 and 2016.[74] The Black ownership was a front for the Watson brothers to make money, allegedly using their contacts in the government, civil service and even the courts to bribe their way into a fortune.

A Black front for White corruption is the perfect metaphor for the state capture of South Africa. As the Bosasa case demonstrates, Black economic empowerment is based on imposing neoliberalism on the post-apartheid economy. If it is not making money from government contracts it is making it in deals with multinationals involved in the same colonial relationship as on the rest of the continent. South Africa's elite is not a sign of progress, especially when over half of all Black South Africans live below a poverty line that we could never imagine in the West.[75]

South Africa was once a beacon of radical politics on the continent, with the anti-apartheid struggle committed to land reform that would have put the wealth of the country into the hands of the people. But like most of Africa, in order to end apartheid South Africa's leaders compromised, accepting the basic political and economic framework that was already in place. The threat of violence was one of the key drivers of this, with the apartheid state being one of the most visceral reminders of the brutality of the West. But the West's claws were so deep into the country that even if a revolutionary struggle had succeeded, it would have been difficult to survive without outside support. The biggest limitation of the revolutionary movements in Africa was that they each settled on a national struggle, winning control of the existing levers of power. But this was doomed to failure because the real power in the system is in the West, with the controls in Africa mostly being for show. Apartheid was *a* problem in South Africa but it was not *the* problem. Merely changing the colour of some of those at the wheel of the ship, or sitting on the top decks, was never going to be enough to change course, because it is a vessel that works by remote control.

*

The logic of empire has always depended on a Black and Brown elite to administer Western domination across the globe. So we should not be surprised about a growing class filling their bellies from the misery of the poor in the underdeveloped world. The rise of China and other nations, somewhat higher up on the ladder of White supremacy, is only causing a stir because of how badly understood the racial dynamics of the system are. Anti-Black racism was a lynchpin in the establishment of Western global dominance, using the profits from the Atlantic system to finance the exploitation of the East. By using Africa as a stepping stone, countries like China are employing the codes of colonial logic embedded in the operating system. The wealth of these emerging economies is also based on the brutal exploitation of their own poor, whose bodies are sacrificed on the altar of progress. The West continues to enrich itself by leaching off the Black and Brown, but can now hide behind the rulers of its former colonies.

The emergence of a non-White elite in the underdeveloped world collaborating with Western imperialism could be seen as an incentive to embrace a global politics of class solidarity. The elite can be viewed as the problem regardless of their colour and there is certainly no shortage of scholars and activists (mostly in the West) yearning for a politics that unites the global proletariat against the bourgeois ruling classes. Unfortunately, the left has always been incapable of coming to terms with both the centrality of racism to their position in the West and the extent to which the logic of Western imperialism radiates through their own politics.

7

Imperial Democracy

Sitting on a plane on the way to São Paolo is not the most guilt-free way to watch a lecture about the dangers of climate change. But the poor movie selection had led me to the documentary section where I stumbled across *The Third Industrial Revolution*, a filmed lecture and Q&A delivered by the economist Jeremy Rifkin. Apocalyptic images of flooding and extreme weather events jarred me enough to keep me awake and feeling bad about my carbon footprint, if not guilty enough to rethink my next trip. Rifkin's message was clear: the world is on the brink of annihilation, the sixth extinction-level event, due to our pollution of the atmosphere, and a radical new alternative is essential in order to save it. Thankfully for us all, he had come to deliver the plan to rescue humanity, embodied in what he called the third industrial revolution.

According to the lecture, existence has been brought to the brink because of the previous two industrial revolutions. First, British ingenuity in the eighteenth century created the technology that became the engine behind rapid industrial progress, urbanization and factory labour. In the early twentieth century it was the United States' turn to be the fulcrum behind progress with a second industrial revolution based on the exploitation of electricity, oil and the motor engine. While these revolutions both brought unprecedented development, they also created the climate crisis by polluting the air. But, fear not, we are at the cusp of a third industrial revolution that not only promises to bring even greater bounties than the first two but to do so in a completely carbon-neutral fashion that will pull humankind from the edge of the abyss.

The third industrial revolution is based on the digital transformation to the 'internet of things', which opens up possibilities that can transform the world. For Rifkin, the key is the 'zero marginal cost' of producing innovations that the new interconnected world creates. He argues that in the future we will be able to sustain our energy needs for relatively little. The example that makes the most sense is electricity from solar power. The cost of producing solar power has been rapidly declining over the years and will shortly be cheaper than fossil fuel energy. If houses and other buildings were fitted with solar panels they could produce their own energy and, once connected to a grid, could feed back surpluses into the system. By connecting across a digital network that would manage the flow of electricity we could create a free source of power for everyone. Imagine the grid powering the train system or driverless electric car apps and you are beginning to imagine the dream that is the third industrial revolution. A networked, digital, green economy providing untold efficiency and therefore wealth for all. Given the setting of the plane I wondered if I had drifted off to sleep, but no, Rifkin had given the technological version of Martin Luther King's 'I have a dream' speech. It was full of all the same hope and promise but also contained the basic limitations present any time someone is picturing a fantasy, if not an outright delusion. Rifkin is not the only one to offer such a revolutionary mirage. A cottage industry has developed around imagining salvation in the form of Western technological development, and Rifkin's lecture contained all the key ingredients.

ENLIGHTENMENT 2.0

Barely distinguishable from Rifkin's ideas is the notion that we are currently embarking on a fourth industrial revolution, which will transform both the political sphere and the very fabric of the economy.[1] In this narrative Britain and the steam engine are still at the foundation of industry but the second revolution is thought to have taken place between 1867 and 1914, with greater scientific advancements and progress in manufacturing. Computing is said to mark the third major shift, after the Second World War. Klaus Schwab, founder of the

World Economic Forum, is a key proponent, arguing that this fourth industrial revolution will bring 'profound and systemic change' in global power relations.[2] Zero marginal costs mean that in theory everyone with an internet connection can plug in and benefit from the new economy. Rifkin actually argues that the underdeveloped world is at an advantage because of its lack of infrastructural development. Whereas the West is designed for an earlier system of production and needs to be retrofitted, the lack of infrastructure in developing countries will make it cheaper to just equip the nations with the hardware needed to exploit the next industrial revolution. I am sure those living in grinding poverty feel reassured.

Both the third and fourth industrial revolutions are ideas generated from relatively mainstream political centres. Rifkin cites his experience of working with governments including Germany and China, and companies like the energy giant EDF and Daimler; and the fourth industrial revolution has been picked up by policy makers around the world and the United Nations.[3] These are the classic Enlightenment progress narratives: more science, reason and technology will lead to a fairer, more just world.

But we can also see very similar ideas about saving the world coming from newer, left-wing voices. Saving the planet from the impending climate catastrophe has rightly become a central issue in progressive politics. If drastic action is not taken shortly to reduce emissions there may well be little of the world left to save. Climate change is also decimating countries in the underdeveloped world, with extreme weather events set to create millions of climate refugees whose homelands will be uninhabitable.[4] It seems even the climate has embraced the logic of White supremacy, punishing those in the Rest for the excesses of the West.

Activists around the globe are protesting, with one of the most notable mobilizations being the climate strike movement led by children and young people. The third strike in 2019 spanned 150 countries, with over 4 million people estimated to have taken part. As valuable as this grassroots activism is, it remains strictly within the framework of empire. The strike was timed to coincide with the UN Climate Summit, and as powerful as figures like climate protestor Greta Thunberg are, they spend their time appealing to the heads of nation states. Once we locate the system as the problem then it should be clear that no matter how many Extinction Rebellion protestors stage nude protests in the British parliament, they will not dismantle the colonial logic of the world order. The concern for the under-developed world fits firmly within the framework of so-called universal rights, as developed in the Enlightenment. Sure, they have a right not to be flooded, burnt or starved out of their homes, but that remains the limit of their humanity.

In fairness, there are attempts to formulate the climate debate in terms of the need for a transformative political agenda. Naomi Klein has been dubbed the 'intellectual godmother' of the push for a Green New Deal, an ambitious policy agenda for reducing carbon emis-sions to zero and reforming capitalism.[5] Klein makes it abundantly clear that reducing emissions is not enough, and connects the climate struggle to her earlier work exposing conditions in sweatshops in the underdeveloped world. Climate goals can only be reached by ending an economy that seeks constant growth and luxuries, the pursuit of which exploits workers in the poorest parts of the world.[6] The Sunrise Movement, who have been campaigning for the realization of the Green New Deal, sum up its vision as being 'to stop climate change, achieve environmental sustainability, create millions of good jobs, and realize economic prosperity for all'.[7]

So successful have the campaigns been that the Green New Deal forced its way into the political debate. Bernie Sanders put the pro-posals at the centre of his presidential campaigns and rising star of the Democratic Party Alexandria Ocasio-Cortez helped introduce a resolution in Congress to support this policy agenda. Ocasio-Cortez represents a younger, more diverse and more progressive slate of pol-iticians in the United States, who are determined to change the policy agenda. As part of the campaign for the Green New Deal she voiced a video with *The Intercept* and Naomi Klein called 'A Message from the Future' that imagines herself looking back at the world created after achieving the Green New Deal. It is a beautifully realized utopia where the green economy has created jobs, shifted the debate on uni-versal healthcare and inspired more women and minorities into office. Unfortunately, it contains much of the short-sightedness we should by now be used to.

The Green New Deal takes its name from Franklin D. Roosevelt's package to counteract the Great Depression of the 1930s. As important as these reforms were, providing housing, jobs and welfare for millions of Americans, they did not tackle the problems of racism in the United States. In fact, the New Deal was racially unjust in its application, particularly in the extremely segregated housing boom it induced.[8] Klein admits that the Green New Deal metaphor is somewhat limited by its predecessor and that delivering on climate justice is 'not a magic cure for racism or misogyny or homophobia or transphobia'.[9] The problem is that nowhere in the agenda is there any real attempt to address these issues. They remain on the margins in the classic mode of believing that the economy is somehow separate from issues of identity. Much of Sanders' platform sounds like a direct appeal to the White working classes languishing in the rust belt of the Midwest, the alleged real victims of globalization, with promises of American jobs 'with strong benefits, a living wage, training . . . and protecting the right of all workers to form a union'.[10] These are all noble pursuits but they would not deal with racism in the United States and, crucially for understanding the implications of the new age of empire, they depend on the exploitation of the underdeveloped world.

Proposals to tax the rich sound progressive, but the rich make their money from a system that brutally exploits Black and Brown bodies. Using that wealth to retrofit the West and provide high-quality jobs and healthcare depends on the very same colonial logic. The left in Britain is no different: Jeremy Corbyn's Labour Party represented the resurgence of the left and embraced the politics of the Green New Deal. Underlying the promise of these new endeavours is a promise of equality for all; the liberation of society by technology. But it is telling that on neither side of the Atlantic is there any real effort to address the problems of global inequality. In keeping with colonial logic, 'equality for all' really means improving the lives of those in the West, which remain the central concern in the latest version of Western empire. The uncomfortable reality is that the new intellectual left is lining up to retrofit the Enlightenment for the present day.

Dutch historian Rutger Bregman went viral when he attacked billionaires for not paying tax at the World Economic Forum in Davos in January 2019. He diagnosed the problem of inequality as being about 'taxes, taxes, taxes. All the rest is bullshit in my opinion' – much to the disappointment of the assembled tax dodgers. But in his book *Utopia for Realists* Bregman outlines a vision so deeply steeped in Enlightenment thinking that he argues that all we need to do is to 'reclaim the language of progress' in order to 'rehoist the sails!' to a brighter future. The idea of picking up a fallen mantle is only possible because he somehow believes that 'historically, politics was the preserve of the left'.[11] As we have seen throughout this book, the truth is the complete opposite, at least with regard to the West. If we conceive of the left as broadly about redistributive politics and fighting for the rights of workers, then the only real period that was the preserve of the left was the social democratic era after the Second World War. But that settlement has already melted away in Britain and the United States, and is fraying even in the more progressive parts of Europe. Even during the heady days of the welfare state, the period was still characterized by White supremacy. Racism, sexism and labour exploitation have, in reality, been the preserve of Western politics.

Bregman's argument manages to get even more absurd when he names the historical figures we should look to for inspiration. He lavishes praise on the sixteenth-century Spanish priest Bartolomé de las Casas for advocating equality between the colonial masters and the indigenous people of the Americas and for attempting to found a colony where everyone received a comfortable living. Las Casas might ring a bell: in Chapter 2 I discussed how his ruling on the natives having souls also provided the justification for the enslavement of Africans, who were deemed incapable of salvation. John Stuart Mill also gets a shout-out for his belief in the equality of women. That would be the same Mill we encountered earlier who justified 'despotism' in attempting to improve the 'barbarians' in the colonies. For Bregman, without these 'wide-eyed dreamers we would all still be poor, hungry, afraid, stupid and ugly'.[12] This is just a more palatable version of lionizing Hitler for building motorways. Bregman was invited to the World Economic Forum in the first place, so perhaps it is unfair to put too much faith in his progressive credentials, but we see this same kind of thinking across the political spectrum.

Novara Media has become an important source for alternative news for the left in Britain, with a major online presence. Co-founder Aaron Bastani has become a key figure on the left but he offers the same basic blueprint for technological progress freeing humanity. Rather than seeing three or four industrial revolutions, he acknowledges only two previous so-called 'disruptions'. First, the emergence of *Homo sapiens*, who started agricultural development, and second, the sacred British-led Industrial Revolution of the eighteenth century. We are supposedly in the midst of a third disruption that promises all the bounties that we have already spoken of. If anything, Bastani is even more optimistic, imagining that under 'fully luxury automated communism . . . we will see more of the world than ever before, eat varieties of food we have never heard of, and lead lives equivalent – if we so wish – to those of today's billionaires'. As if sensing the scepticism of the reader, he declares that 'our ambitions must be Promethean because our technology is already making us gods – so we might as well get it.'[13] Such hubris is not just reminiscent of Enlightenment thinking but lies at the very heart of the Eurocentric intellectual project.

The greatest lie underpinning the Enlightenment is embedded in its name. Knowledge did not spread out of Europe to bring light to the uncivilized parts of the world. In fact, it was the very opposite: Europe took knowledge produced around the globe and Whitewashed it, pretending it was theirs. Science has certainly contributed much to the world but to pretend it is the possession of the West is only possible due to the conceits of Whiteness. A parallel in all the various progress narratives is that they imagine the modern world only begins with the Industrial Revolution in Britain in the eighteenth century. I suppose we should give some credit to Bastani for locating his first disruption outside the West with the emergence of *Homo sapiens* in Africa. But development is then apparently frozen in time until James Watt came onto the scene with his steam engine. To discount the thousands of years of history and development around the globe that laid the foundation for the Western Industrial Revolution is not just short-sighted but deeply offensive. Worse still is the complete lack of any acknowledgement of the dark side of the emergence of Western industry.

The whole purpose of this book is to counter the dominant mythology around the progressive West. By now I hope you are convinced that genocide, slavery and colonialism were just as important, if not more so, as the emergence of science and industry to everything that we have today. You simply do not have the technological advances without the violence that underpinned them. Reading the new so-called radicals is just a reminder that the mythology of progressivism is endemic today even in the circles of the left. In none of the above accounts of history are any of the atrocities of the West even mentioned, let alone given their rightful strategic place. If Europeans colonizing almost the entire globe to exploit labour and resources does not meet the threshold for a disruption then we are in dire need of a new measuring stick.

It is by no means a surprising development that the supposed new radicals are replicating the intellectual exclusions of the Enlightenment; it is just how they were raised. There is a reason that in 2015 students in Britain launched the #WhyIsMyCurriculumWhite campaign. Western thought is still dominated by the notion that knowledge springs forth from the foundation laid by the supposed founding fathers we are told to revere. It may be jarring for me to read a whole body of work written in the twenty-first century that almost exclusively cites White men, but that is just the currency for those producing ideas today.

We have come to expect too much from the left because we have neglected to understand that its intellectual heritage is just as rooted in the progress narratives as neoliberalism's. Marx remains at the core of radical Western thought, but he was just as much a product of the Enlightenment as Kant. Marx saw capitalism as an evil that needed to be overturned, but a necessary one to bring about communism (even its luxury automated form). Just as we are seeing with the arguments today, Marx thought that the technological progress brought about by capitalism was essential to providing the abundance necessary for human liberation. Ideas of White supremacy and scientific progress led by the West are absolutely integral to Marxism and remain its greatest limitation. Marx's inability to understand that the underdeveloped world was inhabited by fully human people capable of struggle led him to completely misidentify the revolutionary class. He could see no further than the Western industrial worker created by the contradictions of capital and labour, and theorized that it was from here that the proletariat would arise to overthrow the unjust system. But history has shown that those who have embraced Marxism and committed successfully to revolution have resided almost exclusively in the underdeveloped world. In Cuba, China, North Korea, Guinea, Grenada, Mozambique, Angola, North Vietnam, and even in beloved Mother Russia the revolution was largely led by the peasantry rather than the workers.[14]

Marx's principal failing was that he 'imagined that the industrial proletariat was the hero of capitalism and had invented a history whose narrative justified this'.[15] It was his roots in the Enlightenment that led him to this conclusion. If knowledge and progress spread out from Europe then so must the revolution. Rather than representing a break from intellectual White supremacy, Marxism is just the flipside of the coin of its logic. It is a paradox of Marxism that the Western industrial worker never managed to produce a communist revolution whilst across the underdeveloped world Marx inspired the overthrow of the state from Cuba to China, via Guinea-Bissau and many stops in between.[16] Marx was so blinded by White supremacy that he was (and far too many of his disciples remain) unable to understand that the most oppressed, the true revolutionary class has always resided outside the West because of the racist nature of capitalism. The new so-called radicals today are no different, presenting alternative visions of the future clouded by Whiteness.

WHOSE ECONOMY IS IT ANYWAY?

Faith in technological progress stands out from the various alternative conceptions of the world because of how the left has typically been resistant to mechanization due to its impact on the workforce. Since the beginning of automation, workers have had an inherent fear of being replaced by machines. The word Luddite, used for someone sceptical of technology, comes from the followers of Ned Ludd who would break factory machinery in early nineteenth-century England. One of the strongest narratives shaping current social policy is the idea that (White) workers in the West are being left behind because of the disappearance of manufacturing jobs either overseas or because of the sinister sounding 'rise of the robots'. There is no doubt that the economy is changing. Globally, factories employed 163 million people in 2003, but that number is likely to dwindle to 'a few million' in the near future.[17]

In the West the decimation of the manufacturing base played no small part in the election of Donald Trump, although it was on the outsourcing of so-called 'American' jobs to foreigners that he laid the blame. Robotics and artificial intelligence are replacing human labour at an alarming rate. But this circle can be squared by the promise of abundance that comes with the third/fourth industrial revolution, which is supposed to be more efficient, and therefore could provide greater levels of wealth to be distributed in the economy. Manufacturing output actually increased by 60 per cent between 1997 and 2005 even though 4 million jobs vanished from the sector.[18] It is the promise of abundance that holds the progress narrative together.

The massive infrastructure development needed to complete the technological revolution when society commits to it will depend on millions of workers being trained, and paid to lead the charge into the new age. Robots are not equipped to install solar panels, cables and all the hardware necessary to network the internet of things together. This promise of employment is one of the key appeals of the Green New Deal, which will engage workers in the raft of new industries necessary to decarbonize the world. It is not that work will disappear, just that it will change. In the progressive utopia, due to the amount of wealth and efficiency, labour itself will become obsolete as the robots do all the dirty work, leaving us humans free to embrace our leisure time. Bregman has a whole section on the pursuit of leisure, quoting Marx's desire to be free to 'hunt in the morning, fish in the afternoon, rear cattle in the evening, criticize after dinner'.[19] Central to the new left in Britain, underpinning Corbynism's political programme, is this desire for leisure time, expressed in the demand to shorten the working week.

Such faith in technological development to provide is a key feature of the progress narrative: science will create abundance that frees us all. There are a myriad of problems with the idea of creating an automated society where we are freed from the mundane. For one, the dystopia of the *Terminator* series of movies hangs over this whole concept, where the artificial intelligent network created to improve the world decides to eliminate the human race once it is switched on. Creating a world run by intelligent machines may actually be the ultimate version of building our own gravediggers. There's an ancient South African legend about the evil Za-hu-Rrellel who created creatures out of the earth, and who did everything for the people, including transfer the food into their stomachs. The population got so used to everything being done for them that they got fat and forgot how to walk or speak, allowing Za-hu-Rrellel to take over the land.[20] Despite the nightmarish quality of these visions of the future they both offer warnings. *Terminator* is about the unintended consequences of trying to master technology. The cautionary tale of Za-hu-Rrellel is about how technology can be used for nefarious purposes by the powerful. This is one of the principal limitations of the idea of utopia through technology.

While pioneers like Rifkin are keen to point out the free products of the internet of things, like Wikipedia or open-source software, they are working with governments and corporations. Hardware for the networks that are building the future cannot be built for free, or by plucky start-ups. Governments and corporations are leading the charge and China is one of the principal forces in developing the third/fourth industrial revolution. China's 'belt and road' initiative aims to bring the old trade routes into the new age by building digital hardware and capacity across much of Asia, Africa and Europe.[21] While the nation may clothe itself in the red of Communism and fond memories of Chairman Mao, it is now a firmly capitalist country. The only aspect of old-style Communism left is a very large and authoritarian state. One of the key mechanisms to maintain the power of the Chinese state is the very same internet of things that Rifkin is so proud of. For instance, China's Muslim minorities are under constant surveillance and attack. Since 2017, more than 1 million have been placed in detention centres because they have been deemed 'unsafe'. By monitoring smartphone use the authorities have built algorithms to detect 'un-Chinese' behaviours and flag Muslims, using their Integrated Joint Operations Platform. China has created a 'web of surveillance' with facial recognition cameras and mobile phone tracking that records the movement of its ethnic Muslim populations.[22] The internet of things has created a virtual prison for Muslims in China.

Technology in the West has always been used to suppress the population as much as to free it. The FBI's counter-intelligence programme (COINTELPRO) of surveillance, wire-tapping and more mundane activities such as using spies undid groups like the Black Panthers in the sixties and seventies. It is terrifying to imagine what the modern-day version of that programme looks like, with the sheer access to our lives that technology allows the powerful. Your phone, computer, digital speaker, smart car, television, the internet, the cameras everywhere, can all be turned against you to curtail your freedom. The mechanisms of our supposed freedom very easily become the tools of oppression. Less violent but equally sinister accusations are already made against the uses of this technology, from algorithms personally tailored to get you to buy goods you do not need, to the targeting of fake news to convince you to support a political party that means you harm.

In terms of employment, the outlook is potentially just as bleak. For all the talk of changing the nature of work, the reality is that there is a steep class divide in who has benefited from automation. Those in middle-class professions, which are less easy to mechanize, have prospered, whilst unemployment has befallen millions of those with low or no skills who could previously have worked in manufacturing. Digitization has also led to worsening conditions for low-wage workers, who are subject to monitoring and targets.

On a different plane journey (carbon footprint alert!) I was watching a Vice documentary, *The Future of Work*, that had a whole segment on the role of automation in warehouses (please let's refrain from calling them 'fulfilment centres'). The company was proud of their efforts to synchronize the work of humans and machines. But the workers were less enthusiastic because of the demands involved in keeping pace with the automated schedule. Rather than liberating the workers, the results of automation have largely been to cut the workforce along with their wages and working conditions, while increasing surveillance and allowing an ever-shrinking minority to amass untold wealth.[23] Amazon represents the embodiment of all those forces, with its warehouse workers surveilled every moment to the point they are afraid to take bathroom breaks whilst doing back-breaking work to keep up with the targets mandated by an algorithm.[24] Meanwhile founder Jeff Bezos is on the way to becoming the world's first trillionaire, making roughly $2,489 every second, more than double the average US worker's earnings in a week.[25] Bezos and his ilk are the emperors in the new age of imperialism and the corporations are their fiefdoms. For those hoping for the liberating impact of technology, be warned: it is these corporations that are laying the foundation for the third/fourth industrial revolution. There is no reason to believe that the new system will differ from the old, in fact we should expect more of the same.

Due to the liberation of capital from nation-state control, national governments find it almost impossible to regulate global corporations, for the obvious reason that they simply do not have the jurisdiction. More could certainly be done, but corporations pour their wealth into politicians precisely so they can influence inaction. Look at the difficulty in getting Facebook to stop sharing fake news stories. In 2019 Microsoft beat Apple to a $10 billion contract to host the cloud services for the US Department of Defense. Good luck regulating a company that stores your nation's classified documents.

The biggest flaw in the argument that abundance will save us is that we already live in the land of plenty. Just sixty-two people hold the wealth of an entire third of the world. There is more than enough food to feed everyone, yet millions die every year while tons of food rot in the West. Scarcity is not the problem, inequality is, and if the new system is built by the same people who profit from the old then it is lunacy to expect better technology to liberate the poor. It is particularly delusional to think that global inequality, or White supremacy in the flesh, could possibly be remedied by a reboot of Enlightenment narratives of progress.

Greater than all other influences over your life chances is where you reside. Living in one of the top 10 per cent wealthiest areas of Britain could put ten more years on your life than if you are trapped in one of the most deprived.[26] Meanwhile, a child born in Somalia today has a one in five chance of dying before their fifth birthday, more than the chances of a soldier being killed in the US Civil War, the Second World War, Vietnam or any other major conflict of the last two centuries.[27] While we complain about our dodgy wi-fi connections most people in the world do not have an inside toilet. There is literally no parallel between our lives in the West and those of most around the globe. On average the poverty line is seventeen times higher in the West than the underdeveloped world. This is the greatest conceit of the supposedly radical new thinkers. By ignoring the dark side of history that created the modern world they have also neglected any serious analysis of how to repair the damage that has been done. Science and technology can never be the solution to the problem of racism.

Absent from any of the analyses of the social order in the alternatives presented is any question about just where the West gets the money and resources needed to develop the next industrial revolution. Slavery and colonialism produced the first two/three revolutions. There is now a new scramble for Africa's resources, which are being plundered for the green revolution. Africa is the most mineral-rich continent, home to the raw materials necessary for the solar panels and efficient batteries that are set to power the globe. As we have seen, the West has the wealth to steal these resources and develop them because of the racial global imbalances in power. If it is highly unlikely that the poor in the West will benefit from technological innovation it is unimaginable that the underdeveloped world, and in particular Africa, will. Bastani fantasizes about being able to mine asteroids for the bounties we will need to retrofit the globe. In the meantime Africa is being stripped of its wealth, and if it ever becomes possible to feast from the stars it remains to be seen how the continent will benefit.

So that everyone can gain from the land of plenty, Bregman proposes tearing down the iron gates that are national borders and allowing those in the underdeveloped world to freely travel into the Garden of Eden that is the West. Apparently global freedom of movement would grow the world economy by between 67 and 147 per cent, bringing huge benefits to the underdeveloped world. He argues that 'if all the developed countries would let in just 3 per cent more immigrants the world's poor would have $305 billion more to spend.'[28] At least Bregman recognizes that most of the world is locked out from the fruits of Western progress and proposes a mechanism for sharing the dividends. It is just a shame that he presents such a short-sighted solution.

Global freedom of movement would certainly lead to more money in the underdeveloped world. Jamaica is the perfect example of the power of migration, with the nation kept afloat by the reality that there are more Jamaicans in the diaspora than on the island. A reduced population means there are fewer mouths to feed, but the main benefit is the money made by those in the diaspora in places like Britain, the United States and Canada. Remittances, money sent back to Jamaica or claimed in foreign pensions, represent 15 per cent of the overall GDP of the nation, a number that somehow manages to mask Jamaica's dependence on foreign payments.[29] When accounting for the amount of money that actually remains in the country (more than 60 per cent of tourism dollars immediately disappear to the foreign entities that own the resorts), remittances are the largest source of foreign income in the country.[30] Outward migration has therefore massively boosted Jamaica's economy. But after all these years of remittances Jamaica still remains extremely poor, unable to overcome its colonial legacy. Whilst the closing-off of migration routes to Britain and the United States makes the future look even bleaker, if they reopened the plight of the average Jamaican would not greatly improve.

For a start, although freedom of movement sounds liberating in principle, only those who can afford to travel, and their families, receive any benefit. The poorest will stay exactly where they are and, worse still, migration encourages the so-called 'brain drain', where those with skills leave an underdeveloped nation to take advantage of opportunities in the West.[31] The impact on an economy is obvious, particularly on those that already lack infrastructure and services. Migration as the solution also suggests that the onus should be on the poor to migrate to countries in the West in order to live a better life. No one should *want* to come to Britain with its miserable weather, dodgy infrastructure and brutal inequalities. We should be trying to make the places people migrate from secure and wealthy enough so that there is no desperation to flee in the first place. But the bigger problem with the idea of open borders as a solution is the intellectual arrogance of the progress narrative.

Only by pretending that the abundance in the West is produced by legitimate means can anyone suggest inviting those in the former colonies to feast. The fruits we are inviting them in to dine on are derived from the exploitation of their home countries. To take back any of that wealth the system of racism that exploits them *has* to stay intact. That is why Jamaica stayed poor even after it had sent half its population out to raise its fortunes. Jamaicans are in effect cannibalizing their own wealth when they cash a remittance cheque. It is no different for any of the many other countries dependent on remittances for their survival. 'No borders' would just keep the underdeveloped locked in dependency on the forces of neo-colonialism.

Using GDP as a measure of progress is nonsensical in any case. GDP measures only certain contributions to the economy, missing out things like domestic labour whilst highlighting aspects like debt.[32] I covered this mirage in the discussion of the illusion of Africa rising through loans from foreign sources. More money certainly does not mean more equality: it is often the opposite. For example, since Thatcherism in the eighties Britain has got a whole lot richer, but the gap between rich and poor has turned into a chasm. Growing global GDP is meaningless if we do not account for where the wealth ends up. Given both the history and present of how the abundance in the West is produced it should now be glaringly obvious that the spoils can never be equitably shared with the underdeveloped world.

Troublesome as the idea of no borders as the solution is, it at least makes an attempt to include those in the underdeveloped world. This is rarely the case when imagining the new utopias. In response to the crisis of work and rise of the robots, one of the most fashionable ideas is that of a universal basic income (UBI). Rather than implementing welfare states based on various entitlements, the idea here is for the state to provide every citizen with a set level of guaranteed income. There are various proposals of how much this should be, but for the idea to work it would need to be a significant amount, set to cover subsistence.[33] Providing enough to survive deals with the decline of available work and also the increased leisure time that we are all pursuing. But the point is not for the income to replace work, just to eradicate poverty by making sure everyone can survive.

The aversion of policy makers to UBI is the narrative that it will make people lazy and workshy. When trialled the result has usually been that people spend the money wisely and work harder, and it vastly improves their lives and economies. Many of the pilots have taken place as development projects and there are suggestions that directly giving people aid would be better than dispensing it through Western agencies. But it is in the underdeveloped world that we can see the severe limitations of the entire project.

The West is bloated with enough wealth to fund a generous basic income. One of the bastions of progressive left democracy, Finland, launched a two-year UBI experiment in 2017, making unconditional payments of around $590 a month to 2,000 randomly selected unemployed individuals in order to research the impact on outcomes and their participation in the workforce. Contrast this to a similar experiment in Kenya, where the US charity GiveDirectly selected 44 villages to make unconditional payments of $23 a month per adult for twelve years in order to study the effects. The yawning chasm between the amounts tells us the scale of racial global inequality and how UBI does absolutely nothing to solve it.[34] Providing enough money to allow people to survive in Kenya is useful but it is never going to be able to overturn the steep global inequalities that the nation is subject to.

Eradicating absolute poverty may be a good thing, but UBI would actually lock in the logic of empire. Remember, the West only has such a disproportionate amount of wealth *because* of poverty in places like Kenya. A world in which a basic income is universal and paid for by no borders, where the Black and Brown poor can make money by doing low-paid migrant work in the West, is the definition of a dystopia. Everyone may be able to eat but the political and economic system would be frozen in the image of White supremacy, with the underdeveloped world unable to ever catch up. The problem for places like Kenya is a global economic system that exploits them, draining out their resources so that the standard of living is so low that a Western charity can afford to pay subsistence to 4,966 villagers for twelve years. Whilst it may make those in the West feel better, the fact that charities have the resources to do UBI experiments on the best way to spend their benevolence *is the problem*.

UBI is not a new or radical idea: one of its proponents is the arch-neoliberal economist Milton Friedman. There is a world in which UBI is 'Thatcherism on steroids', where the welfare state is replaced by payments to the individuals who constitute the myth that is society.[35] Given how unequal Western societies are, welfare spending is a major part of all Western budgets. In addition to further costs caused by poverty in areas such as criminal justice and the health service, UBI may actually present as a far more cost-efficient way of delivering a welfare state.

Accounting for police, courts and prison, criminal justice alone costs an estimated $182 billion a year in the United States.[36] This does not include the impacts of crime on the economy, just the price of dealing with the problem. This figure pales in comparison to estimates of how much poverty overall costs the US economy. Child poverty alone is estimated to cost $1.03 trillion a year.[37] Overall poverty could cost the economy $4 trillion, which is more than the $3.8 trillion a UBI of $1,000 a month would entail.[38] It should not be unimaginable that the right wing may seize on the opportunity to end welfare by bringing in an individualized system of payments, especially because it has already happened.

In 1968 Richard Nixon almost enacted unconditional payments to poor families, which would have been the equivalent of $10,000 to a family of four in today's money. Millions of dollars were spent on experiments involving thousands of families, with the results showing benefits and no huge decline in working hours. Nixon's plan was eventually derailed by the ideological zeal of neo-conservatives who worshipped at the altar of Ayn Rand and the free market, consigning the dream of UBI to the dustbin of history.[39] But the fact that Nixon was in favour should give us a big reason to think twice about the idea. UBI is basically a conversation about how to share out the spoils of empire and to mitigate the extreme inequality that capitalism creates.

IMPERIAL DEMOCRACY

What ultimately undermines the Enlightenment is the claim to the universal when its theories are based on the particular. Whiteness is at the heart of Enlightenment thinking and this is no different in the supposedly radical new approaches. All are fundamentally incapable of even naming the racism that is the basis of the global political and economic system, let alone able to offer any actual solutions. We can see this in the distorted Enlightenment progress narratives that underpin the new utopias, but also in the genesis and creation myths of the social movements that have informed the theory.

The sparks that lit many of the new social movements were the financial crisis in 2008, the election of Trump and the vote for Brexit, which created, in Bregman's words, 'more and more people hungry for a real radical antidote to both xenophobia and inequality . . . for a new source of hope'.[40] Ground zero in this narrative is the birth of neoliberalism, ushered in by Thatcherism and Reaganomics in the eighties. Dismantling the social democratic settlement unleashed the forces of capital and sowed the seeds for the economic crash in 2008. The unemployment, insecurity and austerity that followed led to the inevitable rise of the new right as people looked for causes of their poverty. It also exposed the inherent contradictions of capital and stoked the embers of protest by revealing their oppression to the oppressed. One of the first and most high-profile responses to this crisis was the Occupy movement, which swept the globe.

On 17 September 2011, protestors occupied Zuccotti Park in downtown Manhattan near the financial district in order to protest at the cause of the financial crisis. The movement grew rapidly, spreading to a thousand cities and racking up 6,500 arrests within its first six months.[41] The occupation was prompted by the Canadian anti-capitalist magazine *Adbusters* which 'issued a call to action for a "revolution," a "people's revolt in the West"' in response to the crisis of capitalism.[42] Occupy took inspiration from previous movements like the Indignados in Spain, who had occupied public space in response to rising unemployment, austerity and other structural adjustments enforced by external financial institutions.[43] The Arab Spring, highlighted by the occupation of Tahrir Square in Egypt in 2011, had a large influence on Occupy as the images of mass occupation of a public space took hold in the imagination. Thousands occupied Zuccotti Park for almost two months, until police raided and shut down the protest on 15 November.

Occupy's reach was such that President Obama gave the movement his approval in his 2012 re-election campaign. By focusing on the economic crisis Occupy changed the political language and 'income inequality' became the 'crisis du jour', something that all the 2016 presidential candidates at least had to address.[44] The power of the economic message was its simplicity. The Occupiers declared that they were the 99 per cent standing up to the evil 1 per cent who hoarded the wealth. The only problem is that this idea is a delusional fantasy and a continuation of the universalizing of the White particular that we have seen from both left and right.

Global inequality is so stark that those on the poverty line in the United States are still in the top 14 per cent of earners worldwide. The average US salary puts you in the top 4 per cent of earners. There is simply no comparison between the conditions facing the poorest in the world and those who are at the bottom in the United States, or in the rest of the West. Only by focusing on a national analysis could the '99 per cent' rhetoric make any sense. By looking at its demands, or at least its articulation of the problem, it is abundantly clear that Occupy was focused on those in the West, not the victims of it.

The *Declaration of the Occupation of New York City*, collectively produced by Occupiers, is a laundry list of national demands around healthcare, jobs and student debt. The most telling line is the complaint that the 1 per cent 'have consistently outsourced labor and used that outsourcing as leverage to cut workers' healthcare and pay'.[45] No prizes for guessing which 'workers' they are referring to here. Presumably, bringing back those jobs and further impoverishing the underdeveloped world would be acceptable as long as the true 'workers' had access to unskilled and well-paid work. The declaration does include a line condemning the elite because 'they have perpetuated colonialism at home and abroad.' But this is so vague and contradictory to the rest of the declaration that it makes a mockery of their plea for the 'people of the world' to join the struggle. In the same vein as the Enlightenment thinkers, the centre of Occupy's world was the West because it contained the fully formed workers, the movers of history.

Even within the West the movement faced criticism for its tendency to 'exclude minority voices'[46] and faced serious issues of misogyny.[47] There were also marked class differences, with the people who could afford to sleep in Zuccotti Park in protest brushing up against those who had already made it their home because of poverty. The classed differences also spread into tactics. Occupy Seattle angered working-class dock workers by closing down the port in protest against commercialism; their principled stance meant the people they were supposed to be fighting for, the 'workers', lost valuable income. Occupy prided itself on democratic decision-making but it was 'limited by failures to build alliances beyond those implicit inside its inner community'.[48] Democracy matters very little if your electorate is highly exclusive, a lesson that the left needs desperately to learn.

It might be tempting to see Occupy as 'a global movement (inspired by the Arab Spring)', but the reality is that it was in a long tradition of Western social movements which broke out in the United States and spread into Europe and the rest of the world.[49] In claiming to represent the 99 per cent, Occupy, perhaps unwittingly, followed in the path of Enlightenment universalism, speaking for the entire world through the very narrow lens of Western privilege.

Occupy's other main accomplishment is said to be its commitment to horizontal, leaderless organization and a democratic style of decision-making. It is commendable that although 'Occupy' itself is extremely memorable the names of its leaders do not immediately come to mind. This was done on purpose, with painstaking efforts taken to build consensus. During speeches the rest of the protestors could respond with hand signals and interject to make their points known. Due originally to lack of technology, they used a 'human microphone' to communicate, where the audience in earshot of the speaker would shout out their words to those behind and so on. With such commitment to participation it must have been almost impossible to come to any consensus. The declaration that came from the occupiers of Zuccotti Park is frustratingly vague, but given the circumstances it is miraculous that anything was produced at all. The looseness of its political goals was one of the strengths of Occupy but also its primary weakness. Due to its very broadly stated aims the movement had a wide range of support from figures 'including Noam Chomsky, Michael Moore, Kanye West, Russell Simmons, Alec Baldwin and Susan Sarandon'.[50] But with a tent that large it could never hope to articulate a coherent platform.

There were attempts to produce a more defined agenda, particularly by those at *Adbusters* who had put out the call for action in the first place. Micah White and Kalle Lasn, both from the magazine, tried to put together a manifesto to send to Obama three days after the start of the occupation, including the threat to 'to stay here in our encampment in Liberty Plaza' until their demands were met.[51] The only problem was that they were thousands of miles away in Canada at the time. Credit to Occupy, although a lot of its success was found in digital networks, it relied on people on the ground coming together to form bonds and consensus. Given the broad range of people, ideas and motivations involved it is not surprising that the loose-knit coalition eventually splintered, but many of the protestors would argue that although occupation ended it achieved much of what it set out to do.

It would be wrong to judge the movement by conventional metrics because it set out to subvert them. The most obvious way Occupy was effective was as a 'communications success', utilizing social media to spread its messages across the world and making truly global links.[52] Using these networks to bring people together during occupations allowed those gathered to think through how they could address social problems, to engage in 'DIY politics' in the space.[53] During occupations, tent city universities sprang up offering seminars and workshops, food was delivered to the hungry, medical advice was dispensed and successes were had in buying people out of their debt. To truly see the power of Occupy you have to view it through a different lens:

> it is not a media object or a march. It is first and foremost, a church of dissent, a space made sacred by a community. But like Medieval churches, it is also now the physical center of that community. It has become many things. Public square. Carnival. Place to get news. Daycare center. Health care center. Concert venue. Library. Performance space. School.[54]

In many ways Occupy was 'the idealist moment, the performance rather than permanence'.[55] In Zuccotti Park, or in their hundreds of other locations around the world, they were performing the ideal. Occupy was performance art, a grand piece of 'utopian theatre' dramatizing the other world that is otherwise out of reach.[56]

Here we see the White left at its most stomach-churning. Reading through some of the misty-eyed reflections on the movement, they have the feeling of romantic holiday diaries. Nothing may have changed and the movement may have collapsed but no fear, we will always have Zuccotti Park. Occupy's horizontal organization involved both a deep narcissism – with slogans such as 'we are our demands' – and a way of building community that relied on 'people forming loose connections quickly' which fit perfectly into current times.[57] It was the swipe-right of social movements, with no deep ideological commitments, loose connections, and the ability to find some fun elsewhere without feeling guilty. Performance over permanence is only an option to those in the land of plenty who have jobs or at least a welfare state to fall back on.

What made Tahrir Square a completely different sort of movement was that the protestors had a clear demand, which was life or death, and they refused to move until it was met. We can debate how much difference came about when the military took over from President Mubarak in Egypt but not the organic commitment of the people to their struggle, nor that they risked their lives for their cause. The stakes in the West are of a different nature and therefore so are the politics.

Democracy as a principle runs through the new left agenda. In Britain the new left is pushing for a more inclusive economy, similar to the demands of Occupy. Neoliberalism is diagnosed as the source of the ills of society, with the rich taking too much of the economic pie. We are promised that by a 'democratic revolution' we can transform the institutions of governance and society at large.[58] Not only is this struggle about income but it is also about reducing the social distance between people in society so that 'everyone can share a common life as citizens'.[59] The Labour Party under the leadership of Jeremy Corbyn embraced these ideals when he was unexpectedly voted leader in 2015. Prior to this, Labour had been in a period of mimicking Conservative policy on the economy, fully embracing neoliberalism with the idea that the spoils could be shared across society. After Labour's surprising success (but not victory) in the general election of 2017, Corbyn launched what he called Labour's 'radical and ambitious' manifesto for the 2019 election, promising to transform both society and the economy.[60] Labour's plans mirrored much of the New

Economic Foundation's recommendations for policy reform (the NEF is a key think-tank for the new left).

The NEF hits all the key notes with the goal to build a society where all people are 'paid well, have more time off to spend with their families, have access to affordable housing, know there is a decent safety net if they need one, and are provided with a high level of care throughout their lives'.[61] In order to do this they propose a four-day week, a living wage, boosting trade union membership and fashioning a 'well-being state' where targets are not simply economic but relate to the mental and physical health of the nation. They stopped short of a universal basic income, instead suggesting a far more modest national allowance of £50 a week that counts when calculating benefit entitlements. But they are in favour of universal basic services, nationalizing key industries and providing free childcare to support families. The Green New Deal is of course embraced as a motor for both saving the world and job creation. They are also keen on 'people's participation in decision making' in both policy-making and business.[62] One of the NEF's and Labour's main focuses is on establishing workers' cooperatives as a model for sharing wealth.

Preston, a small city in the north of England, has an outsize importance in the new economy, since it has become a model for local-government led cooperatives. The council's decision to source more locally and create cooperatives in the city has both boosted income and dispersed that extra money somewhat more fairly. Other large local employers like the university have followed suit by engaging with local suppliers, and the city is improving. But we should be wary of celebrating a radical new dawn.[63] For a start it is nothing new, with democratic reforms being part of the left-wing imagination for 'at least a century'. Labour governments and councils attempted such projects before neoliberalism took over in the Thatcher era.[64] John McDonnell, the architect of Corbyn's economic policy, served his political apprenticeship in the eighties under Tony Benn, who developed a series of cooperative projects.

The major flaw with these concepts of participation is who is included and who remains firmly on the outside. For all the talk of participation there is scant regard for the fact that those in the under-developed world are equally stakeholders in the economic life of the

West. One of the cooperatives so praised in Preston is a coffee shop, and while we celebrate the benefits to the worker in Britain, the shop's success is only possible because of the racial exploitation of the poor people farming the coffee beans it uses for next to nothing (it may be a surprise, but coffee does not grow in the north of England). This is Cadbury World all over again but on a societal scale. The wealth the left wants to share with those in their nations is derived in large part from global, racial exploitation. What the new left are offering is just a modified version of social democracy. A return to the days of high taxes, social housing, reduced inequality and the guarantee of a decent wage . . . but only in the West. In reality it is not a social but an imperial democracy they are yearning for.

My grandmother came to Britain during the wonderful days of social democracy and found a nation even more overtly racist than the one I grew up in under neoliberalism. Malcolm X visited Birmingham in 1965 and his trip to Smethwick is remembered because of his comments on the racial situation in the town, which he heard was similar to how the 'Jews were [being treated] under Hitler'.[65] This was in large part because he visited the year after what has been dubbed the most racist election in British history, when the Conservative Party candidate Peter Griffith won with the unofficial slogan 'If you want a nigger for a neighbour, vote Labour'. But people often forget that the Labour club in the area was for Whites only; and there is a long tradition of the trade unions barring people of colour from membership.[66] Imperial democracy cannot deal with the problem of racism because it limits the collective to the citizens of the West, allowing them to participate in economic decisions and to increase their access to the bounty stolen off the backs of the Black and Brown. It took the financial crisis in 2008 to spark this new so-called radicalism, and the uncomfortable truth is that if some of the wealth generated from the new age of empire was distributed fairly enough to provide stability and comfort to everyone in the West, calls for the transformation of society would swiftly end.

The rebooted version of Western imperialism updated the colonial logic embedded in the progressive left. Undoubtedly, the inclusion of Black and Brown activists in the West has meant that there is currently more awareness of issues of racial justice. We have always organized, resisted and ensured that there was a spotlight on White supremacy. But if we are honest, activism for the most part remains one of the most segregated social spaces. Green issues have always formed a part of Black and Brown activism in the West and in the Rest because we are more likely to feel the impacts. But whilst the Green New Deal offers at least a view on racial justice, it is a partial and unfocused one. Solving the climate crisis is an existential priority, but doing so will not end the logic of empire.

Enlightenment narratives of science and progress as the solution to the world's ills are still the foundation of the various branches of the left. A narrow focus on full humanity for workers in the West, and merely the right to life for the those in the Rest, prevents any serious reckoning with the scale of injustice upon which global wealth disparities are built. Bernie or Trump, Corbyn or Boris, are decisions that matter, but the degree to which they end Western imperialism is the same. Heads the West wins, tails the Rest loses. Those of us lucky enough to be in the land of plenty will benefit from a return to social democratic values. But nothing short of a revolution that overturns the very foundations of empire can ever undo the problem of racism.

8

Chickens Coming Home to Roost

Britain and the United States came towards the top of the death charts from Covid-19 in 2020 in an unwelcome demonstration of the much-vaunted 'special relationship'. Given the history there is a dark irony in a virus tearing through the past and present centres of Western imperialism. Unlike the genocide in the Americas and Caribbean this illness was never an existential threat, but the death toll is a reminder that imperialism has unintended consequences. Britain and the United States were not hit hard due to historical karma, but because they are at the most advanced stage of development of the new age of empire: neoliberalism. The deadly prescription of austerity, privatization and unrestrained private capital for the underdeveloped world is now being firmly implanted in the West, with Britain and the United States leading the way. The United States has a disastrous private health-care system that fails to manage its normal load, so it is no surprise the pandemic was so catastrophic. Britain has the much cherished National Health Service, but decades of privatization and cuts have led to a service unable to effectively mobilize against the virus. Prioritiz-ing profit and the individual over services and society is deadly at the best of times but utterly ruinous during a pandemic.

The financial regimes inflicted on the Rest coming home to roost in the West was a likely but not inevitable result of the new age of empire. Once the nation state lost its centrality in coordinating empire, and business was free to exploit with no restraints, it was only a matter of time before neoliberal forces would try to bang down the door. Social democracy was a vital element in rebuilding the West after the dev-astation wrought by the Second World War. The post-war settlement shared the spoils of colonial plunder more fairly in the West, easing

THE NEW AGE OF EMPIRE

internal inequality and tying its White majorities firmly to the imperial project. High taxes, public ownership and restraints on financial markets were the status quo until the 1980s. In order for the floodgates of neoliberalism to open, people had to be convinced to vote for an agenda that would reduce the quality of their lives. More than anything else it was the racist logic of empire that opened the floodgates to imposing the Washington consensus in the West.

Brexit unleashed the rabid dogs of neoliberalism, hell-bent on maximizing their profits from liberating the United Kingdom from the regulation (or protection) of the European Union. The ironically named European Research Group, made up of a segment of Conservative members of parliament, made it impossible to get a deal done, effectively forcing the resignation of Prime Minister Theresa May in 2019. Let us be clear: May was part of one of the most racist British governments of recent times, creating a 'hostile environment' for illegal immigrants that included vans with 'go home' written on them driving around the capital, mass-deportation flights, and withdrawing support for search-and-rescue missions for predominantly African migrants trying to cross the Mediterranean Sea into Europe. If that wasn't enough, she was also the architect of the 'Windrush Scandal', which left thousands of people with every legal and historic right to live in Britain subject to losing their jobs and to deportation if they could not provide documentation to prove they had migrated before 1973, when Commonwealth citizens were legally entitled to enter. Bear in mind that there was no need for documentation at the time and the only official proof of entry held by the government was destroyed in 2010 because they ran out of office space. Thousands of those encouraged to migrate to Britain because of a labour shortage, who had grown up in Britain, were deemed illegal and subject to removal to countries they had often never previously returned to.[1] May's response to the Grenfell Tower tragedy, in which more than seventy mostly Black and Brown people were killed, was so disgraceful and lacking humanity she later admitted that failing to meet the families in the immediate aftermath was something she would 'always regret'.[2]

I despised her politics to the point I argued that she was 'more dangerous than Donald Trump'.[3] May was more problematic because she represented what Malcolm X called the 'Northern foxes' of racism who 'show their teeth to the Negro but pretend that they are smiling'.[4] May shrouded herself in the pretence of social justice, making all the right noises about racial discrimination and the police, and commissioning reports into inequality, without making any changes and continuing policies of austerity that made everything worse. Trump is Malcolm's Southern 'bloody jawed wolf', one of those who 'show their teeth in a snarl' by being openly racist in both word and deed.[5]

Theresa May's departure opened the door to Britain's Trump, Boris Johnson, who has in the past referred to Black young people as 'piccaninnies' with 'watermelon smiles', claimed Obama had an 'ancestral dislike for the United States because he is part Kenyan',[6] and compared Muslim women in the veil to 'letterboxes'.[7] Comparisons to Agent Orange – sorry, I mean President Trump – do not stop there. He is also a highly mediocre White man born into a wealthy family, with all the sense of entitlement that comes from growing up with a silver spoon in one's mouth. Lies flow so effortlessly from both their mouths it is as if they feel that they are not bound by the rules of the poor and unwashed. They create their own realities, including the one where they represent the will of the people. I was never a fan of May but celebrating her decline was premature. Her replacement is not only an openly racist buffoon who is allergic to the truth but a cheerleader for the forces of unrestrained neoliberalism that are due to be unleashed on Britain.

The new reality that Johnson and the hardcore Brexiteers have created is that people voted for a hard Brexit, a clean break from the EU. Although even the most extreme of those advocating to leave, including the vile Nigel Farage (another Trump favourite), assured voters in the referendum campaign that there would be a deal that maintained substantive EU links, they went on to pretend that leaving without a deal was what the people really wanted. No economist or sensible politician believes that leaving the EU without a deal is a practical strategy. So dire are the consequences that it would likely mean food shortages, the end of whole industries that rely on frictionless trade with the EU; and according to the government's own watchdog, the Office for Budget Responsibility, could cost the UK £30 billion a year.[8] The truth is no one knows the potential impact but the prospects are so bleak that the government allocated over £6 billion to prepare for the disaster that would ensue if Britain left without a deal.[9] None of this mattered to the hardcore Brexiteers, who were perfectly happy to risk the wellbeing of others if it means the creative destruction necessary to build the kind of society they can maximize profits from. They may even make a fortune off the chaos. There have been plenty of people with money making a profit from betting against the pound, whose value has fallen to historic lows due to the Brexit turmoil.

Johnson's Brexit promises to shed regulations and workers' rights and open up the economy to even more privatization than Britain is currently defined by. Some of the biggest fears raised during the so-called 'Brexit election' in December 2019 were the looming impact of a trade deal with the United States that would allow weaker food standards and protections. Under a 'Trump Brexit', as the leader of the opposition dubbed it, we could expect to be flooded with chlorinated chicken, currently banned by EU regulations due to the unsanitary nature of the process. Worse still, the much-loved National Health Service, which provides free-at-the-point-of-delivery care to the population is on the table to be carved up by US healthcare companies. Britain has always been far closer to the United States than most of Europe in its economic policy and the fear is that Brexit will push the nation more towards the neoliberal extremes of life across the Atlantic. If, and when, Britain tips fully into the neoliberal abyss it will be the result of 'chickens coming home to roost', the inevitable conclusion where the logic of imperialism returns to wreak havoc at home.

WAGES OF WHITENESS

The ground zero for the emergence of the new left is the wrecking ball that Thatcher and Reagan took to the welfare state in the eighties. Destroying the post-war social democratic settlement led to the unrestrained greed of bankers, which resulted in the 2008 financial crisis and the ensuing misery of austerity. Steep declines in living standards, the casualization of work and whole communities being 'left behind' in the new economy led to the rise in populism that elected Trump and gave the charlatan Brexiteers the opportunity to argue that it was the EU that was to blame for society's ills.

Neither President Trump, Prime Minister Johnson or Brexit would be possible without the support of millions of poor (White) people for agendas that are diametrically opposed to their interests. There is no way to understand this phenomenon separate from the racism that underpins society. It is not an issue of class consciousness but the delusions of Whiteness that have allowed the harbingers of the neo-liberal apocalypse to rise to power.

African American intellectual W. E. B. Du Bois theorized that even the poorest of White people in the United States during the period of Reconstruction after the Civil War received a 'public and psychological wage' from their Whiteness.[10] Even though they were being exploited by the same people as African Americans, their status as Whites gave them limited privilege, which they clung to. For Du Bois, this was the principal reason that Black and White workers did not unite against their common enemy and overthrow American capitalism. We see similar arguments throughout the critical literature on Whiteness, with historian Noel Ignatiev arguing that 'White people must commit suicide as Whites in order to come alive as workers, or youth, or women.'[11] This is a classically Marxist notion that race (Whiteness) is an inauthentic identity enacted by the ruling class to divide the workers. As should hopefully now be evident, it is not that simple. Whiteness is not a mirage, there are actual benefits to being in the category that White workers have fought, and continue to fight, very hard for. Still, Whiteness is a tool used by those in power to control poor Whites, to tie them to the project of imperialism. The rise of neoliberalism is the perfect case study.

Social democracy distributed wealth, at least within places like Britain and the United States, reducing inequality between the rich and poor. Conditions for the poor in the early twentieth century were horrendous and there were almost no vehicles for social uplift. Providing housing, infrastructure, transport, social security benefits, healthcare and schooling vastly improved the lives of the poor. We should never forget that the wealth to do this was achieved through colonial exploitation, but at least within the bubble of the West social democracy transformed social conditions. The only problem with the model of state-led, protectionist economies is that they represented the outdated political and economic model of the original version of Western empire. In the new 'globalized' world the state has less power and lacks sovereignty over the corporations that manage the new imperialism. Once capital is liberated from national constraints it becomes impossible for nation-state governments to control. High taxes on individuals and corporations cannot work because capital is mobile – often stored and registered offshore. There is no longer any such thing as a British or American corporation because they are now all global entities spread across disparate tax regimes.

In order to impose neoliberal regimes internally the White masses, including the poor and the workers, needed to be convinced they were in their interests so that they would vote them into being. The oil crisis in the 1970s destabilized the West and provided just the opportunity. Prior to ruining underdeveloped economies, the IMF was primarily used to support the West. Britain's economy was so damaged by the crisis that it not only sought help from the fund in 1976 but also accepted some of the conditions that have been such a bane to the rest of the world, cutting back some of its more left-wing programmes.[12]

The oil crisis was a result of the United States establishing its central role at the heart of empire. In 1971 Nixon broke the Bretton Woods agreement by removing the dollar from the gold standard, which had underpinned global trade. The result was a devastating loss of revenue for the oil-rich countries of the Middle East, who put an embargo on selling their most valuable commodity to the United States.[13] A global recession took hold that made the costs of social democracy in the West exceedingly difficult to meet and forced Britain into the conditional IMF loan. The country's economic crisis led to wage freezes in the public sector and a showdown with the trade unions, who organized a series of strikes, which included bin collectors and gravediggers. The chaos is seared into the political imagination as the 'winter of discontent' of 1978–9 and provided all the impetus necessary for the Thatcherite takeover in the election of 1979. Social democracy was scapegoated as too expensive given the financial crisis; inefficient; and as having given far too much power to the unions who could bring the country to a halt. Privatization, individualism and a small state were the obvious solutions to the stat-ist former model. But remember that this economic context existed in large part because the United States was laying the foundations of the new age of empire. They eventually won the battle with the Middle East and liberation from the gold standard allowed for rapid expan-sion of finance capitalism, the boom on Wall Street and the eventual financial crash of 2008.

It was not only economics that allowed the rise of neoliberalism. In Britain, Margaret Thatcher stormed to power in 1979 in large part because she was able to secure the support of some traditional Labour, working-class voters whose aversion to the Tory party was deeply ingrained. An area that Thatcher could exploit was the issue of immigration. Due to labour shortages, post-war Britain had opened its doors to immigration from the colonies. Millions of people from the Caribbean, South Asia and Africa had settled in the UK by the time of the momentous election in 1979. My family were part of that migration and the reason I am writing this book in Britain. There were also millions of immigrants from Eastern Europe and the Old Commonwealth (Australasia, Canada, White South Africans) but they did not concern Thatcher, who openly spoke about the 'four million people of the new Commonwealth or Pakistan' flooding into Britain, in a nationally televised interview.[14] She argued that

> people are really rather afraid that this country might be rather swamped by people with a different culture and, you know, the British character has done so much for democracy, for law and done so much throughout the world that if there is any fear that it might be swamped people are going to react and be rather hostile to those coming in.

This was by no means the first time that the Conservatives had engaged in such racist political language. Thatcher was mobilizing a more polite version of Peter Griffiths' 'If you want a nigger for a neighbour, vote Labour' tactic. 'Swamped' is important because it suggests there are too many darkies and that we are a corrupting influence on British institutions and values.

Social democracy only works if society feels that everyone *should* have a stake in sharing the wealth. The idea that foreigners, Black ones at that, should be able to jump the queue for housing or doctor's appointments undermines the idea of universal service provision. Notions of being 'left behind' are intrinsically tied up in this idea. White workers are supposedly being short-changed by multicultural- ism, which is privileging the darkies who are swamping the country and demanding special protections under anti-racist legislation. Brit- ain's embrace of individualism was in large part driven by its rejection of diversity.

There can be no 'we' if that includes the uninvited foreigners des- troying the so-called British way of life. Thatcher's famous declaration that 'there's no such thing as society' must be seen in this context. She continued, 'there are individual men and women and there are fami- lies . . . It is our duty to look after ourselves and then, also, to look after our neighbours.'[15] Given the context of steep racial segregation in housing it is clear who the neighbours are that she is referring to. In this logic, mass migration has torn down the fabric of what once were the shared British values that held the country together. Old ideas of community, nation and class are broken down with the idea that the uniqueness of Britain is being lost and the neoliberal individual is free to come into being, fending for themselves against the hordes of foreigners swamping the country.

The anti-immigration rhetoric of Thatcher was key to her appeal and to being able to maintain a Conservative government for the following eighteen years. In that period taxes were slashed, public utilities privatized, and social housing sold off to those individuals with enough money to be able to afford to buy them. Finance cap- ital was also set free to dominate the economy, and neoliberalism flourished in Britain. Of course, inequality soared and public services became run down through lack of investment, whilst the rich kept on getting filthier and richer.

We saw the same use of racist logic in the campaign for Brexit. The expansion of the EU in 2007 to include Eastern European countries meant that freedom of movement within member states was open to those poorer citizens of the former Communist bloc. As a result, large numbers of migrants began to come to Britain to work, which became an increasing source of discontent for many. Right-wing rac- ists like Nigel Farage came to prominence, with his United Kingdom Independence Party (UKIP), focused on the single issue of leaving the

EU, with fears of uncontrolled immigration being its major talking point. Farage made clear the limits of the social democratic dream with his declaration during an election debate that the beloved NHS was 'our National Health Service, not the International Health Service'.[16] Extending the protections of the welfare state to bloody foreigners was not what the decent hardworking British people had signed up to.

Fearing that the rise of UKIP, who did very well in the EU elections, could be dangerous for his party, Prime Minister David Cameron sought to outflank them on Europe by offering the referendum on membership of the EU. It worked to depress the UKIP vote in the 2015 general election but he was then left with the prospect of having to deliver on this promise. He made a massive miscalculation when he assumed that people would not 'vote themselves poorer because they don't like the Poles living next door'.[17] But by voting in the Conservatives for ever more austerity, that is precisely what a large chunk of the British electorate had already done.

Cameron's Brexit gamble was no doubt in part influenced by the history of racial politics and immigration. As we discussed earlier, migration from Eastern Europe is not a new phenomenon in Britain. In fact, Cameron's opposite number in the Labour Party in 2015, Ed Miliband, was the son of Polish Jewish migrants.[18] There was certainly some questionable coverage in the largely morally deficient right-wing press about his inability to eat a bacon sandwich and how his refugee Marxist father hated Britain.[19] But his background did not receive any of the fanfare, for good or ill, that would have been made had his parents migrated from Jamaica. White migrants are still White and their children melt into the population in a way that we never can. In many ways freedom of movement from Europe was just a continuation of the long-held immigration policy to encourage White migration whilst discouraging those who are Black and Brown. But the pace and scale of migration had an impact on the debate.

Between 2004 and 2017 the proportion of the UK population from Europe, excluding Ireland, rose from 1.5 per cent to 5 per cent. It is not incredibly surprising that the xenophobic backlash against EU migrants coincided with the financial crash and austerity. When people are struggling it is easy to pin the blame on the newly arrived, even when they are migrating from worse conditions. But Cameron should have seen this writing on the wall because it had his fingerprints all over it.

Farage has been ridiculed for his blaming of all things on immigrants, including too much traffic,[20] but Cameron's government was just a more sophisticated version of the UKIP spin machine. During the 2015 general election campaign Cameron warned that a Labour government would massively increase immigration. His immigration minister James Brokenshire declared that 'uncontrolled mass immigration makes it difficult to maintain social cohesion, puts pressure on public services and forces down wages.'[21] Shifting the blame for poverty and lack of investment away from their root cause of neoliberalism and onto immigrants has been key to the Conservatives' electoral success. Millions have been duped into believing that their problem is poor people from other countries looking for a better life, rather than the rich and politicians who are robbing the population of the opportunities to succeed.

Even when immigration is not about race, it still is. EU migrants are overwhelmingly White but this did not stop the campaigners looking to leave the EU during the Brexit referendum invoking race. Farage consistently invoked the spectre of Turkey joining the EU, with its 75 million Muslims supposedly threatening to invade Britain. This is ironic because Turkey has basically zero chance of EU membership *because* it is not a White country. The EU has always been an exclusive club. Farage also unveiled an infamous poster that depicted a long line of Syrian refugees crossing into Croatia from Slovenia with the slogan 'Breaking Point: The EU has failed us all'. So egregious was the imagery that even Boris Johnson denounced it; the imagery was reported to the police and even evoked comparisons to Nazi propaganda. But the message was clear: immigration is always a racial issue.

The result of all of this has been the vote for Brexit and the rise of Boris Johnson, who threatens to complete the neoliberal project. There should be no more worrying prospect for the average Brit. The problem is that the nation voted for all of it in no small part because they bought into the racial politics that underpin the system.

Immigration, in and of itself, is the chickens of imperialism coming home to roost. By conquering a quarter of the globe Britain incorporated hundreds of millions of Black and Brown people into its Empire. For all the fantasies of Britain being great, the reality is that as a little, insignificant island, it was the Empire that established the role of the nation in the world. Colonial subjects were born *in* Britain, not outside it. Our blood, sweat and tears lay at the foundation of British progress. After the War, when the mother country needed labour to rebuild it naturally turned to the source it had been exploiting for centuries. It was seen as your duty to do your part for Queen and country in the same way as supporting the war effort had been.

Often forgotten in the anti-immigration debate is that we were invited. In fact, Enoch Powell, who became infamous for his racist, anti-immigration 'Rivers of Blood' speech, was one of the first health secretaries to reach out to the colonies for nurses. More than any other cherished institution, the NHS has always relied, and still very much continues to rely, on the labour of doctors and nurses from the former colonies to exist. Farage's quip about it not being the International Health Service is as ignorant as it is racist. The truth is that the British welfare state has heavily relied on the former colonies for both the wealth necessary to exist and the labour to run it. Fears of 'swamping' and 'losing' the country are entirely imagined and frankly ridiculous. But if immigration has been seen as a problem and has led to the embrace of the neoliberal individual, then this was a problem of Britain's own making. As the late intellectual Ambalavaner Sivanandan put it, 'we are here because you were there.'[22] Had the West not colonized and then underdeveloped the world there would not be millions of former colonial subjects trying to migrate into their former mother countries for a better life. The dark chickens of the colonies coming home to roost happened later in Europe because of the nature of empire, with indirect rule and slavery in the Caribbean, but the United States had to deal with this issue from its foundation.

The rise of neoliberalism in the United States was no different, driven by the same forces of White supremacy. Donald Trump's victory has been seen as an outlier because he is so ill-suited and unprepared for the role of president, but his election was decades in the making. He is the poster boy for neoliberalism and the silver-spoon-in-the-mouth elite, posing as the friend of the people; and his election was driven by the same basic factors as we saw in Britain. Poor Whites supposedly being left behind by multiculturalism. Fear of the immigrants taking control. A wish to return to the glory days when racism could openly form public policy. Trump's embrace of 'law and order' is the classic racialized language of the right: that the dark inner cities need to be heavily policed to keep the savages in the jungle in check.

Following his tragicomic handling of the Covid-19 outbreak, the rise of the Black Lives Matter protests unfortunately gave Trump the opportunity to play to his strengths and his base. As well as threatening to use the army to quell the unrest, Trump has described Black Lives Matter as a 'symbol of hate'[23] and vowed to defend the monuments to the slave-owning 'patriots' who built the United States that he described as 'heroes' rather than villains.[24] Doubling down on his appeals to Whiteness was undoubtedly the best call in the lead-up to the presidential election. He may have ultimately lost but more voters voted for him than did for Obama in his historic victory of 2008. Millions of voters are seduced by the wages of Whiteness even in the absence of actual wages to support them.[25] Just as in Britain, the real problem is the rich and the politicians who support them, while the blame for inequality is shifted to immigrants and Black folk.

Du Bois declared that the issue of 'the twentieth century was the problem of the color line',[26] and the so-called race problem has been a focus of attention, both well-meaning and mendacious, since emancipation. Having to deal with millions of African Americans is the definition of chickens coming home to roost, the result of stolen bodies, lives and labour. The wages of Whiteness can be traced to the development of the United States, to which the issue of the enslavement of African people was central. We should not delude ourselves with the mythology that the Civil War was about ending slavery. Lincoln made it clear that if he could 'save the Union without freeing any slave' he was perfectly happy to do so.[27] To win the battle with the South, the North ended up issuing the emancipation proclamation in order to enlist the support of the enslaved. During the war so many African Americans had liberated themselves from bondage that if he wanted victory Lincoln had no real choice but to support emancipation.

After the war the first solution to the 'problem' of living with millions of free Black folk was, in effect, to deport them to another country. The more polite term of 'colonization' was used, and Lincoln and his successors pursued the idea of ejecting their Black population to another place, possibly Haiti or Liberia.[28] It is in the Reconstruction period that Du Bois' phrase 'wages of Whiteness' was applied to the inability of White workers to find comradeship with the formerly enslaved. This dynamic only got worse with the immigration of millions of Europeans into the nation who 'became White' in large part by embracing the racism of the United States and directing hatred towards African Americans.[29]

By being openly racist and segregationist wolves, politicians in the South were able to maintain their power whilst the cunning foxes in the North gave nods to racial equality while presiding over de facto Jim Crow through housing segregation, police brutality and institutional racism. In his 1964 'The Ballot or the Bullet' speech Malcolm X declares that he is 'not a Democrat, nor a Republican, nor even an American' because of how misused the votes of Black people had been by politicians.[30]

Like Thatcher, when Reagan wanted to usher in neoliberalism he knew the perfect scapegoat. During both his presidential campaigns, and while in office trying to dismantle the welfare state, he invoked the tale of a Black woman in Chicago who had been gaming the system to the extent that her 'tax-free cash income alone had been running at $150,000 a year'.[31] Reagan's tale of the 'welfare queen' hit all the right notes with certain segments of the electorate. A freeloader, living off the backs of the hardworking. It was abundantly clear that this was a stereotype built on the longstanding racist idea that Black people are workshy. The United States is so racially segregated that nodding to the 'woman in Chicago', one of the cities where the problem of segregation is most acute, created a clear picture of exactly whom Reagan was talking about. Just as in Britain, social democratic principles can only hold if everyone feels everyone else is an equal part of the nation. African Americans, and immigrants, were the perfect weapon to break the New Deal consensus.

Welfare reform was ushered in on the myth of the undeserving Blacks, and the 'war on drugs' sparked mass incarceration as an alternative to welfare provision for African Americans, as well as hugely expanding the role of the private sector in prisons. Trump's election, on a tide of anti-Black and anti-immigration rhetoric, is not an aberration but the logical conclusion of the resentment at neoliberalism being turned onto those perceived as alien to the nation.

We have seen the same process of neoliberal structural adjustment wreak havoc across Britain and the United States, enabled by the same colonial logic that remains deeply written into the political calculus. When covid struck with Trump on one side of the Atlantic and Johnson on the other, we were stuck in the middle, with the chickens that well and truly came home to roost.

LOOK TO THE EAST

Much has been made about the rise of the East as a major change in the global political and economic system. There is no doubt that 'we are living in the Asian century', with dramatic increases of both wealth and standards of living across the continent.[32] China's influence, in particular, is being increasingly felt on the world stage, with the trade war with the United States being just one example. There has undoubtedly been a shift in the balance of power to the East that is not set to reverse. With rising standards of living come greater economic influence, China and India alone hold more than a third of the world's population. In India between 1990 and 2014 the number of households with more than $10,000 a year in disposable income leapt from 2 to 50 million.[33] China has become the new workshop of the world, manufacturing goods for global consumption, while the region is also at the forefront of technological and communications innovations. It is not difficult to see why the West would be worried about China hosting both the means of production and a mass consumer base. But the reality is that the emergence of Asia neither ends the Western imperial project nor calls for a system update. What we are seeing today is the logic of the current version of the system, and 'the sun rising in the east does not mean that it is setting on the west.'[34]

In order to deliver its remarkable economic growth the East has ingrained itself into the Western political and economic system. It is not a coincidence that it is not Mao's China that is poised to become the centre of the global political and economic system; China holds that position *because* the Chairman's legacy has been abandoned. The collapse of Communism led to the infamous declaration of the 'end of history' by Francis Fukuyama, who theorized 'that liberal democracy may constitute the end point of mankind's ideological evolution'.[35] No one could accuse China of being a liberal democracy, but its surrender to market capitalism is almost total. While certainly not neoliberal, the country is remarkably comfortable with billionaires for a supposedly Communist nation. As China depends on the West for its prosperity there is nothing to be gained from trying to foment revolution. Fukuyama's argument is wrong-headed because it is steeped so deeply in Enlightenment principles he forgets that actors, particularly in the former colonies, have agency. But he is right about the extent to which the Western economic model has erased almost all alternatives.

Just as New Labour was Margaret Thatcher's greatest achievement, China is the ultimate success of the West: a potential successor to the seat of power that maintains the relations and exclusions of the old system. This is an absolute defeat of the revolutionary principles that the nation was founded upon. In fact, because China has yet to embrace liberal democracy, let alone neoliberalism, it may end up representing a better form of Western imperialism. With its population of over 1 billion led firmly by the state it is able to mobilize and plan its economy with military precision in a way the rest of the world should equally envy and fear.

The fact that there are non-White faces at the head of the latest version of empire does not mean the system has changed. It is perfectly possible to maintain racism whilst diversifying those in charge of dispensing it. It was precisely by exploiting racial political and economic systems that the region grew. Asia's growth depends on the extreme poverty of hundreds of millions of its own citizens and the continued evisceration of Africa in order to plunder the continent's resources. There are no signs of this changing, and a collection of crazy rich Asians does not alter reality for the majority of people on the continent. One of the most disappointing arguments for the decline of racism is the presence of rich Black and Brown folk. A Black middle class is no more evidence of racial salvation than the existence of many more rich White people means that the class struggle is over.

There have always been some who were better-off than others, even under the brutally violent version of Western imperialism. The current edition has meant that there are now far more opportunities for a limited elite, both in the West and the former colonies, to enjoy the fruits of the system. But we should not delude ourselves into believing that means that the nature of the system itself has changed.

Rather than seeing the emergence of Black and Brown elites as a break from Western imperialism, we should understand them as one of the logics of the new system. The new age of empire is based on moving away from formal colonialism, breaking down the power of the state and delivering racial exploitation through economic, not physical, coercion. This meant granting so-called independence and relying even more on local elites to manage their countries. There are classes of the wealthy from the former colonies who owe their lifestyles and positions to Western imperialism. To be in the elite in the former colonies is to inhabit a position beyond most of those in the West. This also tends to come with Western education, offshore bank accounts and truly being able to access the world as a global citizen.

Occupy's 1 per cent certainly includes some of those who are not White, but we are mistaken if we think that their positions are not defined by Whiteness. To gain that level of wealth in economies that include some of the poorest people on the planet tells us the scale of the inequalities in the system. Even for those of us who are by no means rich but still successful, our relative prosperity remains built on the same colonial logic that keeps the masses of the Black and Brown in poverty. The most painful development of the new age of empire is that we have now become part of the problem, with our hands stained with the blood of the victims of our success.

When the architects of the new age of empire were designing the update to the system they doubtless did not predict the emergence and potential takeover of China and the East. Belief in White supremacy has a tendency to override common sense, and they more than likely thought that the impoverished East could be contained. But taking the boot directly off the neck of the underdeveloped world allowed space for the changes that have occurred. One of the biggest factors has been offshoring as part of the neoliberal project. Due to the racist political and economic system, wages are far lower in the underdeveloped world and therefore when capital and technology were free to be global it made economic sense for companies to move their production overseas. China has been adept at using its cheap labour to become the workshop of the world. This labour was off-shored precisely because of the wealth in the West: it became too expensive to pay the workers here for it, and the work is mundane.

Consumption, technology and services replaced manufacturing as the basis of Western economies. In the pursuit of the middle-class dream this makes some kind of sense, but it is also a big driver of the 'left behind' narrative because it means that unskilled manual jobs are in short supply. Ceding production to the underdeveloped world always had the potential for the rapid development we are seeing. For all the hype about consumption, it is impossible without production. China in particular, but also the region in general, has become expert at making the most of owning substantial elements of the means of production.

When the centre of empire shifts to China, or robots take over production, it may well mean the West moves to its next stage. None of these developments will mean ending the racist political and economic system, and at best they only offer a slightly more bearable format.

END OF EMPIRE

No matter how many of the chickens come home to roost in the West they will never erase the racism at the heart of the global political and economic system. As Malcolm X warned us, 'this system can no more provide freedom, justice and equality . . . than a chicken can lay a duck egg.'[36] But history tells us that all empires end. They either collapse under their own contradictions or are brought crashing down by rebellion or conquest. We may have been told that there is no alternative, but Western imperialism will at some point come to a conclusion. The West has only been truly dominant for 250 years, a blip on the timeline of human history. But despite diagnosing racism as a fundamental sequence in the DNA of the current social order, the premise of this book is deeply optimistic. We do not need to placate the powers that be by limiting our vision to reforming a system that is not broken. Police brutality, health inequalities, thousands of children dying a day are all symptoms of the disease of racism caused by the machine of Western imperialism. Once we recognize that this racism is a necessary a by-product of the political and economic system then we have the freedom to imagine what comes after we have torn it down.

Revolution is possible, but we have to accept that it will not come from those who benefit from Western imperialism. There are centuries-long traditions of radical politics emerging from the oppressed. The bulk of my work is about developing the politics of Black radicalism, which centres on uniting Africa and the African diaspora to create a true revolution, which remains the only solution to the problem of racism.[37] The oppressed never accept their condition and will always struggle to overturn the system that holds them down. Enslaved Africans in Haiti cast off their shackles and took their freedom. Black Power movements changed the conditions of possibility for Black people in the belly of the beast. It was revolutions across the Third World that forced the West to abandon the brutally violent forms of colonial domination. This book is a reminder of the stakes, to not accept edits to the status quo as some kind of progress. Revolution is not only possible but it is absolutely essential if we truly want freedom.

The protests sparked by the murder of George Floyd are deeply rooted in the histories of Black resistance but offer a new hope in one regard. In the sixties there was a struggle between the agendas of revolution and reform: overturning the system or trying to fix it. Reform won out in the shape of civil rights movements in the West and independence for nations in the underdeveloped world. These were some of the most successful movements in history, gaining access to voting rights, changes to legislation and even representation in the halls of power. For fifty years we have been promised we are on a path to freedom, but it is more than just symbolic that Black Lives Matter first came into existence with a Black man in the White House. No amount of editing or inclusion to this racist system will ever give us freedom, and we now have a generation who should no longer be persuaded we are on the right path. The future is now, and it is one in which we can watch a police officer kneel on the neck of a Black person in public for almost nine minutes. If that does not remove the scales from our eyes then nothing will.

The question that I get asked the most, and have no answer to, is 'What can White people do?' If you got to the end of this book hoping there would be a magic bullet, some quick fix or anti-racist potion that could build meaningful allyship then you will leave disappointed. The quest for allyship is in itself misguided. The problem is that society is built on a White supremacy that permeates every institution, intellectual framework and interaction within it. If you have come this far and believe that White people offering a meaningful hand of friendship is the solution then you have entirely missed the point. It is not the place of the oppressed to suggest a progressive role for those who benefit from their oppression. My hope is that understanding the scale of the problem and the limits of the solutions offered can spark a genuine conversation about how to overhaul this wicked system. In one of Malcolm X's most famous speeches he offered a seeming olive branch to mainstream White society, arguing that America was 'the only country in history in a position to actually become involved in a bloodless revolution'.[38] All it had to do was give Black people 'everything they're due', in order to repair the damage done over the centuries. Malcolm did not hold out much hope, and busied himself with organizing the Black masses. If anything should be clear by now, it is that we cannot wait for White allies to join the struggle to end their systemic privilege.

The glimmer of hope for true transformation in the West is that if the system is left to collapse under its own weight it may well end human existence as we know it. The pile of Black and Brown bodies stacked up since Columbus, to millions each year dying from poverty, is of an unimaginable scale. But the West has not shied away from White-on-White violence when vying for the leadership of its empire. Millions of European and American lives were lost in the two World Wars, and we were on the brink of Armageddon more than once during the Cold War. One of the consequences of the rise of a non-White power such as China threatening to take control of the reins is the increased likelihood of nuclear holocaust. It was not by chance that the Japanese were used as guinea pigs for the atomic bomb. Black and Brown bodies are far easier to erase in the logic of empire. Violence consuming the West (and the entire globe in the process) would be the ultimate example of chickens coming home to roost, but there is an even more likely existential threat to humanity.

Over-consumption is killing the planet. The constant pursuit of growth at all costs is polluting the atmosphere to the point where the world may become uninhabitable. If drastic action is not taken to reverse global warming soon then floods of a biblical nature are coming to not only wash away the sins of the West but also its victims. Solar panels, electric cars and planting trees are not enough to undo the damage that has been done. It is the very nature of Western consumption that is due to melt the ice-caps.[39] Climate justice is not just a matter of life and death for those who are Black and Brown; a radical rethink is necessary for humanity to continue.

Maybe it is in this moment, standing on the cliff-edge of annihilation, staring into the abyss caused by Western so-called civilization, that the depth of the problem and scale of the solution can be grasped. Perhaps we can wipe away the illusions of progress based on the distorted vision of Whiteness we are brainwashed into. This is the chance to refuse the next system update of imperialism, destroy the hard drive and create an entirely new framework for the world's political and economic system. But make no mistake, whether spurred by revolution or tipped into collapse under its own weight, the West will eventually fall. Malcolm was right when he warned that it will be 'the ballot or the bullet, liberty or death, freedom for everybody or freedom for nobody'.[40]

Notes

FOREWORD

1   Public Health England (2020) *Disparities in the Risk and Outcomes of COVID-19*. London: Wellington House; Schwitz, M. and Cook, L. (2020) 'These N.Y.C. neighborhoods have the highest rates of virus deaths'. *New York Times*, 18 May.

2   Office for National Statistics (2020) 'Coronavirus (COVID-19) related deaths by ethnic group, England and Wales: 2 March 2020 to 10 April 2020'. 7 May. Available at https://www.ons.gov.uk/peoplepopulationand community/birthsdeathsandmarriages/deaths/articles/coronavirusrelated deathsbyethnicgroupenglandandwales/2march2020to10april2020

3   SA Stats (2015) 'Mortality and causes of death in South Africa: findings from death notification, 2015'. Available at http://www.statssa.gov.za/ publications/P03093/P030932015.pdf

4   Boseley, S. (2019) 'The children labouring in Malawi's fields for British American Tobacco'. *Guardian*, 31 October.

INTRODUCTION

1   Robinson, C. J. (1983) *Black Marxism: The Making of the Black Radical Tradition*. London: Zed Books, 83, 2.

2   The Sentencing Project (2018) 'Report to the United Nations Special Rapporteur on contemporary forms of racism, racial discrimination, xenophobia, and related intolerance regarding racial disparities in the United States criminal justice system'. Available at https://www.sentencingproject. org/publications/un-report-on-racial-disparities/

3   Melamed, J. (2015) 'Racial capitalism'. *Critical Ethnic Studies* 1(1): 77.

4   Alexander, M. (2016) *The New Jim Crow: Mass Incarceration in the Age of Colorblindness*. New York: The New Press.

5 Morrison, T. (1998) 'Talk of the town: comment'. *New Yorker*, 28 September.

6 Alexander, *New Jim Crow*.

7 Campbell, A. (2018) 'The federal government markets prison labor to businesses as the "best-kept secret"'. *Vox*, 24 August. Available at https://www. vox.com/2018/8/24/17768438/national-prison-strike-factory-labor

8 Prison Bureau (2018) 'Annual determination of average cost of incarceration'. *Federal Register*, 30 April. Available at https://www.federal register.gov/documents/2018/04/30/2018-09062/annual-determination-of-average-cost-of-incarceration

9 Gilmore, R. (2002) 'Fatal couplings of power and difference: notes on racism and geography'. *Professional Geographer* 54(1): 16.

10 Dahlgreen, W. (2014) 'The British Empire is "something to be proud of"'. YouGov, 26 July. Available at https://yougov.co.uk/topics/politics/articles-reports/2014/07/26/britain-proud-its-empire

11 Malcolm X (1962) 'Black man's history'. Speech at Muslim Mosque No. 7, New York, 12 December.

12 Malcolm X (1964) 'The ballot or the bullet'. Speech at Cory Methodist Church in Cleveland, Ohio, 3 April.

13 Andrews, N. (2017) 'Blackness in the Roundabout'. Paper at *Blackness at the Intersection* workshop, 8 June, Rugby, UK.

14 Crenshaw, K. (2021) *On Intersectionality: Essential Writings*. New York: The New Press; Taylor, K. (2019) *Race for Profit: How Banks and the Real Estate Industry Undermined Black Homeownership*. Chapel Hill: UNC Press; Hill Collins, P. (2019) *Intersectionality as Critical Social Theory*. Durham, NC: Duke University Press; Kendall, M. (2020) *Hood Feminism: Notes from the Women that a Movement Forgot*. New York: Viking.

15 Perez-Pena, R. (2017) 'Woman linked to 1955 Emmett Till murder tells historian her claims were false'. *New York Times*, 27 January.

16 Wells, I. (2014) *The Light of Truth: Writings of an Anti-Lynching Crusader*. London: Penguin.

17 Davis, A. (1981) *Women, Race and Class*. New York: Random House.

18 Wolfers, J., Leonhardt, D. and Quealy, K. (2015) '1.5 million missing black men. The upshot', *New York Times*, 20 April. Available at https://www.nytimes.com/interactive/2015/04/20/upshot/missing-black-men.html?smid=pl-

19 Crenshaw, K. (2017) 'Say her name'. Paper at *Blackness at the Intersection* workshop, 8 June, Rugby, UK.

20 Olusoga, D. (2016) *Black and British: A Forgotten History*. London: Macmillan.

21 Hill Collins, *Intersectionality.*

22 Crenshaw, K. (2011) 'Postscript' in Lutz, H. Herrera Vivar, M. and Supik, L. (eds) *Framing Intersectionality: Debates on a Multi-Faceted Concept in Gender Studies.* Farnham: Ashgate: 221–33.

23 Hall, D. (1999) *In Miserable Slavery: Thomas Thistlewood in Jamaica, 1750–86.* Houndmills: Macmillan.

24 Roser, M. (2018) 'When will we reach "peak child"?' Our World in Data. Available at ourworldindata.org.peak-child

25 Harris, P. (2010) 'Martin Luther King's spirit is claimed by Fox TV's Glenn Beck and Sarah Palin'. *The Observer*, 29 August.

26 Dolak, K. (2010) 'Alveda King speaks at Glenn Beck's DC rally'. *ABC News*, 28 August. Available at https://abcnews.go.com/Politics/alveda-king-speaks-glenn-becks-dc-rally/story?id=11504453&page=2

27 Malcolm X (1963) 'Message to the grassroots'. Speech at the Negro Grass Roots Leadership Conference, Michigan, 10 November.

28 King, M. (1963) 'I have a dream'. Speech at the March on Washington for Jobs and Freedom, Washington, DC, 28 August.

29 Crenshaw, K., Gotanda, N., Peller, G., and Thomas, K. (1995) *Critical Race Theory: The Key Writings that Formed the Movement.* New York: The New Press, 85–102.

30 Andrews, K. (2018) *Back to Black: Retelling Black Radicalism for the 21st Century.* London: Zed Books.

31 Cabinet Office. (2017) *Race Disparity Audit: Summary Findings from the Ethnicity Facts and Figures Website.* London: Cabinet Office.

32 Green, L. (2019) *Children in Custody 2017–18: An analysis of 12–18-year-olds' perceptions of their experiences in secure training centres and young offender institutions.* London: HM Prison Inspectorate.

33 Bell, D. (1992) *Faces at the Bottom of the Well: The Permanence of Racism.* New York: Basic Books, 12.

1 I'M WHITE, THEREFORE I AM

1 Whyman, T. (2017) 'Soas students have a point. Philosophy degrees should look beyond white Europeans'. *Guardian*, 10 January.

2 Turner, C. (2017) 'University students demand philosophers such as Plato and Kant are removed from syllabus because they are white'. *Telegraph*, 8 January.

3 Collins, D. (2017) 'UNI KANT TOUCH THIS: Barmy SOAS students try to ban classical philosophers like Plato, Aristotle and Voltaire from their courses . . . because they are white'. *Sun*, 9 January.

4 Bhambra, G., Gebrial, D. and Nişancıoğlu, K. (2018) *Decolonising the University*. London: Pluto Press.

5 Turner, 'University students'.

6 Hill, T. and Boxill, B. (2001) 'Kant and race' in Boxill, B. (ed.) *Race and Racism*. Oxford: Oxford University Press, 455.

7 Kant, I. (1777) 'On the different human races' in Bernasconi, R. and Lott, T. (eds) (2000) *The Idea of Race*. Indianapolis: Hackett, 17.

8 Eze, E. (1997) 'The color of reason: the idea of "race" in Kant's *Anthropology*' in Eze, E. (ed.) *Postcolonial African Philosophy: A Critical Reader*. Oxford: Blackwell, 116.

9 Allais, L. (2016) 'Kant's racism'. *Philosophical Papers*. 45(1–2): 2.

10 Kant, 'On the different races', 11.

11 Ibid., 12.

13 Eze, 'The color of reason', 116.

13 Ibid., 108.

14 Kant, 'On the different races', 17.

15 Hund, W. (2011) 'It must come from Europe: the racisms of Immanuel Kant' in Hund, W., Koller, C. and Zimmerman, M. (eds) *Racisms Made in Germany*. Berlin: Lit Verlag, 81.

16 Eze, 'The color of reason', 117.

17 Kant, 'On the different races', 16.

18 Hill and Boxill, 'Kant and race', 452.

19 Rutherford, A. (2020) *How to Argue with a Racist: History, Science, Race and Reality*. London: Weidenfeld and Nicolson.

20 Bernasconi, R. (2003) 'Will the real Kant please stand up: the challenge of Enlightenment racism to the study of the history of philosophy'. *Radical Philosophy* 117: 13–22.

21 Allais, 'Kant's racism'.

22 Bernasconi, R. (2011) 'Kant's third thoughts on race' in Elden, S. and Mendieta, E. (eds) *Reading Kant's Geography*. Albany: State University of New York.

23 Hund, 'It must come from Europe', 79.

24 Hill and Boxill, 'Kant and race', 452.

25 Allais, 'Kant's racism', 19.

26 Hund, 'It must come from Europe', 81.66

27 Olusoga, D. (2016) *Black and British: A Forgotten History*. London: Macmillan, 272.

28 Goldberg, J. (2018) 'Was the Enlightenment racist?' *National Review*, 21 June.

29 Voltaire (1765) 'On the different races of man' in Bernasconi and Lott, *The Idea of Race*, 6.

30 Hegel, G. (1830) 'Encyclopaedia of the philosophical sciences'. Ibid., 40.

31 Kendi, I. (2017) *Stamped from the Beginning: The Definitive History of Racist Ideas in America.* London: Bodley Head.

32 Ibid., 96.

33 Ibid., 109.

34 Niro, B. (2003) *Race.* Houndmills: Palgrave Macmillan, 65.

35 Dover, C. (1952) 'The racial philosophy of Johann Herder'. *British Journal of Sociology* 3(2): 124–33.

36 Ibid., 128.

37 Voltaire, 'On the different races', 6.

38 Kendi, *Stamped.* 86.

39 Darwin, C. (1871) 'On the races of man' in Bernasconi and Lott, *The Idea of Race*, 75.

40 Dubois, L. (2006) 'An enslaved Enlightenment: rethinking the intellectual history of the French Atlantic'. *Social History* 31(1): 5.

41 Halberstam, J. (1988) 'From Kant to Auschwitz'. *Social Theory and Practice* 14: 45.

42 Darwin, 'On the races of man', 70.

43 Hegel, 'Encyclopaedia of the philosophical sciences', 43.

44 Muthu, S. (1999) 'Enlightenment anti-imperialism'. *Social Research* 66(4): 965.

45 Dover, 'Racial philosophy', 128.

46 Grosfoguel, Ramón (2013) 'The structure of knowledge in westernized universities: epistemic racism/sexism and the four genocides/epistemicides of the long 16th century'. *Human Architecture: Journal of the Sociology of Self-Knowledge* 11(1:8), 73–90.

47 Eze, 'The color of reason', 122.

48 Grosfoguel, 'Structure of knowledge'.

49 Moller, V. (2019) *The Map of Knowledge: How Classical Ideas Were Lost and Found: A History in Seven Cities.* London: Picador, 66.

50 Ibid., 112.

51 Ibid., 150.

52 Ibid., 114.

53 Ibid., 133.

54 Henrik Clarke, J. (1977) 'The University of Sankore at Timbuctoo: A neglected achievement in Black intellectual history'. *Western Journal of Black Studies* 1(2): 142–6.

55 Diop, C. (1974) *The African Origin of Civilization: Myth or Reality?* Chicago: Lawrence Hill Books, 4.

56 Ibid., 230.

57 Ibid., 168.

58 Dabiri, E. (2019) *Don't Touch My Hair*. London: Allen Lane, 209.

59 Moller, *Map of Knowledge*, 55.

60 Moller, *Map of Knowledge*, 2.

61 Dabiri, *Don't Touch*, 218.

62 Kendi, *Stamped*, 109.

63 Jefferson, T. (1853) *Notes on the State of Virginia*. Virginia: J. W. Randolph.

64 Wright, J. (2007) *The Trans-Saharan Slave Trade*. Abingdon: Routledge, 5.

65 Hill and Boxill, 'Kant and race', 470.

66 Ishay, M. (2004) *The History of Human Rights: From Ancient Times to the Globalization Era*. Berkeley: University of California Press, 65.

67 Kendi, *Stamped*, 116.

68 Ishay, *History of Human Rights*, 96.

69 Muthu, 'Enlightenment anti-imperialism', 997.

70 Allais, 'Kant's racism', 19.

71 Eisenman, S. F. (1996) 'Triangulating racism'. *Art Bulletin*, 78(4): 607.

72 Walby, S. (2003) 'The myth of the nation-state: theorizing society and polities in a global era'. *Sociology* 37(3): 529–46.

73 Ting, H. (2008) 'Social construction of nation: a theoretical exploration'. *Nationalism & Ethnic Politics* 14(3): 453–82.

74 Andrews, K. (2018) *Back to Black: Retelling Black Radicalism for the 21st Century*. London: Zed Books.

2 GENOCIDE

1 Hitchman, S. (2020) 'Columbus statues are coming down – why he is so offensive to Native Americans'. *The Conversation*, 9 July. Available at https://theconversation.com/columbus-statues-are-coming-down-why-he-is-so-offensive-to-native-americans-141144

2 Trump, D. (2020) 'Remarks by President Trump at South Dakota's 2020 Mount Rushmore fireworks celebration' at Keystone, South Dakota. 4 July.

3 (1992) 'Columbus Day parade canceled to avoid protests'. *LA Times*, 11 October.

4 Doumar, K. (2018) 'Goodbye, Columbus Day'. *Citylab*, 8 October.

5 Bigelow, B. (1992) 'Review: once upon a genocide: Christopher Columbus in children's literature'. *Social Justice* 19(2): 106–21.

6 Sertima, I. (1976) *They Came Before Columbus: The African Presence in North America*. New York: Random House.

7 Balababova, S., Parsche, F. and Pirsig, W. (1992) 'First identification of drugs in Egyptian mummies'. *Naturwissenschaften* 79: 358.

8 Kehoe, A. B. (1998) *The Land of Prehistory: A Critical History of American Archaeology*. London: Routledge.

9 Wiener, L. (2012) *Africa and the Discovery of America: Volume 1*. Philadelphia: Innes and Sons, 34.

10 Thornton, R. (1987) *American Indian Holocaust and Survival: A Population History Since 1492*. Norman: University of Oklahoma.

11 Hinton, A. (2008) 'Savages, subjects and sovereigns: conjunctions of modernity, genocide and colonialism' in Moses, D. (ed.) *Empire, Colony and Genocide: Conquest, Occupation and Subaltern Resistance in World History*. Oxford: Berghahn Books.

12 Tinker, G. E. and Freeland, M. (2008) 'Thief, slave trader, murderer: Christopher Columbus and Caribbean population decline'. *Wicazo Sa Review* 23(1): 25–50.

13 Thornton, *American Indian Holocaust*, 79.

14 Hinton, 'Savages', 442.

15 Tinker and Freeland, 'Thief, slave trader'.

16 Ibid., 41.

17 Beckles, H. (2013) *Britain's Black Debt: Reparations of Caribbean Slavery and Native Genocide*. Kingston: University of the West Indies Press.

18 Ibid., 33.

19 Washington, G. (1985) *The Papers of George Washington: Revolutionary War Series, Volume 20*. Charlottesville: University of Virginia Press, 717.

20 Thornton, *American Indian Holocaust*, 110.

21 Ibid., 199.

22 Wolfe, P. (2006) 'Settler colonialism and the elimination of the native'. *Journal of Genocide Research*, 8(4): 388.

23 Thornton, *American Indian Holocaust*.

24 Madley, B. (2004) 'Patterns of frontier genocide 1803–1910: the Aboriginal Tasmanians, the Yuki of California, and the Herero of Namibia'. *Journal of Genocide Research* 6(2): 168–9.

25 Ibid., 179.

26 Rogers, T. and Bain, S. (2016) 'Genocide and frontier violence in Australia'. *Journal of Genocide Research* 18(1): 85.

27 Barta, T. (1987) 'Relations of genocide: land and lives in the colonization of Australia' in Wallimann, I. and Dobkowski, M. (eds), *Genocide and the Modern Age*. New York: Greenwood, 238.

28 Moses, D. (2008) 'Moving the genocide debate beyond the history wars'. *Australian Journal of Politics and History* 54(2): 248–70.

29 Barta, 'Relations of genocide', 243.

30 Rogers and Bain, 'Genocide and frontier violence', 87.

31 Ibid., 88.

32 Moses, 'Moving the genocide debate', 253.

33 Tatz, C. (1999) 'Genocide in Australia'. *Journal of Genocide Research* 1(3): 325.

34 Markus, A. (2001) 'Genocide in Australia'. *Aboriginal History* 25: 63.

35 Tatz, C. (2001) 'Confronting Australian genocide'. *Aboriginal History* 25: 23.

36 Barta, 'Relations of genocide', 245.

37 Ibid.

38 O'Malley, P. (1994) 'Gentle genocide: the government of aboriginal peoples in Central Australia'. *Social Justice* 21(4): 1.

39 Ibid., 4.

40 Batrop, P. (2001) 'The Holocaust, the Aborigines, and the bureaucracy of destruction: an Australian dimension of genocide'. *Journal of Genocide Research* 3(1): 75–87.

41 Elinghaus, K. (2009) 'Biological absorption and genocide: a comparison of indigenous assimilation policies in the United States and Australia'. *Genocide Studies and Prevention* 4(1): 67.

42 Ibid., 68.

43 (1997) *Bringing Them Home: Report of the National Inquiry into the Separation of Aboriginal and Torres Strait Islander Children from Their Families* [Commissioner: Ronald Wilson]. Human Rights and Equal Opportunity Commission: Sydney, 368.

44 Tatz, 'Confronting Australian genocide', 19.

45 Davis, J. (2001) 'American Indian boarding school experiences: recent studies from native perspectives'. *Magazine of History* 15(2): 20–22.

46 Batrop, 'The Holocaust, the Aborigines', 87.

47 Madley, 'Patterns of frontier genocide', 183.

48 Ibid., 187.

49 Ibid., 188.

50 Schaller, D. (2008) 'From conquest to genocide: colonial rule in German Southwest Africa and German East Africa' in Moses, *Empire, Colony and Genocide*, 309.

51 Sarkin, J. and Fowler, C. (2008) 'Reparations for historical human rights violations: the international and historical dimensions of the Alien Torts Claims Act genocide case of the Herero of Namibia'. *Human Rights Review* 9: 331–60.

52 Kössler, R. (2005) 'From genocide to Holocaust? Structural parallels and discursive continuities'. *Afrika Spectrum* 40(2): 313.

53 Ibid.

54 Lemkin, R. (1946) 'Genocide'. *American Scholar* 15(2): 227.

55 Bauman, Z. (1989) *Modernity and the Holocaust*. Cambridge: Polity, 16.

56 Ibid., 17.

57 Grosfoguel, Ramón (2013) 'The structure of knowledge in westernized universities: epistemic racism/sexism and the four genocides/epistemicides of the long 16th century'. *Human Architecture: Journal of the Sociology of Self-Knowledge,* 11(1/8): 83.

58 Badru, P. (2010) 'Ethnic conflict and state formation in post-colonial Africa. A comparative study of ethnic genocide in the Congo, Liberia, Nigeria and Rwanda-Burundi'. *Journal of Third World Studies* 27(2): 149–69.

59 Hochschild, A. (1999) *King Leopold's Ghost: A Story of Greed, Terror, and Heroism in Colonial Africa*. New York: Mariner, 44.

60 Ibid.

61 Ward, T. (2005) 'State crime in the heart of darkness'. *British Journal of Criminology* 45(4): 439.

62 Kevorkian, R. (2011) *The Armenian Genocide: A Complete History*. London: I. B. Tauris.

63 Ward, 'State crime', 437.

64 Presse, A. (2017) 'Germany to investigate 1,000 skulls taken from African colonies for "racial research"'. *Guardian*, 6 October.

65 Saini, A. (2019) *Superior: The Return of Race Science*. Boston: Beacon Press, 47.

66 Painter, N. (2011) *The History of White People*. New York: W. W. Norton Company, 268.

67 Semujanga, J. (2003) *Origins of Rwandan Genocide*. Montreal, Canada.

68 Clinton, B. (1998) 'Rwanda speech' at Kigali International Airport. 25 March.

69 Carrol, R. (2004) 'US chose to ignore Rwandan genocide'. *Guardian*, 31 March.

70 Epstein, H. (2017) 'America's secret role in the Rwandan genocide'. *Guardian*, 12 September.

71 Mamdani, M. (2001) *When Victims Become Killers: Colonialism, Nativism, and the Genocide in Rwanda*. Princeton: Princeton University Press.

72 Ibid., 88.

73 Nubia, O. (2019) *England's Other Countrymen: Black Tudor Society*. London: Zed Books.

74 Mamdani, *When Victims Become Killers*, 79.

3 SLAVERY

1 Hall, C., Draper, N., McClelland, K., Donnington, K. and Lang, R. (2014) *Legacies of British Slave-Ownership: Colonial Slavery and the Formation of Victorian Britain*. Oxford: Oxford University Press, 140–41.

2 Sir Charles Grey in ibid., p. 140.

3 Olusoga, D. (2016) *Black and British: A Forgotten History*. London: Macmillan.

4 Ibid.

5 Hunter, T. (2019) 'When slaveowners got reparations'. *New York Times*, 16 April.

6 Darity, W. (2008) 'Forty acres and a mule in the 21st century'. *Social Science Quarterly* 89(3): 656–64.

7 Visit https://www.ucl.ac.uk/lbs/ for the searchable database.

8 Mason, R. (2015) 'Jamaica should "move on from painful legacy of slavery", says Cameron'. *Guardian*, 30 September.

9 Hall *et al.*, *Legacies*, 101.

10 Malachy Postlethwayt in Williams, E. (1964) *Capitalism and Slavery*. London: Andre Deutsch, 51.

11 Ibid., 104.

12 Rawlinson, K. (2020) 'Lloyd's of London and Greene King to make slave trade reparations'. *Guardian*, 18 June.

13 Groark, V. (2002) 'Slave policies'. *New York Times*, 5 May.

14 Beckles, H. and Downes, A. (1987) 'The economics of the transition to the black labour system in Barbados, 1630–80'. *Journal of Interdisciplinary History* 18: 505–22.

15 Thomas, H. (2006) *The Slave Trade: The History of the Atlantic Slave Trade, 1440–1870*. Chatham: Phoenix.

16 Batie, R. (1976) 'Why sugar? Economic cycles and the changing staples of the English and French Antilles'. *Journal of Caribbean History* 8: 1–41.

17 Walvin, J. (1992) *Black Ivory: A History of British Slavery*. Washington, DC: Howard University Press.

18 Rodney, W. (1972) *How Europe Underdeveloped Africa*. London: Bogle-L'Ouverture Books, 99.

19 Satchell, V. (2000) 'The early use of steam power in the Jamaican sugar industry, 1768–1810' in Beckles, H. and Shepherd, V. (eds) *Caribbean Slavery and the Atlantic World*. Kingston: Ian Randle, 518–26.

20 Olusoga, *Black and British*.

21 Williams, *Capitalism and Slavery*.

22 Rodney, *How Europe*, 96.

23 Engerman, S. (1972) 'The slave trade and British capital formation in the eighteenth century: a comment on the Williams thesis'. *Business History Review* 46(4): 430–43.

24 Thomas, *Slave Trade*.

25 Williams, *Capitalism and Slavery*.

26 Thomas, R. and Bean, R. (1974) 'Fishers of men: the profits of the slave trade'. *Journal of Economic History* 34(4): 885–914.

27 Diouf, S. (2004) 'The last resort: redeeming family and friends' in Diouf, S. (ed.) *Fighting the Slave Trade: West African Strategies*. Athens: Ohio University Press.

28 Ibid.

29 Ekiyor, H. (2007) 'Making a case for reparations'. *Journal of Pan African Studies* 1(9): 103–16.

30 Thomas, *Slave Trade*.

31 de Kok, G. (2016) 'Cursed capital: the economic impact of the transatlantic slave trade on Walcheren around 1770'. *TSEG* 13(3): 1–27.

32 Williams, *Capitalism and Slavery*.

33 Eltis, D. and Engerman, S. (2000) 'The importance of slavery and the slave trade to industrializing Britain'. *Journal of Economic History* 60(1): 123.

34 Williams, *Capitalism and Slavery*.

35 Ibid.

36 Ibid., 82.

37 Ibid., 84.

38 Eltis and Engerman, 'Importance of slavery', 135.

39 Thomas and Bean, 'Fishers of men'.

40 Clarke, J. H. (1998) *Christopher Columbus and the Afrikan Holocaust: Slavery and the Rise of European Capitalism*. Buffalo: E-World Inc., 15.

41 Russell-Wood, A. (1995) 'Before Columbus: Portugal's African prelude to the middle passage and contribution to discourse on race and slavery' in Beckles and Shepherd, *Caribbean Slavery*, 11–32.

42 Thomas, *Slave Trade*.

43 Klein, H. (1972) 'The Portuguese slave trade from Angola in the eighteenth century'. *Journal of Economic History* 32(4): 894–918.

44 Thomas, *Slave Trade*, 185.

45 Batie, 'Why sugar?'.

46 Kopperman, P. (1987) 'Ambivalent allies: Anglo–Dutch relations and the struggle against the Spanish empire in the Caribbean, 1621–1641'. *Journal of Caribbean History* 21(1): 55–77.

47 Rodney, *How Europe*.

48 James, C. L. R. (2001) *The Black Jacobins*. London: Penguin.

49 Rodney, *How Europe*.

50 James, *Black Jacobins*, 47.

51 Evans, C. and Rydén, G. (2013) 'From Gammelbo Bruk to Calabar: Swedish iron in an expanding Atlantic economy' in Naum, M. and Nordin, J. (eds) *Scandinavian Colonialism and the Rise of Modernity*. Springer: New York.

52 Thomas, *Slave Trade*.

53 Anderson, A. (2013) '"We have reconquered the islands": figurations in public memories of slavery and colonialism in Denmark 1948–2012'. *International Journal of Political and Cultural Sociology* 26: 69.

54 James, *Black Jacobins*.

55 Thomas and Bean, 'Fishers of men', 892.

56 James, *Black Jacobins*.

57 Dadzie, S. (2020) *A Kick in the Belly: Women, Slavery and Resistance*. London: Verso.

58 Knight, F. (1970) *Slave Society in Cuba during the Nineteenth Century*. Madison: University of Wisconsin Press.

59 Thomas, *Slave Trade*.

60 Wright, M. (2015) *Physics of Blackness: Beyond the Middle Passage Epistemology*. Minneapolis: University of Minnesota Press.

61 Walvin, *Black Ivory*, 34.

62 Krikler, J. (2007). 'The Zong and the Lord Chief Justice'. *History Workshop Journal* 64: 37.

63 Walvin, *Black Ivory*.

64 Inkiori, J. (2003) 'The struggle against the Atlantic slave trade: the role of the state' in Diouf, *Fighting the Slave Trade*, 170–98.

65 Anievas, A. and Nişancıoğlu, K. (2015) *How the West Came to Rule: The Geopolitical Origins of Capitalism*. London: Pluto Press, 155.

66 Wright, J. (2007) *The Trans-Saharan Slave Trade*. Abingdon: Routledge, 167.

67 Ibid., 5.

68 Russell-Wood, 'Before Columbus', 25.

69 Wright, *Trans-Saharan Slave Trade*, 167.

70 Ibid., 20.

71 Olusoga, *Black and British*.

72 Ibid.

73 Beckles, H. (2007) '"Slavery was a long, long time ago": remembrance, reconciliation and the reparations discourse in the Caribbean'. *ARIEL* 38(1): 22.

74 Ibid.

75 Darity, W. and Frank, D. (2003) 'The economics of reparations'. *American Economic Review* 93(2): 326.

76 Beckles, 'Slavery'.

77 Craemer, T. (2018) 'International reparations for slavery and the slave trade'. *Journal of Black Studies* 49(7): 694–713.

4 COLONIALISM

1 Mondelez (2018) 'Cadbury 2017 fact sheet'. Available at https://au. mondelezinternational.com/~/media/MondelezCorporate/Uploads/down loads/cadbury_fact_sheet.pdf

2 Cadbury (n.d.) 'Fact sheet – Bournville site'. Available at https://www. cadburyworld.co.uk/schoolandgroups/~/media/CadburyWorld/en/Files/ Pdf/factsheet-bournville-site.pdf

3 Ibid.

4 Nieburg, O. (2018) 'How will the chocolate industry approach cocoa farmer "living income"?' *Confectionery News*, 3 May. Available at https://www.confectionerynews.com/Article/2018/05/03/How-will-the-chocolate-industry-approach-cocoa-farmer-living-income

5 Nkrumah, K. (1998) *Africa Must Unite*. London: Panaf Books, 27.

6 Nieburg, 'How will the chocolate industry'.

7 Rodney, W. (1972) *How Europe Underdeveloped Africa*. London: Bogle-L'Ouverture Books.

8 Ibid., 29.

9 Ibid., 228.

10 Ayokhai, F. and Rufai, B. (2017) 'West African women and the development question in the post World War Two economy: the experience of Nigeria's Benin province in the palm oil industry'. *Journal of Global South Studies* 34(1): 72–95.

11 Rodney, *How Europe*, 182.

12 Ibid.

13 Kemp, K. (2019) 'Unilever turnover dips in "challenging market conditions"' *Insider.co.uk*, 31 January. Available at https://www.insider. co.uk/company-results-forecasts/unilever-shares-dove-vaseline-profits-13932365

14 Rodney, *How Europe*, 182.

15 Li, T. (2017) 'The price of un/freedom: Indonesia's colonial and contemporary plantation labor regimes'. *Comparative Studies in Society and History* 59(2): 245.

16 Koh, L. P. and Wilcove, D. S. (2007) 'Cashing in palm oil for conservation'. *Nature* 448(30): 993–4.

17 Li, 'Price of un/freedom', 250.

18 Ibid., 253.

19 Ibid., 269.

20 Nkrumah, *Africa Must Unite*, 35.

21 Rodney, *How Europe*.

22 Lassou, P., Hopper, T., Tsamenyi, M. and Murinde, V. (2019) 'Varieties of neo-colonialism: government accounting reforms in anglophone and francophone Africa – Benin and Ghana compared'. *Social and Environmental Accountability Journal* 39(3): 207–8.

23 Kieh, G. (2012) 'Neo-colonialism: American foreign policy and the first Liberian civil war'. *Journal of Pan African Studies* 5(1): 164–84.

24 Rodney, *How Europe*.

25 Lassou *et al.*, 'Varieties of neo-colonialism', 17.

26 Rodney, *How Europe*, 287.

27 Nkrumah, *Africa Must Unite*.

28 Rodney, *How Europe*.

29 Malcolm X (1963) 'Message to the grassroots'. Speech at the Negro Grass Roots Leadership Conference, Michigan, 10 November.

30 Nzongola-Ntalaja, G. (2011) 'Patrice Lumumba: the most important assassination of the 20th century'. *Guardian*, 17 January.

31 Schama, S. (2009) *A History of Britain: The Fate of Empire 1776–2000*. London: The Bodley Head, 196.

32 Tharoor, S. (2016) *Inglorious Empire: What the British Did to India*. London: Penguin.

33 Frankopan, P. (2015) *The Silk Roads: A New History of the World*. London: Bloomsbury.

34 Ibid., 227.

35 Huntingdon, S. (1996) *The Clash of Civilizations and the Remaking of World Order*. London: Simon and Schuster.

36 Said, E. (1979) *Orientalism*. New York: Vintage Books, 3.

37 Ibid.

38 Tharoor, *Inglorious Empire*.

39 Frankopan, *Silk Roads*, 277.

40 James, C. L. R. (2001) *The Black Jacobins*. London: Penguin.

41 Tharoor, *Inglorious Empire*.

42 Arnold, D. (1986) 'Cholera and colonialism in British India'. *Past & Present* 113: 118–51.

43 Tharoor, *Inglorious Empire*, 55.

44 Mukerjee, M. (2010) *Churchill's Secret War: The British Empire and the Ravaging of India During World War II*. New York: Basic Books, 347.

45 Tharoor, *Inglorious Empire*, 155.

46 (2017) 'Good news! India will win over illiteracy by 2021'. *India Today*, 7 August. Available at https://www.indiatoday.in/education-today/news/story/illiteracy-removed-by-2021-1028222-2017-08-07

47 Unicef (n.d.) 'India: country profile'. Available at https://data.unicef.org/country/ind/

48 Bennett, J. (1999) 'The confederate bazaar at Liverpool'. *Crossfire: The Magazine of the American Civil War* 61. Available at http://www.acwrt.org.uk/uk-heritage_The-Confederate-Bazaar-at-Liverpool.asp

49 Olusoga, D. (2016) *Black and British: A Forgotten History*. London: Macmillan.

50 Guyatt, N. (2016) *Bind Us Apart: How Enlightened Americans Invented Racial Segregation*. Oxford: Oxford University Press.

51 Kieh, 'Neo-colonialism', 169.

52 Adogamhe, P. (2008) 'Pan-Africanism revisited: vision and reality of African unity and development'. *African Review of Integration* 2(2): 1–34.

53 Kieh, 'Neo-colonialism'.

54 Turse, N. (2018) 'U.S. military says it has a "light footprint" in Africa. These documents show a network of bases'. *The Intercept*, 1 December. Available at https://theintercept.com/2018/12/01/u-s-military-says-it-has-a-light-footprint-in-africa-these-documents-show-a-vast-network-of-bases/

55 Arimatéia da Cruz, J. and Stephen, L. (2010) The U.S. Africa Command (AFRICOM): building partnership or neo-colonialism of U.S.–Africa relations?' *Journal of Third World Studies* 27(2): 194.

56 Stiglitz, J. and Bilmes, L. (2008) *The Three Trillion Dollar War: The True Cost of the Iraq Conflict*. New York: W. W. Norton and Company.

57 McCulloch, J. and Pickering, S. (2005) 'Suppressing the financing of terrorism: proliferating state crime, eroding censure and extending neo-colonialism'. *British Journal of Criminology* 45: 478.

58 Ibid., 480.

59 Crawford, N. (2018) 'Human cost of the post-9/11 wars: lethality and the need for transparency'. Available at https://watson.brown.edu/costsofwar/papers/2018/human-cost-post-911-wars-lethality-and-need-transparency.

60 Bureau of Investigative Journalism database, 'Drone wars: the full data'. Available at https://www.thebureauinvestigates.com/stories/2017-01-01/drone-wars-the-full-data

61 Zabci, F. (2007) 'Private military companies: "shadow soldiers" of neo-colonialism'. *Capital and Class* 31(2): 1–10.

62 Fifield, A. (2013) 'Contractors reap $138bn from Iraq war'. *Financial Times*, 18 March.

5 DAWN OF A NEW AGE

1 Ferguson, N. (2004) *Colossus: The Price of America's Empire*. New York: Penguin Press, 198.

2 United Nations (1941) The Atlantic Charter. Available at: https://www.un.org/en/sections/history-united-nations-charter/1941-atlantic-charter/index.html

3 Malcolm X (1964) Speech at the 2nd Founding Rally of the OAAU. New York, 28 June.

4 Peet, R. (2007) *Unholy Trinity: The IMF, World Bank and WTO*. London: Zed Books, 28.

5 Boughton, J. M. (2004) 'The IMF and the force of history: ten events and ten ideas that have shaped the institution', 6. Available at elibrary. imf.org

6 Pahuja, S. (2000) 'Technologies of empire: IMF conditionality and the reinscription of the north/south divide'. *Leiden Journal of International Law* 13(4): 757.

7 Peet, *Unholy Trinity*.

8 Ibid., 73.

9 Forster, T., Kentikelenis, A., Reinsberg, B., Stubbs, T. and King, L. (2019) 'How structural adjustment programs affect inequality: A disaggregated analysis of IMF conditionality, 1980–2014'. *Social Science Research* 80: 83–113.

10 Ball, J. (2004) 'The effects of neoliberal structural adjustment on women's relative employment in Latin America'. *International Journal of Social Economics* 31: 974–87.

11 Goulas, E. and Zervoyianni, A. (2016) 'IMF-lending programs and suicide mortality'. *Social Science & Medicine* 153: 44–53.

12 Abouharb, M. and Cingranelli, D. (2009) 'IMF programs and human rights, 1981–2003'. *Review of International Organizations* 4: 47–72.

13 Harvey, D. (2005) *The New Imperialism*. Oxford: Oxford University Press, 67.

14 Pop-Eleches, G. (2008) *Crisis Politics: IMF Programs in Latin America and Eastern Europe*. Princeton: Princeton University Press.

15 Harvey, *New Imperialism*, 66.

16 Bergoeing, R., Kehoe, P., Kehoe, T. and Soto, R. (2002) 'A decade lost and found: Mexico and Chile in the 1980s'. *Review of Economic Dynamics* 5: 167.

17 Pop-Eleches, *Crisis Politics*, 134.

18 Ibid., 158.

19 Stone, R. (2004) 'The political economy of IMF lending in Africa'. *American Political Science Review* 98(4): 577–91.

20 Dreher, A. and Sturm, J. (2012) 'Do the IMF and the World Bank influence voting in the UN General Assembly?'. *Public Choice* 151: 363–97.

21 Stiglitz, J. (2017) *Globalization and its Discontents Revisited: Anti-globalization in the Era of Trump*. London: Penguin, 185.

22 Ibid., 191.

23 Collins, C. and Rhoads, A. (2010) 'The World Bank, support for universities, and asymmetrical power relations in international development'. *Higher Education* 59: 184.

24 Williamson, J. (2004) 'The Washington consensus as policy prescription for development'. Lecture at the World Bank, January 2004, 13.

25 Glewwe, P. and de Tray, D. (1989) 'The poor in Latin America during adjustment: a case study of Peru'. *Living Standards Measurement Study Working Paper No. 56*. Washington, DC: World Bank.

26 Stiglitz, *Globalization*.

27 Hardt, M. and Negri, A. (2000) *Empire*. Cambridge, MA: Harvard University Press, 175.

28 Easterly, W. (2006) *The White Man's Burden: Why the West's Efforts to Aid the Rest Have Done So Much Ill and So Little Good*. Oxford: Oxford University Press.

29 Ibid.

30 United Nations (2015) *The Millennium Development Goals Report*. New York: United Nations.

31 Pinker, S. (2019) *Enlightenment Now: The Case for Reason, Science, Humanism, and Progress*. New York: Penguin, 6.

32 Harris, S. (2010) *The Moral Landscape: How Science Can Determine Human Values*. New York: The Free Press.

33 Rosling, H. and Rosling, O. and Rönnlund, A. (2008) *Factfulness*. London: Hodder and Stoughton.

34 World Bank (2019) *Poverty*. Available at https://www.worldbank.org/en/topic/poverty/overview

35 UN, *Millennium*, 8.

36 Ayres, R. (1983) *Banking on the Poor: The World Bank and World Poverty*. Cambridge, MA: MIT Press, 81.

37 Warner, M. (2017) 'Is development aid the new colonialism?'. *Foundation for Economic Education*, 28 September.

38 Williams, Z. (2017) 'The UK peddles a cynical colonialism and calls it aid'. *Guardian*, 23 July.

39 Pahuja, 'Technologies of empire', 751.

40 Chakrabortty, A. (2016) 'A death foretold: watch as Priti Patel trashes our proud record on aid'. *Guardian*, 23 August.

41 Elliott, L. (2017) 'Impact of UK foreign aid diluted by pursuing national interest, says IFS'. *Guardian*, 8 May.

42 Noxolo, P. (2011) 'Postcolonial leadership: a discursive analysis of the Conservative Green Paper "A Conservative agenda for international development"'. *Area* 43(4): 509.

43 Williams, 'UK peddles a cynical colonialism'.

44 Provost, C., Dodwell, A. and Scrivener, A. (2016) *The Privatisation of UK Aid: How Adam Smith International Is Profiting from the Aid Budget*. London: Aidwatch.

45 Department for Business, Energy and Industrial Strategy (2017) *Policy Paper: Global Challenges Research Fund (GCRF): How the Fund Works*. Available at https://www.gov.uk/government/publications/global-challenges-research-fund/global-challenges-research-fund-gcrf-how-the-fund-works

46 UK Research and Innovation, 'Global Challenges Research Fund, funded projects'. Available at https://www.ukri.org/research/global-challenges-research-fund/funded-projects/

47 Easterly, *White Man's Burden*, 239.

48 Hardt and Negri, *Empire*, 175.

49 Bush, G. W. (2005) Speech at Fort Bragg, North Carolina. 29 June.

50 Easterly, *White Man's Burden*, 273.

51 Mearsheimer, J. and Walt, S. (2009) 'Is it love or the lobby? Explaining America's special relationship with Israel'. *Security Studies* 18(1): 58–78.

52 Green, E, (2016) 'Why does the United States give so much money to Israel?'. *The Atlantic*, 15 September.

53 Syal, R. and Asthana, A. (2017) 'Priti Patel forced to resign over un-official meetings with Israelis'. *Guardian*, 8 November.

54 Hiernaux, J. and Banton, M. (1969) *Four Statements on the Race Question*. Paris: UNESCO.

55 Pappé, I. (2008) 'Zionism as colonialism: a comparative view of diluted colonialism in Asia and Africa'. *South Atlantic Quarterly* 107(4): 617.

56 Text available at https://avalon.law.yate.edu/20th_century/balfour.asp

57 Ibid., 66.

58 Ibid., 77.

59 Chomsky, N. (1999) *Fateful Triangle: The United States, Israel and the Palestinians*. London: Pluto, 95.

60 Ibid., 96.

61 Little, D. (1993) 'The making of a special relationship: the United States and Israel, 1957–68'. *International Journal of Middle East Studies* 25(4): 575.

62 Mearsheimer, J. and Walt, S. (2006) 'The Israel lobby'. *London Review of Books* 28(6): 4.

63 Roth, A. (2009) 'Reassurance: a strategic basis of U.S. support for Israel'. *International Studies Perspectives* 10(4): 379.

64 Mearsheimer and Walt, 'Israel lobby'.

65 Little, 'Making of a special relationship', 580.

6 THE NON-WHITE WEST

1 United States Census Bureau (2019) 'Trade in goods with China'. Available at https://www.census.gov/foreign-trade/balance/c5700.html

2 McNally, C. (2012) 'Sino-capitalism: China's re-emergence and the international political economy'. *World Politics* 64(4): 741–76.

3 Adem, S. (2010) 'The paradox of China's policy in Africa'. *African and Asian Studies* 9(3): 334.

4 Ikenberry, J. (2008) 'The rise of China and the future of the West: can the liberal system survive?'. *Foreign Affairs* 87(1): 24.

5 Lumumba-Kasongo, T. (2011) 'China–Africa relations: a neo-imperialism or a neo-colonialism? A reflection'. *African and Asian Studies* 10(2): 248.

6 Pinghui, Z. (2019) 'Chinese in disbelief that a US$295 monthly salary makes them "middle class"'. *South China Morning Post*, 27 January.

7 Archberger, J. (2010) 'The dragon has not just arrived: the historical study of Africa's relations with China'. *History Compass* 8(5): 368–76.

8   Kelley, R. and Esch, B. (1999) 'Black like Mao: red China and black revolution' in Ho, F. and Mullen, B. (eds) *Afro Asia: Revolutionary and Political Connections Between African Americans and Asian Americans*. Durham, NC: Duke University Press, 98.

9   Seale, B. (1970) *Seize the Time: The Story of the Black Panther Party*. New York: Random House.

10 Newton, H. P. (1974) *Revolutionary Suicide*. London: Wildwood House, 333.

11 French, H. (2014) *China's Second Continent: How a Million Migrants are Building a New Empire in Africa*. New York: Vintage Books.

12 French, H. (2014) 'Why 1 million Chinese migrants are building a new empire in Africa'. *Quartz Africa*, 10 June. Available at https://qz.com/ 217597/how-a-million-chinese-migrants-are-building-a-new-empire-in-africa

13 Campbell, H. (2008) 'China in Africa: challenging US global hegemony'. *Third World Quarterly* 29(1): 104.

14 Antwi-Boateng, O. (2017) 'New world order neo-colonialism: a contextual comparison of contemporary China and European colonization in Africa'. *Africology: The Journal of Pan African Studies* 10(2): 191.

15 Moyo, D. (2010) *Dead Aid: Why Aid Is Not Working and How There Is Another Way in Africa*. London: Penguin.

16 Antwi-Boateng, 'New world order neo-colonialism', 191.

17 Kabamba, B. (2015) 'China–DRC: a convergence of interests?' in Wouters, J., Defraigne, J. and Burnay, M. (eds) *China, the European Union and Developing World: A Triangular Relationship*. Cheltenham: Edward Elgar, 417.

18 Olopade, D. (2008) 'China's long march across Africa'. *The Root*, 7 August.

19 Adem, 'The paradox'.

20 Lumumba-Kasongo, 'China–Africa relations'.

21 Nkrumah, K. (1998) *Africa Must Unite*. London: Panaf Books, 27.

22 French, *China's Second Continent*.

23 Burgis, T. (2016) *The Looting Machine: Warlords, Tycoons, Smugglers and the Systematic Theft of Africa's Wealth*. London: William Collins.

24 French, *China's Second Continent*.

25 Ibid., 17.

26 Ibid., 113.

27 Taylor, I. (2014) *Africa Rising?: BRICS – Diversifying Dependency*. Woodbridge: James Currey.

28 Burgis, *Looting Machine*.
29 Wengraf, L. (2018) *Extracting Profit: Imperialism, Neoliberalism, and the New Scramble for Africa*. Chicago: Haymarket, 142.
30 Taylor, *Africa Rising?*, 125.
31 Ibid.
32 World Bank (n.d.) 'Physicians (per 1,000 people)'. Available at https://data.worldbank.org/indicator/SH.MED.PHYS.ZS?locations=ZA
33 Silver, L. and Johnson, C. (2018) 'Majorities in sub-Saharan Africa own mobile phones, but smartphone adoption is modest'. *Pew Research Centre*, 9 October. Available at https://www.pewresearch.org/global/2018/10/09/majorities-in-sub-saharan-africa-own-mobile-phones-but-smartphone-adoption-is-modest/
34 Taylor, *Africa Rising?*
35 Ibid.
36 Phillips, T. (2011) 'Portuguese migrants seek a slice of Brazil's economic boom'. *Guardian*, 22 December.
37 McKinsey Global Institute (2010) *Lions on the Move: The Progress and Potential of African Economies*. Available at https://www.mckinsey.com/~/media/McKinsey/Featured%20Insights/Middle%20East%20and%20Africa/Lions%20on%20the%20move/MGI_Lions_on_the_move_african_economies_Exec_Summary.ashx
38 Robertson, B. and Pinstrup-Andersen, P. (2010) 'Global land acquisition: neo-colonialism or development opportunity?'. *Food Security* 2(3): 271.
39 Li, T. (2017) 'The price of un/freedom: Indonesia's colonial and contemporary plantation labor regimes'. *Comparative Studies in Society and History* 59(2): 245–76.
40 Laishley, R. (2014) 'Is Africa's land up for grabs?'. *Africa Renewal*. Available at https://www.un.org/africarenewal/magazine/special-edition-agriculture-2014/africa's-land-grabs
41 Li, 'Price of un/freedom'.
43 Ibid., 272.
43 Anievas, A. and Nişancıoğlu, K. (2015) *How the West Came to Rule: The Geopolitical Origins of Capitalism*. London: Pluto Press, 145.
44 World Bank (n.d.) 'GDP annual growth (%)'. Available at https://data.worldbank.org/indicator/NY.GDP.MKTP.KD.ZG?locations=ZG
45 World Bank (n.d.) 'Unemployment, total (% of total labor force) (national estimate)'. Available at https://data.worldbank.org/indicator/SL.UEM.TOTL.NE.ZS?locations=ZA

46 International Bank for Reconstruction and Development (2018) *Overcoming Poverty and Inequality in South Africa: An Assessment of Drivers, Constraints and Opportunities*. Washington, DC: World Bank. Available at https://openknowledge.worldbank.org/handle/10986/29614

47 Burgis, *Looting Machine*.

48 United Nations (n.d.) 'Population'. Available at https://www.un.org/en/sections/issues-depth/population/

49 French, *China's Second Continent*.

50 World Bank (2019) 'The World Bank in Africa'. Available at https://www.worldbank.org/en/region/afr/overview

51 Wengraf, *Extracting Profit*.

52 de Maria, B. (2008) 'Neo-colonialism through measurement: a critique of the corruption perception index'. *Critical Perspectives on International Business* 4(2/3): 184–202.

53 Ndikumana, L. and Boyce, J. (2018) *Captial Flight from Africa: Updated Methodology and New Estimates*. University of Amherst: PERI Research Report.

54 Wengraf, *Extracting Profit*.

55 Burgis, *Looting Machine*.

56 Osborne, H. (2020) 'What are the Luanda leaks?'. *Guardian*, 20 January.

57 Burgis, *Looting Machine*, 19.

58 Wengraf, *Extracting Profit*, 208.

59 Ibid., 204.

60 Global Witness (2019) 'New analysis shows Shell and Eni used Nigeria's share of oil to fund alleged billion dollar bribery scheme'. Press release, 25 April. Available at https://www.globalwitness.org/en/press-releases/new-analysis-shows-shell-and-eni-used-nigerias-share-of-oil-to-fund-alleged-billion-dollar-bribery-scheme/

61 Burgis, *Looting Machine*, 190.

62 Angeles, L. and Neandis, K. (2015) 'The persistent effect of colonialism on corruption'. *Economica* 82: 322.

63 Witte, L. (2001) *The Assassination of Lumumba*. London: Verso.

64 Smith, D. (2015) 'Where Concorde once flew: the story of President Mobutu's "African Versailles"'. *Guardian*, 10 February.

65 Burgis, *Looting Machine*.

66 Ibid., 27.

67 Rich, T. and Recker, S. (2013) 'Understanding Sino-African relations: neocolonialism or a new era?'. *Journal of International and Area Studies* 20(1): 61–76.

68 Burgis, *Looting Machine*.

69 Alemazung, J. (2010) 'Post-colonial colonialism: an analysis of international factors and actors marring African socio-economic and political development'. *Journal of Pan African Studies* 3(10): 68.

70 Easterly, W. (2006) *The White Man's Burden: Why the West's Efforts to Aid the Rest Have Done So Much Ill and So Little Good*. Oxford: Oxford University Press, 242.

71 Ibid.

72 Yates, D. (2008) 'French puppet, Chinese strings? Sino-Gabonese relations' in Ampiah, K. and Naidu, S. (eds) *Crouching Tiger, Hidden Dragon?: Africa and China*. Scottsville: University of Kwazulu-Natal Press.

73 Kakar, A. (2017) 'Why is Gabon poor when the country is rich in natural resources?'. *The Borgen Project*, 9 October. Available at https://borgen-project.org/why-is-gabon-poor-despite-natural-resources/

74 Gevisser, M. (2019) '"State capture": the corruption investigation that has shaken South Africa'. *Guardian*, 11 July.

75 Chutel, L. (2017) 'Post-apartheid South Africa is failing the very people it liberated'. *Quartz Africa*, 25 August. Available at https://qz.com/africa/1061461/post-apartheid-south-africa-is-failing-the-very-people-it-liberated/

7 IMPERIAL DEMOCRACY

1 Philbeck, T. and Davis, N. (2019) 'The fourth industrial revolution: shaping a new era'. *Journal of International Affairs* 72(1): 17.

2 Schwab, K. (2016) *The Fourth Industrial Revolution*. Geneva: World Economic Forum, 9.

3 Caruso, L. (2018) 'Digital innovation and the fourth industrial revolution: epochal social changes?'. *AI & Society* 33: 379–92.

4 Sealey-Huggins, L. (2017) '"1.5°C to stay alive": climate change, imperialism and justice for the Caribbean'. *Third World Quarterly* 38(11): 2444–63.

5 Kelly, K. (2019) 'Naomi Klein is not here to make you feel better'. *Vice*, 23 September. Available at https://www.vice.com/en_us/article/3kxvg8/naomi-klein-is-not-here-to-make-you-feel-better

6 Klein, N. (2020) *On Fire: The (Burning) Case for a Green New Deal*. New York: Simon and Schuster.

7 Sunrise Movement (2019) 'Ready for a green new deal: your guide to build an unstoppable movement to bring a new day to America'. Available at https://drive.google.com/file/d/1zYfPG3I8VNKIGsGUGMDhACZT3DGZzKTs/view

8 Taylor, K. (2019) *Race for Profit: How Banks and the Real Estate Industry Undermined Black Homeownership*. Chapel Hill: UNC Press.

9 Klein, *On Fire*, loc 504.

10 https://berniesanders.com/issues/green-new-deal/

11 Bregman, R. (2017) *Utopia for Realists: And How We Get There*. Bloomsbury Audio Book, ch. 11, 8:25; ch. 10, 27:14; ch. 11, 3:29.

12 Ibid., ch. 1, 34:22.

13 Bastani, A. (2019) *Fully Luxury Automated Communism*. London: Verso, 189.

14 Robinson, C. J. (1983) *Black Marxism: The Making of the Black Radical Tradition*. London: Zed Books.

15 Robinson, C. (1992) 'C. L. R. James and the world-system'. *Race & Class* 34(2): 61.

16 Robinson, *Black Marxism*.

17 Bastani, *Fully Luxury Automated Communism*.

18 Ibid., 17.

19 Bregman, *Utopia for Realists*.

20 Mutwa, V. C. (1998) *Indaba My Children: African Tribal History*. Edinburgh: Payback Press.

21 Frankopan, P. (2019) *The New Silk Roads: The Present and Future of the World*. London: Bloomsbury.

22 Byler, D. (2019) 'China's hi-tech war on its Muslim minority'. *Guardian*, 11 April.

23 Caruso, L. (2018) 'Digital innovation', 390.

24 Sainato, M. (2020) '"I'm not a robot": Amazon workers condemn unsafe, grueling conditions at warehouse'. *Guardian*, 5 February.

25 Warren, K. (2020) 'Jeff Bezos is the only one of the world's five richest people who hasn't lost money in 2020. Here are 11 mind-blowing facts that show just how wealthy the Amazon CEO really is'. *Business Insider*, 1 April. Available at https://www.businessinsider.com/how-rich-is-jeff-bezos-mind-blowing-facts-net-worth-2019-4?r=US&IR=T

26 Raleigh, V. (2020) 'What is happening to life expectancy in the UK?'. *The King's Fund*. Available at https://www.kingsfund.org.uk/publications/whats-happening-life-expectancy-uk

27 Bregman, *Utopia for Realists*.

28 Ibid., ch. 9, 45.35.

29 https://data.worldbank.org/indicator/BX.TRF.PWKR.DT.GD.ZS?locations=JM

30 Andrews, K. (2018) *Back to Black: Retelling Black Radicalism for the 21st Century*. London: Zed Books.

31 Dodani, S. and LaPorte, R. E. (2005) 'Brain drain from developing countries: how can brain drain be converted into wisdom gain?' *Journal of the Royal Society of Medicine* 98(11): 487–91.

32 Bregman, *Utopia for Realists*, ch. 5. 12:39.

33 Standing, G. (2017) *Basic Income: And How We Can Make It Happen.* London: Penguin.

34 McFarland, K. (2017) 'Current basic income experiments (and those so called): an overview'. *Basic Income Earth Network*, 23 May. Available at https://basicincome.org/news/2017/05/basic-income-experiments-and-those-so-called-early-2017-updates/

35 Bastani, *Fully Luxury Automated Communism*, 225.

36 Wagner, P. and Rabuy, B. (2017) *Following the Money of Mass Incarceration.* Prison Policy Initiative. Available at https://www.prison policy.org/reports/money.html

37 McLaughlin, M. and Rank, M. (2018) 'Estimating the economic cost of childhood poverty in the United States'. *Social Work Research* 42(2): 73–83.

38 Fri, T. (2019) 'Poverty costs the U.S. more than UBI would'. *The Incomer*, 15 February. Available at https://www.theincomer.com/2019/02/15/poverty-costs-the-u-s-more-than-ubi-would/

39 Bregman, *Utopia for Realists*.

40 Ibid., ch. 11, 16:48.

41 Kavada, A. (2015) 'Creating the collective: social media, the Occupy movement and its constitution as a collective actor'. *Information, Communication & Society* 18(8): 872.

42 Da Silva, C. (2018) 'Has Occupy changed America?' *Newsweek*, 19 September.

43 Castañeda, E. (2012) 'The *indignados* of Spain: a precedent to Occupy Wall Street'. *Social Movement Studies* 11(3–4): 310.

44 Levitin, M. (2015) 'The triumph of Occupy Wall Street'. *The Atlantic*, 10 June.

45 (2011) 'Declaration of the occupation of New York City'. Available at http://uucsj.org/wp-content/uploads/2016/05/Declaration-of-the-Occupation-of-New-York-City.pdf

46 Kerton, S. (2012) 'Tahrir, here? The influence of the Arab uprisings on the emergence of Occupy'. *Social Movement Studies* 11(3–4): 307.

47 Halvorsen, S. (2012) 'Beyond the network? Occupy London and the global movement'. *Social Movement Studies*, 11(3–4): 427–33.

48 Calhoun, C. (2013) 'Occupy Wall Street in perspective'. *British Journal of Sociology* 64(1): 14.

49 Pickerill, J. and Krinsky, J. (2012) 'Why does Occupy matter?'. *Social Movement Studies* 11(3–4): 284.

50 Da Silva, C. (2018) 'Has Occupy changed America?'. *Newsweek*, 19 September.

51 Schwartz, M. (2011) 'Pre-occupied: the origins and future of Occupy Wall Street'. *New Yorker*, 21 November.

52 Piven, F. (2014) 'Interdependent power: strategizing for the Occupy movement'. *Current Sociology Monograph* 62(2): 225.

53 Halvorsen, 'Beyond the network?', 428.

54 Stoller. M. (2011) 'The anti-politics of #OccupyWallStreet'. *Naked Capitalism*, 6 October. Available at https://www.nakedcapitalism.com/2011/10/matt-stoller-the-anti-politics-of-occupywallstreet.html

55 Calhoun, C. (2013) 'Occupy Wall Street in perspective'. *British Journal of Sociology* 64(1): 33.

56 Schwartz, M., 'Pre-occupied'.

57 Ibid.

58 Jones, O. (2014) *The Establishment: And How They Get Away With It.* London: Penguin.

59 O'Neil, M. and Guinan, J. (2019) 'From community wealth building to system change: local roots for economic transformation'. *IPPR Progressive Review* 25(2): 387.

60 Cowburn, A. (2019) 'Labour manifesto: Corbyn vows to take on "wealthy and powerful" and save NHS from privatisation, as election pledges unveiled'. *Independent*, 21 November.

61 New Economics Foundation (2019) *Change the Rules: New Rules for the Economy.* London: New Economics Foundation. Available at https://neweconomics.org/2019/11/new-rules-for-the-economy

62 Ibid., 29.

63 O'Neil and Guinan, 'From community wealth', 384.

64 Beckett, A. (2019) 'The new left economics: how a network of thinkers is transforming capitalism'. *Guardian*, 25 June.

65 Jeffries, S. (2014) 'Britain's most racist election: the story of Smethwick, 50 years on'. *Guardian*, 15 October.

66 Virdee, S. (2000) 'A Marxist critique of Black radical theories of trade-union racism'. *Sociology* 34(3): 545–65.

8 CHICKENS COMING HOME TO ROOST

1 Gentleman, A. (2019) *The Windrush Betrayal: Exposing the Hostile Environment.* London: Guardian Faber.

2   Walker, P. (2018) 'Theresa May calls her response to Grenfell fire "not good enough"'. *Guardian*, 11 June.

3   Andrews, K. (2017) 'Theresa May is more dangerous than Donald Trump – video'. *Guardian*, 12 April.

4   Andrews, K. (2018) '"Beware the northern fox": keeping a focus on systematic racism post Trump and Brexit' in Joseph-Salisbury, R., Johnson, A. and Kamuge, B. (eds) *The Fire Now: Anti-Racist Scholarship in Times of Explicit Racial Violence*. London: Zed Books.

5   Malcolm X (1964) 'The ballot or the bullet'. Speech at King Solomon Baptist Church, Detroit, Michigan, 12 April.

6   BBC (2016) 'Boris Johnson's most controversial foreign insults'. *Newsbeat*, 14 July. Available at http://www.bbc.co.uk/newsbeat/article/36793900/boris-johnsons-most-controversial-foreign-insults

7   Proctor, K. (2019) 'Boris Johnson urged to apologise for "derogatory and racist" letterboxes article'. *Guardian*, 4 September.

8   BBC (2019) 'No-deal Brexit could cause £30bn economic hit, watchdog says'. *BBC News*, 18 July.

9   BBC (2019) 'Brexit: £2.1bn extra for no-deal planning'. *BBC News*, 1 August.

10 Du Bois, W. E. B. (1998) *Black Reconstruction in America: 1860–1880*. New York: The Free Press.

11 Ignatiev, N. (1997) 'The point is not to interpret Whiteness but to abolish it'. Available at https://www.pmpress.org/blog/2019/09/16/the-point-is-not-to-interpret-whiteness-but-to-abolish-it

12 Peet, R. (2007) *Unholy Trinity: The IMF, World Bank and WTO*. London: Zed Books.

13 Harvey, D. (2005) *The New Imperialism*. Oxford: Oxford University Press.

14 Thatcher, M. (1978) Interview for Granada's *World in Action*, 27 January.

15 Thatcher, M. (1987) included in 'Margaret Thatcher: a life in quotes'. *Guardian*, 8 April 2013.

16 Mason, R. (2015) 'Nigel Farage's HIV claim criticised by leaders' debate rivals'. *Guardian*, 3 April.

17 Andrews, K. (2016) 'Brexit and the racial fault line awakened in Britain'. *Ebony*, 29 June.

18 Levy, G. (2013) 'The man who hated Britain: Red Ed's pledge to bring back socialism is a homage to his Marxist father. So what did Miliband Snr really believe in? The answer should disturb everyone who loves this country'. *Daily Mail*, 27 September.

19 Murphy, J. (2014) 'Ed Miliband's battle with a bacon sandwich as he buys flowers for his wife at London market'. *Evening Standard*, 21 May.

20 Rawlinson, K. (2014) 'Farage blames immigration for traffic on M4 after no-show at Ukip reception'. *Guardian*, 7 December.

21 Jones, O. (2016) 'David Cameron's fatal mistakes on immigration threaten our country's future'. *Guardian*, 21 June.

22 Sivanandan, A. (2008) *Catching History on the Wing: Race, Culture and Globalisation*. London: Pluto Press, xi.

23 Cohen, M. (2020) 'Trump: Black Lives Matter is a "symbol of hate"'. *Politico,* July. Available at https://www.politico.com/news/2020/07/01/trump-black-lives-matter-347051

24 Trump, D. (2020) 'Remarks by President Trump at South Dakota's 2020 Mount Rushmore fireworks celebration' at Keystone, South Dakota. 4 July.

25 Narayan, J. (2017) 'The wages of whiteness in the absence of wages: racial capitalism, reactionary intercommunalism and the rise of Trumpism'. *Third World Quarterly* 38(11): 2482–500.

26 Du Bois, W. E. B. (1903) *The Souls of Black Folk*. New York: New American Library, 19.

27 Abraham Lincoln to Horace Greeley, Friday 22 August 1862 (clipping from *New York Tribune* 23 August 1862). Available at http://www.abrahamlincolnonline.org/lincoln/speeches/greeley.htm

28 Guyatt, N. (2016) *Bind Us Apart: How Enlightened Americans Invented Racial Segregation*. Oxford: Oxford University Press.

29 Ignatiev, N. (1995) *How the Irish Became White*. New York: Routledge.

30 Malcom X, 'Ballot or the bullet'.

31 Brockell, G. (2019) 'She was stereotyped as "the welfare queen." The truth was more disturbing, a new book says'. *Washington Post*, 21 May.

32 Frankopan, P. (2019) *The New Silk Roads: The Present and Future of the World*. London: Bloomsbury, 14.

33 Ibid.

34 Ibid., 43.

35 Fukuyama, F. (1992) *The End of History and the Last Man*. New York: The Free Press, xi.

36 Malcolm X (1964) 'Speech at the Militant Labor Forum'. New York, 29 May.

37 Andrews, K. (2018) *Back to Black: Retelling Black Radicalism for the 21st Century*. London: Zed Books.
38 Malcolm X, 'Ballot or the bullet'.
39 Klein, N. (2020) *On Fire: The (Burning) Case for a Green New Deal*. New York: Simon and Schuster.
40 Malcolm X, 'Ballot or the bullet'.

Acknowledgements

I often joke that doing talks is like being on tour as a stand-up comedian. We get to test out our material on an audience, sharpening our arguments. So many people have engaged with the ideas in this book that it feels like a collective effort, so a big thank you to every comment, question and challenge. Lockdown brought home just how much I have been on the road the last couple of years, which has only been possible because of the support of my wife, Dr Nicole Andrews, who has had to put up with a lot and hold everything together. Also a big thanks to my family, particularly my mom and sisters for their support.

The Black Studies family at Birmingham City University have also been a key source of strength. It is not an exaggeration to say that I couldn't have written the book, or stayed sane, without you. I have to send a massive thank you to Dr Dionne Taylor who has helped to nurture Black Studies and been a rock of support.

Thanks also to Sarah Chalfant and Emma Smith from the Wylie Agency who championed the book and helped to shape the ideas. Maria Bedford from Penguin and Katy O'Donnell from Bold Type really helped bring the book together through the editing process, creating something to be proud of. Also a big thanks to Kim Walker and Rik Ubhi who were at Zed Books for all their work on *Back to Black*, which made this book possible.

If you have got this far, then thank you for reading. Another world is possible if we accept the scale of change necessary to build it. Revolution is not just possible, it is essential.

Index

Kehinde Andrews is professor of Black Studies at Birmingham City University, where he founded, and is currently director of, the Centre for Critical Social Research. At BCU he was also one of the team who founded the first undergraduate degree in Black Studies. Andrews regularly writes for the *Guardian* and the *Independent*. He has been featured on Good Morning Britain, Newsnight, Channel 4 News, BBC News Channel, and Under the Skin with Russell Brand. Andrews is the author of *Back to Black: Retelling Black Radicalism for the 21st Century, Resisting Racism: Race, Inequality and the Black Supplementary School Movement,* and he edits *Blackness in Britain* book series. He lives in Birmingham.